PERFECT
ENOUGH

ALSO BY GEORGE ANDERS

Merchants of Debt

Health Against Wealth

PERFECT ENOUGH

Carly Fiorina and the Reinvention of Hewlett-Packard

GEORGE ANDERS

PORTFOLIO

PORTFOLIO
Published by the Penguin Group
Penguin Putnam Inc., 375 Hudson Street, New York, New York 10014, U.S.A.
Penguin Books Ltd, 80 Strand, London WC2R 0RL, England
Penguin Books Australia Ltd, 250 Camberwell Road, Camberwell, Victoria 3124, Australia
Penguin Books Canada Ltd, 10 Alcorn Avenue, Toronto, Ontario, Canada M4V 3B2
Penguin Books India (P) Ltd, 11 Community Centre, Panchsheel Park, New Delhi—110 017, India
Penguin Books (N.Z.) Ltd, Cnr Rosedale and Airborne Roads, Albany, Auckland, New Zealand
Penguin Books (South Africa) (Pty) Ltd, 24 Sturdee Avenue, Rosebank, Johannesburg 2196, South Africa

Penguin Books Ltd, Registered Offices: Harmondsworth, Middlesex, England

First published in 2003 by Portfolio, a member of Penguin Putnam Inc.

1 3 5 7 9 10 8 6 4 2

Copyright © George Anders, 2003
All rights reserved

CIP data available

ISBN 1-59184-003-1

This book is printed on acid-free paper. ∞

Printed in the United States of America
Set in Bembo
Designed by Jaye Zimet

For Betsy,
and for our children,
Matthew and Peter

Contents

Prologue

Ever since Carly Fiorina arrived at Hewlett-Packard in 1999—in a blaze of publicity as the first woman ever to run such a giant enterprise—critics had been predicting she would fail. In their eyes, she was too inexperienced, too slick, too *different* ever to succeed as the chief executive officer of the legendary Silicon Valley company. It was hard enough to guide one of the fifty largest companies in the world. She also needed to be the new face of leadership at an enterprise where everyone talked constantly about "Bill and Dave," two self-effacing billionaires who started Hewlett-Packard in a tiny garage in 1939, soldering together the first products themselves. Retirement and even death couldn't diminish the founders' impact. Some commentators talked delicately about the "tremendous pressures" that Fiorina faced. Others used the taunting language of the playground or the gutter. "Pack it in babe, you stink!" one columnist wrote, before Fiorina had finished her second year in office.

Now Fiorina's opponents were closing in. At the start of her third year in office, she had staked everything on an audacious plan to remake Hewlett-Packard by carrying out one of the biggest takeovers of all time. She planned to acquire archrival Compaq Computer for $20 billion, but she couldn't execute the deal without shareholder approval. As she raced across the United States in the winter of 2001, trying to rally support for her plan, descendants of Bill Hewlett and Dave Packard campaigned just as hard against it, suggesting that a No vote by shareholders could save the company and oust the intruder. "I don't see how Carly could be effective if the merger is voted down," said Walter Hewlett, the fifty-seven-year-old son of HP's cofounder. "It would be better if she left."

Defeat seemed imminent—and she was doomed if she lost. Or was she?

On the evening of Thursday, March 14, Carly Fiorina and six Hewlett-Packard directors pieced together an extraordinary way to strike back. They did it during a late-night dinner at HP headquarters, less than a week before shareholders cast their ballots. Pushing aside half-eaten meals of squab and sugar snap peas, they talked for hours about the possibility of losing the merger vote, a subject that had been taboo for months. They confronted the prospect of chaos at HP and their immense obligations as representatives of all the company's shareholders. It was frightening enough to make people shiver, and that was just what Fiorina desired. Each of the directors in the room believed she was the right leader for Hewlett-Packard, no matter what. Losing her would only make things worse. By the end of the evening, a rescue plan for the embattled CEO was taking shape.

For months, Fiorina had been reaching deep into Hewlett-Packard's history, pulling out black-and-white photos of the founders when they were young men in the 1930s and 1940s. Those photos of Bill Hewlett and Dave Packard inspired nationwide ad campaigns, in which Fiorina argued that she was the rightful heir to their courage and optimism. "This company's history has always been about being daring," she reminded audiences. "It's been about doing things that others said it was not possible to do. Somehow, in the course of time, the daring part of it got lost. It became timid. I came to HP because I have a passion for this company and this business. We negotiated this merger because it is what's necessary to keep the company vibrant and leading."

The directors in the room agreed with every word of her message. They had recruited her three years earlier, believing she was their best hope of reviving a proud, aging company. The only director who opposed her, Walter Hewlett, hadn't been invited to this meeting. And now Fiorina was ready to address failure the way she wanted. If her opponents blocked the merger and squeezed her out, she warned, "This company will not dare again. And that would be a tragedy." Could she stay in office if she lost the merger vote? Fiorina portrayed grave dangers. Dissenters' attacks against her were likely to turn even nastier. Employee morale would be in tatters. "If I lose," she said, "I will be a damaged, even more controversial CEO. Do you understand what that means?" She looked all around the long table. "You must now talk about what happens if we lose."

With that, Fiorina stepped out of the room. For the next ninety minutes, she wanted HP's directors to caucus among themselves. Everyone knew the board faced nerve-wracking questions. Who would run the company? What hope was there of fixing HP's many business challenges without the Compaq merger? Would the company be governable in any form? Or was chaos inevitable and, if so, how long did each director want to stay? Fiorina wanted this to be a raw, painful conversation in which directors faced the apocalypse. Once they had done so, she would rejoin the meeting. Directors could find her in her office, just fifty feet down the hall.

The CEO of Hewlett-Packard would be sitting at her desk, working. Even that late at night, there was a lot to do.

At about 9:30 P.M., director Jay Keyworth walked over to Fiorina's office. He was the longest-serving member of HP's board and one of the earliest champions of the Compaq deal. "We really need you to dig deeper," he said. "Come back in." His tone was friendly, almost pleading. They walked down the corridor together, noticing that all the other offices in the executive wing were dark. Everyone else had gone home. This was the last piece of business for the night.

Once Fiorina sat down, the directors went around the room, telling her, one by one, what they thought. The first to speak was Phil Condit, the gruff, heavyset CEO of Boeing. He had become a strong advocate of the merger, but he also treated Fiorina with the greatest personal reserve. Other directors often greeted her with a hug; he never did. This time, though, he spoke to her as a friend. "We believe very strongly that this company has a very important future," Condit said. "We believe you're the right person to carry this company forward. I'm here because of you. If you're not on this board, I'm not staying."

In rapid succession, the other five directors echoed his remarks. "We didn't hire you to do the merger," Keyworth said. "We hired you to fix the company." Each director vowed to keep Fiorina as chief executive, no matter what. She thanked each board member, by name, for his or her support. She said it meant an enormous amount to her. But she didn't fully accept the offer to stay on as CEO, and she quickly pushed the conversation on to the hardest topics. "If we lose, we cannot retreat," she said. "We have to think about what we can do next. Are you ready for that?"

For the next few minutes, directors talked about the company's strategic direction if it couldn't buy Compaq. Former HP chairman Dick Hackborn, the director widely regarded as the board's wisest strategist, had reluctantly been forming a backup plan. Without the merger, he believed, HP's big computer businesses were in perilous shape. The main hope of preserving overall shareholder value might involve taking HP's renowned printer business and spinning it off as a separate company, safe from whatever turmoil lay ahead for the computer operations. Then the company's leaders would seek the best destiny available for HP's unprofitable personal-computer business and its stumbling enterprise-computing divisions. That wasn't a pretty path. It might involve enormous layoffs or fire-sale divestitures of HP assets. But it was the least dismal of all the alternatives that Hackborn could see.

Could employees rally around Fiorina in such circumstances? "Things have already got very nasty, and they could potentially get much worse," Fiorina said. Walter Hewlett had been spotted in his late father's old office at HP Labs interviewing employees, which unnerved her greatly. She ticked off a series of other challenges to her authority, which she lumped together as "intrusive engagement." If the merger plan failed, Fiorina believed, all those pressures on her would intensify. Yet as she talked through all the perils, directors kept reassuring her. They believed she could win back the confidence of her employees, no matter what.

After nearly an hour of dialogue, Fiorina still wasn't ready to commit herself. "We have to be very clear-eyed about what this means," she said. "This isn't about quitting. This is about being realistic. Let's take a night to think about it and regroup in the morning." Directors filed out of the headquarters building, heading either to a local hotel or to their homes if they lived nearby. On the way out, HP director Bob Knowling puzzled over Fiorina's response. He had jousted with her for many years, going back to the days when both of them were rising young talents at AT&T. He hadn't ever seen her be indecisive about anything. *Carly always knows what she wants*, he told himself. And so, Knowling began to wonder, was Fiorina holding out for something? Was there one more thing she wanted from the board before she would agree to stay?

At first, Knowling thought Fiorina might want more money, or better severance terms if she ultimately were squeezed out. That didn't seem in keeping with her usual concerns, but CEOs were known to fixate on such things. He asked fellow director Sam Ginn, who had deep insight into boardroom pay discussions, but Ginn assured him that pay wasn't at issue. So Knowling pondered further. *There's something she wants to bargain for,* he told himself. *I don't know what the hell it is.*

The next morning, Knowling got his answer. Fiorina was ready to fight harder than ever, but only if she could be surrounded by directors who shared every aspect of her agenda. "It's time to make a break," she said. If the board really wanted Carly Fiorina to stay, Walter Hewlett had to go.

Chapter 1

THE BEST OUTFIT ON EARTH

Nighttime had come. The clatter of screwdrivers at Hewlett-Packard's engineering lab had stopped; the slide rules were tucked away. The barnlike building was utterly deserted, except for one tall man in his late forties. He walked through the facility with authority, as if he owned the place. Moving from bench to bench, he stopped every now and then to examine the engineers' handicraft. Sometimes he would pick up a half-built instrument and hold it in his hands, the fierce hands of a former lineman on the Stanford football team.

At 8 A.M. the next day, a cheery, drawn-out chime announced the start of the workday at Hewlett-Packard's Palo Alto, California, headquarters. It was 1957, and HP was just a small company in the outer suburbs of San Francisco. It would be years before anyone started calling this area Silicon Valley. But the sixty HP engineers heading toward their workbenches regarded themselves as something special. Their head of research, former Bell Labs scientist Barney Oliver, described his men as "a proud, enthusiastic bunch who really believed they were part of the best outfit on earth."

Eric Hammerquist was one of Hewlett-Packard's newer hires, and he liked the place a lot. He was in his midtwenties, with an engineering degree from the University of Washington. His prototype of a new oscilloscope had just passed its internal lab inspections, including a "shake and break" test meant to ensure that the machine was strong enough for industrial use. Hammerquist had gambled a bit on that one, using thinner 16-gauge aluminum for the outside casing to trim weight, instead of the standard 14-gauge metal. But he believed his gamble had worked.

As soon as Hammerquist got to his bench that morning, his jaw dropped. His oscilloscope was ruined. Someone had grabbed the casing and twisted it violently out of shape, leaving the pretzel-shaped wreckage in the middle of his workbench. The young engineer was furious. *Some vandal has broken in and ruined everything,* he thought. Then he noticed a scrap of paper attached to the twisted metal. On it was an eight-word note: "You can do better than this—Dave Packard."

Within minutes, a new legend was born. Engineers crowded around Hammerquist's workbench to marvel at the damage. Some roared with laughter. Others wanted to touch the twisted sheet metal so that they could feel the raw power of a boss who would destroy bad work rather than let it leave the shop. They talked about nothing else for hours. By lunchtime, Hewlett-Packard's lab engineers agreed that Dave Packard was the meanest, toughest, most brilliant boss in America and that they were damn lucky to be working for him. They also agreed it would be wise to use stronger sheet metal from now on.

Decades later, business-school professors and management consultants would flock to Hewlett-Packard in hopes of figuring out what made its corporate culture so distinctive—and so effective. By then it was clear that they were looking at the Mississippi River of corporate America: an enormous force that just kept gathering strength as it went along. Every decade, HP's sales, profits, and stock price climbed another fourfold or more. The company hardly ever had a bad year. The cumulative effect was a company with more than $30 billion a year in sales by the mid-1990s, more than 100,000 employees, and no obvious limits to its growth.

As the experts poked around the company, they extracted a half-dozen or so principles that were, indeed, part of the HP Way. The company believed in technical excellence, teamwork, the importance of the individual, sound finances, and community service. But the more abstract the rules became, the harder it was to see why any intelligently run company wouldn't do the same. The experts could see all the attributes that accompanied HP's success; they couldn't explain why it was unique. The key questions remained: What shaped the soul of HP at its most rudimentary level? And what let the company pull far ahead of its rivals in terms of profitability, public esteem for its products, and a reputation as a great place to work?

Any diligent hunt for answers has to start in two places: the era in which HP came of age—and the two men who founded it.

To a striking degree, World War II defined Hewlett-Packard's values when the company was very young. As historian Stephen Ambrose observed, the war years were a time of sacrifice, common goals, and a belief that everyone could play a part, no matter how small, in helping achieve victory in the highest-stakes battle of all time. Veterans came back from the war with an optimism and passion that they wanted to apply to the rest of their lives. Hewlett-Packard tapped into that desire perfectly, with its constant talk of "making a contribution," rather than pursuing crasser goals of money and power. In the late 1940s and early 1950s, HP hired hundreds of young men who had flown B-29s in the Pacific and marched across war-torn Europe as the army of liberation. The company promoted these men fast and allowed them enormous responsibilities at a young age. Just as in the war, almost everyone handled the new duties superbly. Older, more established companies had a hard time harnessing this spirit. Their cultures had been defined by the labor upheaval of 1880–1920, when bosses ruled with an iron fist and desperate unionists believed that almost any tactic was defensible to fight capitalism. Long after labor violence abated at the likes of U.S. Steel or AT&T, distrust between workers and management lingered. At Hewlett-Packard, everyone got a fresh start.

Dave Packard was the iron-willed leader who made it all work. He was 6-foot-5 and so physically strong that most employees were a little frightened of him. During summer breaks in his college years, he hauled ore at a mining camp, built roads, and delivered huge blocks of ice to taverns. He didn't say much, but when he spoke, he made every word count. "If you can't get the job done, we'll damn well find someone else who can," he told countless subordinates over the years.

Employees called him "Pappy" and "The Mean One." Both nicknames were richly earned. But there was another side to Packard—an extraordinary compassion and sense of public service—that kept his workers and managers coming back for more. He established catastrophic health insurance for employees in the 1940s, when hardly any other company did so, because he felt dreadful that family medical crises had cost two of his workers their jobs. He spent an inordinate amount of the week on the shop floor, asking employees how their work was going and whether HP could do anything to make their jobs more productive. "Management by walking around," he called it—and it took a remarkable blend of self-assurance and humility to pull it off.

Most of all, Dave Packard pushed himself so hard that he inspired everyone else. Retired HP engineer Alan Bagley recalled an encounter with Packard in the early 1950s, when the boss gave him just twenty-four hours to complete a week's worth of product testing. Bagley was furious. He stormed into Packard's office, only to be waved toward an empty chair. Packard was on the phone with officials of the Palo Alto school board, who were so overwhelmed with surging enrollments that they were about to pack double shifts of first graders into tiny, inadequate classrooms. "We can't let this happen," Packard said. For the next ten minutes, he pleaded and cajoled the school board to buy more land, boost its budgets, and do whatever it took to make sure that the little children of Palo Alto got a decent education. Then Packard looked at Bagley and said: "Now what do you want?"

"I'd been planning a whole speech about how it just wasn't any fun to work in those circumstances," Bagley recalled. "But when Dave finally looked at me, all I could say was: 'That's a tough deadline you set. But we'll get it done.'"

Meanwhile, Bill Hewlett was the friendly, zesty inventor: the genius who could see a little farther into the future than anyone else. He was endlessly curious about everything: the way a lock worked, the history of sixteenth-century Mexico, the business goals of HP's best customers. Even after he became an enormously powerful executive, some of Hewlett's favorite moments involved sitting with young engineers, brainstorming about what their sketches and prototypes could become. "Hewlett allowed you to dream with him," onetime protégé Bruce Woolpert recalled. "He would become a twenty-year-old, asking, 'What do you think? Could we do that?'" A few weeks later, Hewlett might bombard the project's champion with all the tough questions that a top executive should ask, but he never lost track of the young inventor's passion that fuels any great company's growth. Even as a middle-aged executive, Hewlett wanted to stay in the game, and he would tiptoe into HP's labs at night to run his own experiments. By the end of his career, Hewlett had won thirteen patents for everything from oscillators to distance-measuring devices. The last one came in 1971, when he was nearly sixty years old.

There was a rumpled, unpretentious quality to Bill Hewlett that made him all the more likable as he grew richer and more powerful. His off-the-rack suits were frayed at times; his fondness for corny puns made even his friends groan. But there was nothing bashful about his attitudes toward HP. Near the end of his life, in an interview with business-school professors James C. Collins and Jerry I. Porras, he declared: "I'm probably most proud of having helped create a company that by virtue of its values, practices, and success has had a tremendous impact on the way companies are managed around the world." The professors used that epigram to open the first chapter of their management classic *Built to Last*.

Hewlett's best ideas were masterful. In the early 1970s, when cheap little calculators were catching on, he ordered HP engineers to build mightier machines that still could fit in a shirt pocket. These calculators wouldn't just add and divide; they would churn out everything from factorials to hyperbolic cosines. It took months to figure out how to cram all the essential circuitry into what seemed like an impossibly tiny shell. Outside consultants couldn't see any meaningful market for such an elaborate device that might cost more than $300. But beginning with the HP 35 calculator, scientists and engineers bought the company's calculators by the millions. For a few years, handheld calculators were HP's most successful and profitable product.

Even Hewlett's worst ideas made people smile for years afterward. At one point, he became enchanted with the promise of electro-anesthesia, in which modified HP instruments would deliver electric shocks that could numb surgical patients. The project made it as far as animal trials in Colorado before stunningly bad results made it clear that Hewlett's idea would never work. As local HP managers tried to disband the project, they were stuck with six baboons that had been purchased as lab subjects. "We tried calling every zoo in Colorado," recalled former HP executive Bill Terry. "None of them wanted the baboons. Finally there was an intense flood on the South Platte River, and all the baboons escaped. We were so relieved."

Dave Packard was born in 1912 in Pueblo, Colorado, the son of a small-town lawyer. By age twelve the boy was an ardent ham-radio enthusiast, thrilled to have built a device that could pick up radio signals from faraway Des Moines, Iowa. His mother and her friends encouraged him to head west for college, and in 1930, he enrolled at Stanford University. There he met Hewlett early in their freshman year, when both tried out for the football team. Packard made the starting lineup; the much smaller Hewlett, at 5-foot-8, was quickly cut from the squad.

The two men became friends in their senior year while studying electrical engineering with legendary Stanford professor Frederick Terman. Packard was the methodical straight-A student. Hewlett was the class cutup. He rigged up contraptions that would dump buckets of water on people's heads, he brought live goldfish into the classroom, and, in his spare time, he practiced his mountaineering skills by scaling the sheer sandstone walls of Stanford's Quad with his bare hands and shoes, like a campus version of Superman. Hewlett started most of his climbs near the faculty parking lot, and he had the effrontery to name his routes after his professors' parking spaces.

Hewlett's energy and quick mind made him great fun to be around, even if he hadn't quite figured out his calling yet. "He could dull more tools in an afternoon than most fellows could in an entire week," Terman later recalled. But Hewlett at age twenty-three could read his professor's landmark textbook on electrical engineering and dash off a note that pointed out several mistakes, including "one that is quite fundamental." Suggested corrections were attached, and Terman gladly made them.

After graduating in 1934, Hewlett and Packard went camping together for two weeks in Colorado's San Juan Mountains, so far in the back country that they rented a horse for a dollar a day to carry their gear. The two men were starting a sixty-year friendship that ultimately became famous because of their astonishing success in business together. But the heart of the friendship was defined well before commerce entered the picture. Near the ends of their lives, when Dave Packard and Bill Hewlett were asked how they had learned to trust and respect each other, they repeatedly alluded to those early wilderness adventures. They kept that spirit alive throughout their careers, crisscrossing the American West on fishing and hunting trips—even buying ranches together that would become second homes for their families. People who wanted to rise at HP learned to enjoy at least a little of the outdoorsman's life with Bill and Dave.

By the summer of 1938, the two Stanford graduates were making plans to launch a business together. Hewlett had picked up a master's degree in electrical engineering at the Massachusetts Institute of Technology. Packard had spent several years in Schenectady, New York, working for General Electric. Terman had kept a close watch on both of them, and he became the unstoppable matchmaker, tugging both of them back to California and coaxing his two best students, again and again, to form a company together. As early as 1937, Packard and Hewlett had proposed forming something called the Engineering Service Company. The next year they decided to use their own names instead, flipping a coin to determine whose name came first. Hewlett won.

Even in the final stages of the Great Depression, there was something wonderfully romantic about starting a company with your best friend. The men set up shop in the garage of 367 Addison Avenue, a rented house in Palo Alto. There, the two founders and Packard's wife, Lucile, chipped in the company's entire capitalization: $538. Simple machine-shop work was done in the garage, with a drill press, a soldering iron, and a few other tools. Heat curing was done in the oven in the Packards' kitchen. No one was quite sure at first what Hewlett-Packard should be making. So the founders became engineers for hire, producing foul-lane indicators for bowling alleys, motor controllers for Lick Observatory, and anything else that would bring in money.

Their first big seller was an audio oscillator that Hewlett designed. Eight units were sold to the Disney movie studio, for use in cleaning up the sound track of *Fantasia*. Packard—in a rare miscalculation—priced it at $54.40, thinking of the nineteenth-century slogan 54° 40' OR FIGHT. That was too low a price to be profitable, and the founders quickly raised the price to $70 or more. By the end of the first year, Hewlett-Packard had taken in $5,369 in sales and tucked away nearly 30 percent of that amount as profits. Those sturdy profit margins, coupled with an ability to use self-generated cash to finance further growth, would be HP hallmarks for the next fifty years.

When World War II broke out, Hewlett was called into the army as a Signal Corps officer. Packard stayed in Palo Alto to run the business, which rapidly swelled with big military contracts. HP alone didn't win the war, but its engineers could take pride that their antenna controllers and other gear helped soldiers and sailors do their jobs a little better. By the war's end, HP had two hundred employees. Packard had jammed them onto his payroll to keep up with military orders, only to be obliged to sack many of them as the country demobilized. It was a deeply unpleasant experience for the thirty-four-year-old company president, and Packard vowed never again to run a "hire-and-fire" operation.

Soon after the war, a sturdier version of Hewlett-Packard took shape. The company began making top-notch technical instruments in every category it could identify, from frequency counters to voltmeters. Packard's perfectionism infused the whole company, aided by the belief that HP's engineers were building for scientists and researchers very much like themselves. The classic HP product of that era was an atomic clock, accurate to one millionth of a second. Before HP entered the market, no one could do any better than one-thousandth-of-a-second accuracy. "You're not here to make the average instrument," new hires were told. "You're going to make a breakthrough in the art of instrumentation—or we're not going to put it in the catalog."

There was no time for nostalgia. As soon as one device came to market, a new team of engineers began devising a better model that would make the first one obsolete. Shortly before Christmas one year, employees gave Hewlett and Packard a mischievous gift for their ranch: a fertilizer spreader packed full of product manuals for old or discontinued HP products. Other companies could start museums lauding past efforts. At HP in those days, the future was too exciting to allow any sentimental looks backward.

There was no room for bureaucracy or excessive hierarchy, either.

Hewlett had returned from his Signal Corps duty, disgusted with the army's command-and-control system. That wasn't how he wanted to run HP. He and Packard insisted on open-plan seating, with vice presidents and factory workers all side by side in one big, open workspace. Everyone was on a first-name basis, starting with "Bill" and "Dave." And when Hewlett walked through the production area, he didn't just shake hands with workers. He sat down at their stations and operated their machines for a few minutes so he could learn firsthand how HP's manufacturing really stacked up.

That left plenty of time to make Hewlett-Packard the best little company in America, with Packard constantly goading his people to do it right. Some of his most scathing memos became collector's items—still treasured forty years later by the people who got them. "Manifestly absurd and evidence of total stupidity," he told finance officials one time. The marketing department got a different broadside: "A waste of money and a violation of policy." And a two-line memo to the earliest computer engineers has disappeared from HP archives but is still referred to as the "Wow! Ouch!" memo—because of the reaction it caused in one recipient.

Why did those memos become HP heirlooms? Alumni have a hard time finding the right words, but eventually they all settle on some variation of the same explanation. The most blistering memos were worth saving because they showed how much Dave Packard cared. In a world where so many companies settled for second best, Packard was the stern parent who wanted his children to push themselves as hard as possible. For employees of his generation—men and women who had grown up in the Depression and come of age in the epic struggle of World War II—his version of tough love really worked. In one confidant's words: "Dave hired ordinary people, and then he found a way to get extraordinary results out of us."

Occasionally Packard went too far. Some of his harshest scoldings left victims so stunned that they couldn't come to work. They stayed home for days, certain that they had been fired. In those cases, it was Packard's wife, Lucile, who told him: "David, you've been too severe on that man." It took the company president a little while to agree that she was right. And then Dave Packard would drive to the employee's home and say he was sorry. He had lost his cool. He had said some things he shouldn't have said. There was still a job open at HP—and wouldn't it be a good idea if everyone gave it another try?

Just when people thought Dave Packard had too much Old Testament vengeance in him, he would show a sweet, warmer side that would make even the surliest men melt. At the dawn of the computer age HP engineer Paul Ely devised a project that would require him to take hold of a $1 million computer that HP was building and divert it to his own use instead of letting it go to a customer. Ely was enormously excited about his project, but fearful that top management wouldn't approve it. He went into Packard's office with an immense presentation of thirty overhead slides, determined to show why his project made sense.

After the third slide, Packard said, "You can have it."

"We've got this whole presentation for you!" Ely interjected. His adrenaline by now was running so strong that he couldn't stop himself. "We can prove to you that we need it!"

"You don't have to," Packard replied. "I can tell by your enthusiasm that it's right for you to have it."

For more than a dozen years, Ely built computer system after computer system at HP, eventually rising to be an executive vice president at the company, in charge of more than $3 billion a year of sales. Whenever people asked what gave him the courage to push ahead so fast in an unproven field, he shared the story of his first exchange with Packard.

In 1957, Packard wanted to codify HP's values. His first public attempt came at an off-site managers' meeting at a Napa Valley, California, resort. Addressing the crowd after dinner, he handed out binders with his text so that managers could follow along, word for word. As his starting point, he picked robust profitability: "the objective which makes all the other objectives possible." Packard wanted pretax earnings equal to 20 percent of sales, even in bad years. It was a rip-roaringly ambitious target that few American companies ever achieved, then or now. But HP so far had been a fountain of profitability, and Packard didn't want the company ever to fall short. Everything else that he and Hewlett wanted to provide—good jobs, state-of-the-art innovation, etc.—depended on turning the profit crank. Anyone who couldn't accept that profit goal, Packard thundered, "has no place either now or in the future on the management team of this company!"

A moment later, Packard introduced his favorite word: *contribution*. HP should make instruments that contributed to the advancement of electronics, and it should produce each one with what he termed "inexpensive quality." (The quality was never in dispute, although outsiders joked that HP stood for High Price.) After that came employee issues: letting workers share in the company's success, providing job security based on performance, and making sure that work was satisfying and fulfilling. HP would be lenient about keeping older workers whose output was slipping, but it wouldn't provide absolute tenure. And finally, HP should show good citizenship and finance its growth internally, without taking on debt.

Managers liked the talk. A few months later, Hewlett-Packard announced plans to go public, selling 10 percent of the company to outside investors. The offering was a big success; in its first year of trading, HP stock nearly doubled in value. When it came time to publish HP's first annual report in early 1958, Packard included some thoughts about his overall business philosophy. Most of the Napa Valley tenets were there: making a contribution, inexpensive quality, and a belief that "profit is a means to everything else that the company does." At the back of the report was a tantalizing allusion to something else: "an informal, friendly atmosphere" for employees.

By now, HP's version of management by walking around was in full swing, and it was a shocking, delicious contrast to the rigid hierarchies of older companies. Both founders loved to roam through their facilities and strike up conversations with anyone who had a minute. Those brief chats with scientists and shipping clerks kept Packard and Hewlett stunningly sharp about their own company. What's more, rank-and-file employees reveled in the belief that their jobs were so important that the top bosses wanted to hear from them. As HP grew ever larger, the original small-company camaraderie stayed alive in large part because Bill and Dave were so accessible.

Hewlett in particular pioneered what later became known as servant leadership. Before a trip to Japan in 1971, he telexed HP's manager in Tokyo, Dick Love, to see if Love needed anything from the United States. "It's hard to find good tortillas here," Love replied. When Hewlett arrived at Tokyo's Narita airport, he brought with him a dozen plastic bags containing twelve tortillas each—and a mild rebuke. "I had to get these at the grocery store," Hewlett told him. "If you had given me more time, I could have gone to the farmers' market in San Jose and brought some really good ones." For the next few years, Love did everything possible to build HP's business in Japan, working at all hours of the day and night to close deals. He was an ambitious manager to begin with, but now he had an extra driving force: He didn't ever want to disappoint his boss and friend, Bill Hewlett.

On their rambles, Packard and Hewlett were such good listeners, and so indifferent to formal rank, that half-informed people believed their system amounted to consensus management. It didn't. As onetime HP marketing manager Dwight Johnson wryly put it: "They told us what consensus was, and we managed to get used to it." On the little things, Packard and Hewlett were humble men, always willing to learn something new. On the big issues, the founders were supremely confident in their own judgment.

What's more, both the founders really liked being patriarchs. At company barbecues, Dave Packard would don an apron that said "The Boss" and hand out sizzling hot, juicy steaks to hundreds of employees. Not only did he provide paychecks and professional fulfillment for all his workers, but on that day he provided their food as well. (Vice presidents got to distribute the potatoes and vegetables.) Hewlett, meanwhile, had bought one hundred acres in the hills above Palo Alto soon after World War II, when land was cheap. Over time, he sold off one- and two-acre lots to new arrivals, including some HP employees. His prices were fair; his message unmistakable. HP would provide everything you needed, thanks to the resources, foresight, and generosity of its founders.

The founders made sure, too, that their moral code infused every aspect of the business. Bragging and deceit weren't allowed; offenders would be fired. An early HP ad in *Electronics News* made the unpardonable mistake of listing a bargain price in the headline and then explaining in fine print that these terms were available only for bulk orders of fifty or more. "I never want to see this kind of advertisement again!" one of the founders wrote, in such anger that his pen broke through the magazine page.

All the same, once employees learned the company code, they realized it was possible to talk back to the founders and get away with it. Packard urged junior executives to put on sassy skits after dinner at off-site retreats, making fun of the top brass. "Pick on anyone you want," he told public-relations manager Dave Kirby, "but be hardest on me and Bill." Sure enough, for one evening it was all right to tease Hewlett about his reckless driving habits, to chide Packard about his mumbling public delivery, and even to have the onstage version of Packard disparage a never-ending stream of people who "can't get this job done right." By the end of the skit, Packard was threatening to fire half the company—and managers in the audience were howling with glee.

Unwittingly, the HP founders had built a foundation for incredible team spirit and trust. Paul Ely noticed it his first week at HP, after joining the company from Sperry Gyroscope, an East Coast engineering company. At Sperry, labor relations were so bad that engineers had dismantled an entire lathe and smuggled it out of the factory, one piece at a time, under their clothes, just to taunt their bosses. At Hewlett-Packard, the central parts depot was open all day long, without any guards or sign-out forms. People took whatever they needed for the job, and no more. "If anyone started cheating even a little bit," Ely recalled, "the other guys in the shop would give them hell. Management didn't need to do a thing. The feeling on the shop floor was: 'You're stealing from us! Don't do that.'"

As HP grew in the 1960s, Packard decided that he didn't want a giant corporate campus in Palo Alto. Instead, he would replicate HP's small-company charm in other towns, expanding into places such as Loveland, Colorado; Corvallis, Oregon; and Boise, Idaho. He created a spectacularly decentralized enterprise with lots of little colonies each championing their own products, each free to make routine business decisions on their own, without much meddling from headquarters. Many of the new locations were out-of-the-way college towns with good hunting, fishing, or skiing nearby. That made it easy to recruit engineers; it also minimized everyone's exposure to the less-noble practices of other big companies. Usually, division managers themselves could infuse the HP Way into these new outposts. If they needed help, Hewlett and Packard would gladly stop by to work their magic. When Hewlett visited a new HP facility in Santa Rosa, California, one weekend, he was startled to find the supply room locked. He left a note saying: "Please do not lock this storeroom again." And soon a new legend was born. In the retelling, Hewlett supposedly bought bolt cutters and snipped through the lock that day. It was an exaggeration, but it was warmly tolerated because it helped everyone get the point.

Overseas markets followed soon afterward, with Hewlett leading the way. He had lived in Paris for a year as a twelve-year-old, and had been stationed in Japan as an army officer in 1945, assessing the status of the enemy's wartime technology. Those experiences made him an internationalist from early on. After European nations took their first steps toward economic unity with the Treaty of Rome in 1957, Hewlett argued strongly that someday non-U.S. markets would be bigger for HP than the company's home country. Skeptics disagreed, but he went ahead anyway and opened a European headquarters in Geneva, Switzerland, started manufacturing facilities in Germany, and struck up friendships with Japanese industrialists who would one day be vital allies for HP in the printer business. By 1975, Hewlett's prediction had come true: 51 percent of HP's sales came from outside the United States.

As HP expanded, Packard's and Hewlett's horizons grew even faster. They joined the Business Roundtable and various high-powered corporate boards. Packard became a director of Boeing and Chevron; Hewlett won directorships at Chase Manhattan and Chrysler. Packard at various points was president or a director of every electronics-industry association that mattered—and some that didn't. The two men believed it was their duty to help their whole industry succeed. Besides, sometimes business networking could be fun. Both men joined the Bohemian Club, a secretive group of San Francisco–area executives whose big summer festival in the woods would run for weeks. There was a frat-house tone to these gatherings, but they were great places to get to know business leaders like George Shultz, president of the Bechtel construction company and a future secretary of state in the Reagan administration.

After the 1968 presidential election, Packard decided to try his luck in what he called public service—and everyone else called politics. As an active backer of Republican candidates, Packard was rewarded with an invitation to be deputy secretary of defense in the first Nixon administration. He lasted two and a half years. To his dismay, techniques that worked beautifully at HP often proved useless in the Pentagon. The Vietnam War was going badly, and instead of building a winning team, Packard spent much of his time helping dismantle a losing effort. Nobody openly resisted his take-charge style, but career military officers could be surprisingly languid about following his directives. There wasn't much he could do about it. As one writer delicately put it in 1970, "He has not always made a strong impression in Congress, where a great premium is placed on subtlety and political skill." When Packard came back to HP in January 1972, he had aged ten years. Asked about his biggest accomplishment in Washington, he said, "I gave up smoking."

While Packard was away, Hewlett finally rose to the top job at HP, after thirty-one years of being the No. 2 man. It was an emotional moment for Hewlett, and he couldn't hide it. Addressing a large group of HP employees on his first day as chief executive, Hewlett wanted them to know that the company was still in good hands. He was in the midst of what seemed like a safe sentence—"We may have slightly different management styles, but our objectives are the same"—when his voice cracked. One witness thought he saw tears forming in Hewlett's eyes. The new CEO gripped the lectern tightly and stopped talking for a few seconds. Only then could he continue.

For the next nine years, Hewlett kept the CEO job. (When Packard returned from Washington, "Pappy" was allowed to reclaim only his old title of chairman.) The company's annual sales burst through the $1 billion barrier during Hewlett's reign. But the two most profound changes were ones that never made it into the financial statements.

First, Hewlett led a campaign to make Hewlett-Packard a great place for women to work—and to be leaders. As early as the mid-1960s, he had been speaking up at company meetings, saying that HP needed to open career paths for women. So many women working on HP's production line were bright, capable people who could aspire to key jobs in engineering or marketing, he contended. "They're so underutilized!" he declared, adding that if HP could get women into management ranks faster than the competition, the company would have an enormous competitive edge.

Transforming HP's old-boy culture wasn't going to be easy. On the job, managers were known to ask attractive secretaries to wear something "sexy" to work the next day, because it might brighten the spirits of some hardworking male engineers. Off-site, frat-house humor prevailed at the all-important managers' meetings. One favorite diversion involved taking Magic Markers to company photos and seeing who could attach the most outrageous caption to an otherwise boring picture. The winning entry one year: a befuddled-looking executive, blurting out a graffiti artist's question: "What is a vagina?"

At the HP Ranch itself, Hewlett and Packard for years had been entertaining their friends with good, hearty male bonding. The founders and their buddies rose before dawn and gulped down coffee and rolls that Packard himself had heated. They went deer hunting all morning, drank a gin concoction known as "moose milk" before lunch, and then napped in the afternoon before resuming the hunt. At night, they gathered around a campfire for steak dinners followed by hours of ballads and bawdy songs. Packard himself would loosen up in ways that would be unthinkable at work, belting out such favorites as: *"Me father was the keeper of the Eddystone light. He slept with a mermaid one fine night."* It was a wonderful, warm ritual to the men involved. They would have been profoundly angry and hurt if anyone suggested it should stop. But from the 1970s onward, such customs became more and more anachronistic.

A revolution in male-female relations was under way, and it's unlikely that anyone at HP fully knew where it was going. Hewlett did tell a newspaper reporter in 1974—with an unmistakable sense of pride—that HP was opening doors for talented female line leaders in its plants. Many of them "had the capability of being supervisors but didn't think they had the leadership skills," he said. "By encouraging them to move up, we have tapped an important resource."

Hewlett's other transformation involved a more systematic change in the kinds of people recruited into HP leadership. Packard had always relied on his intuition, sometimes pushing people with limited formal qualifications into big jobs, just because he felt sure they could handle the responsibility. But Hewlett believed it was time to formalize HP's management track. Inevitably, that meant going to the top business schools and hiring newly minted MBAs, whose budgeting and strategy skills could help Hewlett-Packard stay on course now that it was a multibillion-dollar enterprise. Old-timers griped that the business-school graduates were too detached and too clinical; that they were somehow compromising the HP Way. Hewlett disagreed. The company's key principles were safe, he believed. If new managers overhauled some day-to-day practices, that was simply part of the natural development of the business.

And if the company stumbled, even briefly, Dave Packard was always around to read the riot act. In February 1974, he stormed into the Santa Clara, California, facility to tell managers what he thought about their past year's performance, when sales jumped 38 percent and pretax income advanced nearly as much. "We've made some very bad mistakes," Packard declared. Inventories were too high. Executives were chasing market share in crummy businesses that HP shouldn't even be in. Cash was being squandered. And in some divisions, earnings growth was so feeble that if those bad habits spread to the rest of the company, HP's stock price could tumble fifty points or more. "The market doesn't give a damn about your sales," he thundered. "They don't give a damn about your share of the market. The only thing that counts is rate of growth of earnings." By now Packard had taken off his jacket and rolled his shirtsleeves above his elbow, a sure sign he was incensed. Not until the final moments of his forty-five-minute talk did he let a little compassion seep into his voice. "You're the ones we depend on to get this job done," he concluded. "We want to help you in any way we can." Nearly two hundred managers went back to their cubicles that afternoon and vowed to try harder. Sure enough, HP held strong during the coming months as the 1973–75 recession gouged its way through American industry. Other companies went belly-up; HP squeaked through with lean inventories, frugal use of cash, and financial performance that made its shareholders proud.

Although HP in its early years lacked a formal retirement age, Hewlett decided to step down as president in 1977 and then cede the CEO's job on his sixty-fifth birthday, in early 1978. Packard would remain as chairman for at least several years. The founders had seen this moment coming for a long time, and they had groomed several strong candidates as successors, including marketing chief Bob Boniface, manufacturing boss Ralph Lee, and

John Young, a well-rounded executive with experience in both the computer and instrument businesses. All were homegrown managers a half-generation younger than the founders. As Boniface later put it, "Dave and Bill were deeply committed to promoting from within. To them, it was kind of ridiculous to think about bringing in someone from outside when there was so much knowledge and talent within the company." The appearance of a three-candidate contest lasted briefly. Then, more than a year before Hewlett was ready to leave, the mystery was over.

Everyone knew the next president and CEO would be John Young. He was the youngest of the front-runners, in his midforties, but he was decisive, widely admired, and a master of everything he had tackled in his two decades at HP. Most important, he understood the computer business. Computers were becoming an ever-bigger part of HP's overall revenue, even though Packard never found them totally to his liking. HP had been nudged into computers in the early 1960s because its high-end instruments required more computing power, making it clear that HP effectively *had* to be making computers. Young had an engineering degree from Oregon State University and an MBA from Stanford; he could thrive in both the old and new worlds. What's more, he was a tall, good-looking man who carried himself like a modern CEO. He was a protégé of Ernest Arbuckle, who was both the Stanford business school dean and a frequent deer-hunting guest at the HP Ranch.

At one point in the mid-1970s, Hewlett offered Young the ultimate rite of passage. They both sat down with a grab bag of electronics parts in the middle of the HP Lab. When a referee shouted "Go!" they raced to see who could assemble the jumble into an HP terminal faster. Employees crowded around to watch the contest. The result delighted everyone and proved that Young was a worthy heir. Hewlett finished first. Young took a few moments longer—but his machine worked.

In his first few years, John Young got off to a great start. HP's revenue tripled in his first five years, to $4.3 billion in 1982. Earnings and the stock price did just as well. Most important, Young began repairing a Packard strategy that had been just right for the 1950s and 1960s but was creating constant headaches in the 1980s. Packard had always believed that HP functioned best if it kept splitting off major products into freestanding divisions, with their own manufacturing plants and marketing teams. That decentralization kept the company young, energetic, and free of bureaucracy, Packard contended. What Packard didn't fully foresee, however, was how much the divisions would stumble over one another as HP tried to make headway in the complex, highly intertwined computer industry. In the early 1980s, the company ended up with three divisions in separate cities making some form of personal computer, without any good way of coordinating prices, features, and product launches. HP's fast-growing printer division was excited about some new graphics capabilities, but the graphics wouldn't work on some of the company's own computers. Hewlett-Packard acted "like three or four companies that don't seem to talk to each other," one major customer remarked in 1982.

For the first time in his career, Young had to challenge his old boss Packard on HP's next move. To the business-school-educated new CEO, the cure was obvious: Start making crucial decisions at headquarters and yank power out of the divisions' hands. But to Packard, centralization was repugnant. He loved to think of HP as a loose federation of far-flung divisions, each finding its own way to contribute to the greater good. As Packard told an interviewer in the 1980s: "It's better to stay with something that you know how to manage than to try to do something new." Their fiercest tussles involved HP's computer strategy, which really did need to be different from the highly decentralized approach that worked so well in the instrument business. Young talked about the essence of his job being the development of "a strategic glue and direction for the computer effort." He could see that a relative upstart, Digital Equipment Corporation of Maynard, Massachusetts, had darted past HP in the industrial computing market. Determined to overtake DEC, Young became the company's No. 1 salesman, catching overnight flights to the East Coast to pitch HP's wares himself to America's largest corporations. "When I started visiting AT&T, the guys at DEC had the place locked up," Young later recalled. "By the late 1980s, we had pushed DEC out, and we had most of the business."

But to HP's consternation, the personal-computer revolution was changing the high-tech world even more decisively in the 1980s—and much of its impact seemed horribly antithetical to everything that Packard and Hewlett believed. Cheap desktop machines were making modern computing as accessible as cars or phones. New fortunes were being built in the high-tech industry, and the most successful companies were doing all the things that Packard and Hewlett hated. Companies like Apple Computer, Compaq, Tandy, and even IBM boasted about new models in the press months before they were fully built and debugged. Many of them competed not on technical excellence, but on price, advertising slogans, the aesthetics of their casing, and their ability to become an easy-to-use platform for some other company's software. "Fluff and marketing," the HP executives called it. But it worked.

HP's leaders started to seem old-fashioned with their insistence that products ought to have proprietary technology that no one else could provide. When they pushed into the PC industry in the early 1980s, it was with a touch-screen PC that operated differently from everyone else's machine. Even though HP's engineers loved it, no one else did. The machine was a flop, and at one point later in the decade, Packard argued that HP should just get out of the business. He didn't prevail, but his disdain for the PC business colored the whole company's thinking.

HP's financial conservatism became problematic, too. Like most people who grew up in the Depression, Packard and Hewlett abhorred borrowing. Well into his old age, Packard loved to retell a story of how he raced back from Washington in the early 1970s, after his Pentagon stint, and at the last moment stopped HP from raising money by issuing bonds. He thought that intervention was heroic; with the passage of time, it seemed out-of-step with the ways that modern companies were using the capital markets. In hard times, Packard's advice to managers was: Raise your prices and cut your growth rate. That brought rock-solid profitability, but it also meant moving more slowly than rivals that had more modern (and more permissive) attitudes about raising money from the public.

Increasingly, HP was seen as a great place to start a career, but hardly the fastest-track opportunity in Silicon Valley. The new business heroes were men and women in their thirties who had founded tiny companies, raised some venture-capital backing, and then took the companies public, becoming multimillionaires in the process. A startling number of these new tycoons turned out to be former HP managers or engineers. Among them were Apple Computer co-founder Steve Wozniak; Tandem Computing founder James Treybig; Rolm founder Ken Oshman, and Acuson founder Sam Maslak. "You're making a mistake," Packard told some of them as they headed out the door. They seldom argued to his face; in fact, many of them said they hoped to instill the best parts of the HP Way at their new companies. But in private conversations, the alumni confided that HP had become too slow and too timid for their tastes.

In the late 1980s, all these issues caught up with HP. The company's growth curve flattened. Decision-making stalled out. Meetings seemed to go on forever without any resolution. As a high-tech slump took hold,

HP's stock tumbled more than 50 percent from 1987 to 1990. As Packard and Hewlett watched their company stumble, their initial feelings of concern shaded first into alarm and then into a conviction that they had better jump into action themselves. They were in their midseventies now, without formal offices at HP's sleek new headquarters building. They were part-timers, still using their old desks in what now had been designated the main building for HP Labs. But the founders believed they could come charging back one last time and fix whatever needed fixing.

"Something's wrong at HP and it smells like bureaucracy," Packard told his friends. So in 1989, he and Hewlett embarked on a fact-finding mission. Packard in particular visited dozens of executives in Palo Alto and in the key operating divisions in Colorado, Idaho, Oregon, and Europe. At each stop, he asked two crucial questions: "What is the purpose of your department?" and "What percent of your time is spent doing that?" Frustrated local managers told Pappy about endless distractions and committee meetings that were disrupting their days and making it hard to get things done. To Packard, the remedy was obvious. Disband the committees. Stop trying to centralize HP so much. Let the operating divisions regain control of their own businesses.

Packard was seventy-seven years old now—a white-haired man who would soon need a cane to get around. But he had never shirked hard work. And if some of HP's necessary reforms required painstaking attention to detail, then, by God, Packard was going to stay on the case until things got fixed. A young financial analyst at the time remembers Packard grimly lumbering up the stairs at HP headquarters, clutching two giant binders of internal accounting data. Pappy looked like a relic from a different era, wearing a white shirt and a bolo tie just as the rest of Silicon Valley was embracing the business-casual uniform of chinos and colorful open-neck shirts. But Packard had found an immense snarl in HP's bookkeeping system, and he was determined to get it sorted out, by himself if necessary. *If you can't get the job done right, we'll damn well find someone else who can.*

How did John Young feel about all this? It depends on who you ask. The emergence of two rival accounts—in essence, two versions of the truth—may be the most striking fact of all. Publicly, Young insisted that the dismantling of committees was a good idea, and that in fact it was *his* idea. He told interviewers that as CEO, he had been quick to detect the bureaucratic buildup. It was his decision to invite Packard and Hewlett back into the company to help sort things out, he added. Once he and the founders agreed on the remedies, he led the push to make them happen. A

BusinessWeek profile of the company in 1992 embraced this version of events, portraying Young as a savvy turnaround specialist. To prove his case, Young pointed to HP's remarkable 60 percent improvement in productivity from 1989 to 1992, thanks to some hard-nosed but necessary layoffs in the instrument division, as well as a general rebound in sales. Those were vital accomplishments, and they were truly his. At a more fundamental level, though, Young had been humiliated. He had been a dynamic and effective CEO for more than a decade, but when things got ugly, it was still Dave and Bill's company. What's more, the founders wanted public recognition for their role. When *Forbes* magazine came knocking soon after the *BusinessWeek* piece, Packard and Hewlett told their version of the story, in which they were the heroes. "If something needed to be done, we just had to get in there and do it," Packard declared.

By this time the founders were in the twilight of their careers. Packard's hearing was deteriorating, and even expensive hearing aids didn't fully restore his ability to follow what others were saying. While Packard remained a formidable force in the boardroom, everyone agreed that when his eightieth birthday arrived in early 1992, it would be time to think about stepping down. (Packard finally retired as a director in September 1993, at age eighty-one.) Hewlett had faded even farther from the scene. He was a director emeritus now, having officially resigned from the board in 1987, at age seventy-four. He had suffered two heart attacks, the second of which had occurred on a ski vacation that he took in defiance of doctors' orders. And while everyone treasured Hewlett's counsel, his eyes sometimes drifted shut in board meetings.

Even so, anyone who underestimated the power of two old billionaires was making a serious mistake. The founders together still owned more than one-third of the company's stock, and they absolutely controlled HP's board of directors. Outsiders knew HP's directors as leaders of Ford Motor Company, Chevron, or other giant corporations, but just about everyone in the boardroom also was a hunting or fishing buddy of Bill and Dave. For good measure, the founders' oldest sons, David Woodley Packard and Walter Hewlett, had joined the board in 1987, at ages forty-seven and forty-three, respectively. There wasn't any aggressively independent faction in the boardroom, just men and women who were proud to play whatever advisory role the founders wanted.

In early 1992, Dave Packard decided to show colleagues that he could still crush something he didn't like. As chairman, he exercised his privilege to call a board meeting without John Young or other company executives present. "I've been traveling up and down the entire Hewlett-Packard organization," Packard began. "I've talked with our business people all over. And to a man, they've lost respect for the CEO." A boardroom coup had begun. Packard wanted John Young out. Other directors had been hearing for a while that HP didn't have the leadership that it needed; that it was being overtaken in the marketplace by younger companies like Microsoft and Intel. Now an angry Dave Packard was betting that a different CEO could revitalize HP. "We need to make a change," Packard said. "I want it very clearly understood that this is my decision, and that Bill is not responsible for this." Packard stared at his co-founder. Hewlett stared back. As fellow director Jay Keyworth remembers it, an exasperated look crept over Hewlett's face. Hewlett picked up a yellow No. 2 pencil and flipped it toward the middle of the boardroom table. As he did so, Hewlett said: "Packard, I was there years before you were on this one. And I'm totally there with you now."

Later that year, Hewlett-Packard announced that sixty-year-old John Young would be retiring after fifteen years of service as chief executive. The top job was open at HP for the first time since the 1970s—and Dave Packard knew exactly who he wanted. He would need to visit Boise, Idaho, where the biggest maverick in Hewlett-Packard's history lived. It was a long trip for a seventy-nine-year-old man who needed a cane and a hearing aid to get around. But Packard told fellow directors it would be worth it. He was sure he had identified the right successor. And he was sure his candidate would say yes.

Chapter 2

THE MAN WHO SAID NO

Afew miles southwest of downtown Boise, motorists driving along a four-lane road encounter an endless stream of used-car lots, chiropractors' offices and 7-Eleven stores. Rich people don't shop here. Powerful companies don't put their executives near here. This is Fairview Avenue, a commercial strip where the most popular dinner is a $4.49 special at Popeyes Chicken & Biscuits. On the north side of the street, just past a strip mall, is a one-story office building with aluminum siding on the outside. Stenciled red-and-white signs on the windows identify the tenants: a two-man accounting firm and a car-insurance salesman. Inside the building, blue shag carpeting is interrupted only by cheap desks and a few sickly potted plants.

Overall, the offices are as humble as the original Hewlett-Packard garage—and nearly as significant. During the final years of John Young's tenure, a soft-spoken man in running shoes and chinos moved into one of those shabby offices on Fairview Avenue and did an enormous amount to revive HP. Working largely on his own, 550 miles from the company's Palo Alto headquarters, Dick Hackborn stripped away all the clutter in everyday life and focused on two crucial questions: "What are the biggest market changes occurring in technology today?" and "How can we best make an impact?"

As he nailed down his answers, Hackborn, in the words of one admirer, "built the family fortune." As early as 1982, Hackborn could see that cheap personal computers would change people's homes and workplaces in profound ways. Over the next three years, he rallied Hewlett-Packard scientists and manufacturing specialists to create the first affordable, high-quality laser printers, so that PC users could easily print what they created. By some estimates, nearly half of HP's $18 billion stock market value in 1992 could be ascribed to Hackborn's printer business. With Dave Packard and Bill Hewlett each owning about one-sixth of the company, Hackborn had added more than a billion dollars to each of the patriarchs' personal wealth. The founders adored him. "He was almost like a son to them," director Jay Keyworth observed. "They felt he embodied everything that was important about the HP Way."

Born in Detroit in 1937, Hackborn studied electrical engineering at the University of Minnesota, where he worked part-time for Seymour Cray, the legendary pioneer of the supercomputer. Immediately after college, Hackborn joined Hewlett-Packard as part of the instrument R&D team in Palo Alto. By his own account, he spent nights and weekends partying in San Francisco, but he did well enough at work to become a top project leader in the computer division a decade later. When Hackborn got the itch to run a division himself, Packard in 1977 encouraged him to take HP's disc-drive business out of Silicon Valley and relocate it to Boise. Hackborn made the move, and in a moment of great serendipity, found himself just down the hall from another group of HP-Boise employees dabbling with the earliest laser printers. Their first machines seemed like utter losers: they were bigger than refrigerators, cost $100,000 apiece, and coated the paper with kerosene in a mad-scientist attempt to get pigments to stick. But if Hewlett-Packard could just make these machines smaller, better, and cheaper, Hackborn believed, they could become the wave of the future.

A rebel at heart, Hackborn didn't mind that most printing experts thought HP's approach was stupid. Everything Hewlett-Packard was doing involved squeezing hundreds of tiny dots together to form letters on a printed page. Experts believed this approach couldn't ever produce characters as crisp and elegant as those created by classic methods of dropping fully formed letters onto the page, one after another. But Hackborn and his Boise colleagues believed the experts were wrong. "If we could get the resolution high enough and the dots small enough," Hackborn later explained, "you could print a mighty fine character. Furthermore, you could print graphics, which the other printers couldn't do."

Determined to take the consumer market by storm, Hackborn put together a radically new business model that defied forty-five years of conventional wisdom at Hewlett-Packard. He decided to cut prices aggressively on printers, even though HP had long been a premium-price company, because he correctly believed his approach would pay off in the form of a vastly bigger market. "We give the customer more for less every year," he told his acolytes. He and HP Labs director Don Hammond negotiated to borrow crucial laser-printing technology from Canon of Japan, even though HP traditionally built everything itself, down to the knobs on some of its instruments. Simultaneously, Hackborn and his colleagues prepared to pour millions of dollars into consumer branding and alliances with mass-market retailers such as CompUSA, Circuit City, and Best Buy.

For the rest of HP's leadership, this new approach was a shocking departure from what they knew. At a managers' meeting in 1984, two mid-level executives tried to kill the laser-printer initiative, denouncing it as "a bad idea" and not in keeping with the HP Way. Packard, Hewlett, and Young, however, decided that Hackborn deserved his chance. "You're running the show," they told him. "Just make sure you're right." Before long, it was clear that Hackborn's initiative was a huge winner. Millions of people bought HP printers to go with their new computers. The clunky, costly machines of the late 1970s gave way in the mid-1980s to smaller, faster, easier-to-use models that cost just $3,500. Each year afterward, Hewlett-Packard kept improving performance and cutting prices so aggressively that rivals never caught up. In a mischievous moment, Hackborn declared that printers would be "like toilets. You'll find them in every home." The founders purred about it every time they came to Boise. As HP executive Doug Carnahan remembered it, "Dave and Bill would lean back in their chairs and say: 'Boy, we really won big with that bet on Dick!' "

In all his jobs, Hackborn talked constantly about making a contribution, the magic term that meant so much to the World War II generation. He showed a common man's touch, taking more interest in lab technicians than in famous executives. He had the same restless drive for constant improvement that Packard and Hewlett did. In fact, he encouraged people on his team to think of themselves as smarter and bolder than the bureaucrats in Palo Alto—more in touch with the *real* Hewlett-Packard than someone with a fancy title at headquarters. What's more, Hackborn appreciated the importance of HP's storytelling culture, passing wisdom to each new generation of executives, one parable at a time. Anyone who spent time with Hackborn learned that his first project at HP in the 1960s had been a total failure and that Dave Packard had taught him a vital lesson: Don't build a new machine until you know what the customers want. When Hackborn shared that story, he wasn't just flattering Packard. He was strengthening the modern-day HP by intelligent use of historical precepts.

By early 1992, the founders were so fond of Hackborn that they couldn't see his limits. Hackborn's decision to abandon his regular HP office in the late 1980s in favor of the hermit's lair in Boise wasn't just a mild eccentricity; it was his way of escaping major parts of his job. He was one of Hewlett-Packard's top officers now, a fifty-three-year-old executive vice president in charge of half the company, clearly in line to be the next CEO. Most future leaders at big companies join industry task forces, become known in government circles, and give dozens of speeches, with an eye to widening their authority. Hackborn dodged all those commitments. All he wanted was to run his businesses brilliantly and help develop young leaders within his team. Hackborn avoided public speaking opportunities and routinely sent a more gregarious subordinate, Ray Smelek, instead. Hackborn also skipped many of John Young's management meetings in Palo Alto, explaining that severe earaches made it impossible for him to travel. That excuse brought squeals of delight from colleagues in Boise, who didn't like Young's meetings, either. It infuriated Young, who felt he was being played for a fool.

Within the printer business, people revered Hackborn. He nudged younger people to do mightier work than they had ever expected, sometimes just by asking a single, prophetic question. "Why shouldn't HP own one hundred percent of the scanner market?" he wondered out loud, at a time when the company didn't even make scanners. Protégés listened, nodded, and set out to conquer the scanner business. In their eyes, anyone smart enough to double HP's stock-market value needn't bother with corporate formalities. Hackborn could work on the moon for all they cared. But some of HP's top executives in Palo Alto had a tougher time making peace with Hackborn's habits. "He was a wonderful business manager and a great strategist," one of them remarked. "But beyond that, he contributed nothing to the organization. He didn't like to get his hands dirty in the busy work of the corporation. The rest of us took care of all the crap for him."

The man who probed deepest into Hackborn's psyche was Michael Maccoby, author of a best-selling business book released in 1977 called *The Gamesman*. For seven years, Maccoby roamed around Hewlett-Packard and other companies, interviewing 250 people about their business goals, their innermost fears, and their moral values. Maccoby quickly pegged many HP employees as craftsmen: diligent workers of modest imagination. When he got to Hackborn, Maccoby was fascinated by a much more complex personality. Starting in 1970, Maccoby watched Hackborn's career unfold, asking all the while about his father, his marriage, and his attitudes toward money. What ultimately emerged was a stunningly candid fifty-six-page profile of Hackborn as the title character in *The Gamesman*, masked by the pseudonym Jack Wakefield.

Most of the profile was enormously positive, calling Hackborn "one of the most creative and life-loving of the successful young managers we interviewed." But an early paragraph hinted at something darker. "Jack Wakefield looks like Tom Sawyer grown up," Maccoby wrote. "He is extremely likable and seems open, yet one always feels in danger of being tricked or slightly conned. He is very seductive. He seems gregarious, yet when one knows him better, he is introverted and a little lonely. Like the typical gamesman, he is a collection of seeming paradoxes. He is idealistic, yet shrewd and pragmatic; cooperative, yet highly competitive; enthusiastic, yet detached; earnest, yet evasive."

In other parts of the profile, Hackborn seemed weirdly uneasy with where a corporate career might take him. He admitted to constantly toying with the idea of leaving HP, perhaps to become an environmental lawyer or even a dentist. Hackborn insisted in the early 1970s that he had no interest in being rich or even in rising to be a corporate vice president. Top executives at HP weren't happy people, he observed. Maccoby wrote down every word but figured that Hackborn's talent and verve would propel him far higher than the young manager expected. Reminiscing much later about the time he spent getting to know Hackborn, Maccoby said, "I told him, 'You're going to be CEO of Hewlett-Packard some day.' "

In the spring of 1992, Hackborn's moment arrived. Packard appeared in Idaho to offer the chairmanship, presidency, and CEO title to Hackborn in one glorious package. Dazzled by the prospect, Hackborn spent a week or two imagining himself in command. He told his buddy Ray Smelek to get ready for a move to Palo Alto as a key member of the Hackborn team. Then, abruptly, Hackborn reconsidered. Modern-day CEOs, he realized, didn't just set a company's strategic direction. They were expected to testify in Washington, charm the media, brief Wall Street analysts, and meet foreign heads of state. That half of the job made him shudder. He couldn't do it.

Hackborn phoned Young several times to talk about his qualms. Their memories of those calls differ, but both agree that Hackborn was struggling to reconcile the top job's demands with an awareness of his own personality. They explored a compromise in which Hackborn would become CEO but Young would stay on as chairman and serve as the public face of Hewlett-Packard. Both men were intrigued by that idea, but they knew it could happen only if Packard approved. It didn't take long for them to realize that Packard didn't like it.

On May 13, 1992, Hackborn wrote Packard a three-page letter turning down the job offer. It was an enormous honor to be asked, but Hackborn said he would rather stay in Idaho and retire soon, at age fifty-five. Boise was home. In the third paragraph of the letter, Hackborn added: "I feel tired and burned out." He sent a copy to Young, who told him: "Fine. You understand yourself very well. You're going to make a much more important contribution to the company and to your own health and happiness by doing a great job at what you're doing."

Dave Packard wasn't about to give up. His company was ailing, and he viewed Hackborn as the savior. After getting that letter, Packard flew to Boise a second time, with Hewlett in tow. Sitting in Hackborn's living room, Packard made an astonishing—and rash—offer. If it meant the difference between landing Hackborn or not, Packard said, he was prepared to move HP's headquarters to Boise. That would mean uprooting a Palo Alto institution and transferring key executives to Idaho, so Hackborn could be surrounded by the people he needed to do his new job. Hewlett-Packard would turn its back on Silicon Valley after decades of nurturing California's high-tech boom and being nurtured by it. But Packard wanted Hackborn's assent that badly.

Now Hackborn was caught in an even worse bind. Boise wasn't just a geographic location to him; it was a spiritual sanctuary, with all the privacy he craved. He could hike in the mountains, go quietly to a restaurant, or do anything else he wanted without attracting stares. He and his wife could help their two children through the stormiest parts of adolescence, without needing to justify anything to anyone. Moving HP's headquarters to Boise would be violently disruptive to the company and wouldn't really solve anything. Bill Hewlett sensed this and pulled back. If something else was bothering Hackborn, there was no need to pry. Hewlett left Boise with a pragmatic statement that closed the matter in his mind: "For a job like this, you shouldn't have to talk someone into it."

Dave Packard stayed at Hackborn's house for three hours, trying to win a test of wills. At some level, Pappy must have been angry and bitterly hurt that his protégé would turn down the greatest prize a company founder could offer. Stories circulated for years afterward that Hackborn tried to craft one last compromise, perhaps by becoming chairman but letting someone else be CEO. That would let him steer Hewlett-Packard while keeping his cherished low profile to the world. According to these accounts, Packard said no. If Hackborn didn't want full leadership of the company, another executive would get the chance.

At some point, the two men finally understood each other. "Dave realized that if he pushed any farther, he might destroy a man," HP director Jay Keyworth later said. Packard did invite Hackborn to join the HP board so that the whole company could benefit from his counsel in some form. Hackborn gladly accepted. Eventually, the patriarch let things rest with a gracious gesture that became a face-saving resolution for everyone. On his last visit to Boise, as Packard got ready to leave, he stopped to look at the beautiful wooded landscape just outside Hackborn's home. "I can see why you like to live here," Packard said. "If I were living here, too, I wouldn't want to move."

Now Packard needed to entrust leadership of the company to someone else. Wasting little time, he offered the CEO job to Lew Platt, the company's fifty-one-year-old head of computer systems. Platt couldn't match Hackborn's deep strategic insights—in fact, hardly anyone in America could. But after the emotional roller coaster of negotiating with Hackborn, everyone was relieved to have an alternative as solid and dependable as Platt. He was a stocky, baldish man who struck one writer as looking "more like your favorite bowling buddy" than the head of a 100,000-employee enterprise. But Platt had impeccable credentials: a mechanical engineering degree from Cornell, an MBA from Wharton, and twenty-six years of steady advancement at HP. On his way up the corporate ladder, Platt had supervised everything from the janitors to the medical-instrument divisions. He faithfully attended all of Young's meetings. Most important, Platt wanted the job, and people at all levels of the company felt comfortable with him.

On July 16, 1992, Hewlett-Packard announced that Young would retire in November and that Platt would succeed him. Eager to quiet the rumor mill and get Platt off to the best possible start, everyone in a position of prominence now declared that this was the right choice—and in fact had really been the only choice all along. Hackborn made his way to Palo Alto to congratulate Platt in person. "It was very sincere and very cordial," Platt later recalled. Young was even more generous. He put aside any feelings of bitterness about his ouster and took Platt under his wing for the transition period, introducing the new boss to important senators in Washington and to key customers such as Jack Welch, the head of General Electric.

Dave Packard offered the new CEO some pointers, too, focusing mostly on what was happening to the HP Way. In private talks, Packard said he worried that the company's values were being endangered by secrecy and distrust, which were undermining employees' respect for top management. If Platt wanted to be a great CEO, Packard had one piece of advice: "Pay attention to the people. Get our people believing in the company again."

With Packard's apparent blessing, Platt decided to become known as the man crusading to make Hewlett-Packard a wonderful place to work. Platt had already decided to govern HP's basic businesses with a looser hand than Young had favored. That seemed wise. The instrument, computer, and printing divisions were following such different strategies that there wasn't any obvious way to yoke them together. All the same, Platt needed an overriding mission that would define his time in office. Employee harmony would be his cause. Within his first year in office, Platt required HP's top executives to get diversity training, so they could relate better to black, Asian, Latino, gay, and disabled employees. He sent out memos telling employees that "work/life issues are a top priority." He opened exciting career tracks for parents with small children, letting two people share high-powered jobs by each working thirty hours a week. Together, these managers could get the job done and still have plenty of time at home to help raise their families. Those initiatives won wide admiration inside and outside the company. Throughout Platt's tenure, *Working Mother* magazine hailed HP as one of the best places to work in America.

When outsiders chided him for being too nice and losing track of business priorities, Platt bristled. "People describe this as soft, as if it didn't have any relation to business performance," he told one interviewer. "But I think valuing your employees pays off on the bottom line." Platt could offer his own life story as proof. In 1981, his first wife died of a brain tumor. For the next two years, he tried to be a fast-track executive during the day and a single parent in the evening. After work, instead of socializing with adults or preparing for the next day's meeting, he pushed a grocery cart through a supermarket, looking for simple meals for himself and his two preteen daughters. "Here I was, a white male, who had been doing really well at HP," he later recalled. "I suddenly was thrust into a different role." Platt came away from that experience with a lifelong respect for working parents' juggling act and a conviction that if Hewlett-Packard could help out, everyone would benefit.

Three years into his tenure as CEO, it looked as if Lew Platt had found the winning formula. The great technology boom of the 1990s was under way, and Hewlett-Packard was enjoying its full share of prosperity. Revenue was surging more than 20 percent a year, and HP's stock was climbing even faster. The computer divisions finally overtook Digital Equipment to become the No. 2 computer makers in the United States, behind only IBM. The laser-printer business kept its leading role in the workplace, and cheaper inkjet printers—with full-color capability—became must-have items for home offices. Awards flowed in: Platt was named Technology Leader of the Year in 1994 by *Industry Week* and Hewlett-Packard was named Top Corporate Performer of 1995 by *Forbes*. Platt professed to be wary, telling people that "it would be quite easy for us to bask in the glow too long." But he had every right to believe that his gentle approach was working perfectly.

On his visits to HP facilities worldwide, Platt took a far milder approach than his predecessors, talking mostly about corporate values. "In the HP environment, you really can't order people to do anything," he told one interviewer. "As CEO, my job is to encourage people to work together." He carried on the simple shirtsleeves culture that had defined Packard and Hewlett in their prime. Platt joined lower-ranking employees for lunch in the cafeteria most days, munching on chicken strips and French fries. He drove the standard company car, a Ford Taurus, and flew coach class on commercial carriers, rather than letting himself be cosseted in the luxuries of limousines, executive dining rooms, and private jets. Rank-and-file employees loved him for that, and they gave him standing ovations when he came to visit.

But some senior executives began to chafe. Platt wasn't making tough decisions, they noticed. On something as basic as installing business-process software, Platt let five divisions pick five slightly different versions of the same SAP package. Once the installations were complete, there wasn't any way to standardize. Hewlett-Packard would be stuck forever with incompatible versions across its businesses, pushing up operating costs and making it harder to monitor activities across the entire company. One manager stormed into Platt's office, upset about this lack of control. "Lew," he said, "you need to do something about this. Make them all use the same version. Act presidential!" By this manager's recollection, Platt turned red and declared, "I'm not prepared to do that. Meeting over."

In the hallways of Hewlett-Packard, people talked as much as ever about being true to the HP Way. But somehow, a weird inversion had taken place. Packard's original version of the HP Way had been predicated on strong profitability—"the objective that makes all the other objectives possible." Now explicit financial success had been shunted to the back of the pack. Much of the company's energy was going into the softer values:

community service, respect for the individual, and the creation of a great workplace. There wasn't anything wrong with those values; in the right setting, they were enormously admirable. But they couldn't single-handedly guide a successful company for long. The high-tech sector was too cutthroat to allow any company, even Hewlett-Packard, to coast on its past successes.

Years later, many people would blame Lew Platt for letting HP get soft. But the changing nature of Dave Packard himself may have made the biggest difference. Packard's business genius earlier in his career made him one of the world's richest people in his eighties. He didn't need more money; he needed a way to redirect it to the betterment of society. He began to regard philanthropy as his final mission, and being Dave Packard, he carried it out with awesome effectiveness. At HP, people who had never known The Mean One now told stories about the warmhearted founder who covered employees' catastrophic medical bills from his own pocket when $500,000 of company-sponsored insurance wasn't enough. Long past the age at which he could fathom every technical twist in HP's markets, Packard somehow found out about the widowed employee who had fallen behind on her mortgage payments and was on the verge of selling her house at a distress price. Even though a fast-rising HP executive was about to buy the place, Packard decided that this wasn't right. He paid off the woman's mortgage and left the young hotshot to find a bargain somewhere else. Such stories became legends in their own right, reshaping the corporate culture so that everyone tried to emulate the conduct of a kindly old man.

On March 26, 1996, Dave Packard died of pneumonia at age eighty-three. Even though most employees knew his end was near, people at Hewlett-Packard still burst into tears. Directors were too distraught to hold their regular board meeting that week; they nearly canceled the session but decided instead just to sit in the boardroom and pay tribute to Packard's life. Mourners flocked to Stanford University's Memorial Church soon after his death for an upbeat, moving memorial service. Speakers included HP board member Condoleezza Rice, former Secretary of State George Shultz, and Packard's son, David Woodley Packard. It was the son's finest hour. For much of his life, the younger Packard had been stubbornly charting his own course, becoming a professor of ancient Greek, opening a revival movie theater, and bewildering his famous father all along the way. But on this afternoon, David Woodley Packard was a warm, loving son and a gracious host, paying tribute to the father he admired. Lew Platt spoke partway through the service and praised Packard as "our closest personal experience to greatness."

The next Monday, Platt was back at his desk at HP, with no choice but to begin the company's post-Packard era. Problems abounded, starting with HP's puzzling inability to conquer big new markets anymore. Scientists in HP Labs kept finding exciting prospects, but some projects, like screen-capture printers for video, never amounted to much. Others, like handheld computers, eventually became giant winners for other companies, but HP's versions never caught on with customers. Platt had let HP become so decentralized and fragmented that even when someone had a great idea, "there never was much wood behind the arrow," as one insider put it. It had been a long time since the last big triumphs: Dick Hackborn's laser and inkjet printers of the mid-1980s. Employees knew it, and so did Wall Street analysts.

When pressed, Platt pointed to the personal-computer division's rapid growth as his biggest business achievement. Indeed, HP's market share was climbing steadily. The company had nearly abandoned the PC market before Platt took over; by early 1996, it had climbed to become the sixth-largest shipper of PCs in the United States, surpassing Dell Computer for the next few years. More growth lay ahead, with Hewlett-Packard at one point breaking into the ranks of the top three producers, behind industry leader Compaq Computer. But Hewlett-Packard's profit record in the PC business was erratic. "Making money in this business is like trying to land a man on the moon," HP executive Webb McKinney lamented in 1996. Winning in the PC industry required brutally good operating skills. HP just wasn't that tough-minded anymore.

A myth grew up that Hewlett-Packard hadn't ever had layoffs. That wasn't true; Packard had sacked workers in 1946, and Young had cut the payroll decisively in 1989. The company did regard layoffs as a last resort, and even when it shut down production lines, it tried to find work for idled employees elsewhere. But Platt tried so hard to reassure employees about their job security that many people came to regard a spot on the HP payroll as something akin to a safe, undemanding civil-service career. "People could get dismal performance ratings for four or five years in a row," recalled Gary Fazzino, who ultimately became head of the company's government and public-affairs group. "It was almost as difficult to get rid of them as it was to get rid of a tenured teacher. People felt they were owed lifetime employment."

People who saw Hewlett-Packard in action began rolling their eyes at the company's lack of direction. When California legislators considered a bill to tighten emissions regulations on computer terminals, one branch of HP sent lobbyists to Sacramento to urge passage of the bill. Another HP delegation argued against it. Legislators snickered at the company that lobbied politicians twice and thereby canceled its own message. At one point, Hewlett-Packard had 12 percent of its employees telecommuting from home, a figure seven times higher than industry averages. Some of them may have been extremely productive, but when PBS did a documentary on HP's friendly work policies, it ended up with footage of an HP employee playing the guitar inside his home office, during a "break" from his company job.

Ultimately, employees were taking advantage of Platt's gentle, caring ways. The HP Way had worked brilliantly for the World War II generation, which was filled with people who truly wanted to contribute to a bigger goal. But most of the company's employees by this time had grown up in the more self-centered 1960s, 1970s, or 1980s. It was easy for them to regard HP as nothing more than an endless cookie jar, dispensing whatever resources employees needed to pursue their favorite interests. Increasingly, HP was being defined by the intensity of its recycling program, its community activism, and its after-hours orchestra, rather than by a commitment to win brilliantly and relentlessly in the business arena, year after year.

On one occasion in 1997, Platt was a guest of honor at a CEO lunch in Denver. He tried to explain Hewlett-Packard's unique approach to a tablemate, Malik Hasan, head of a fast-growing health plan with $9 billion in revenue. Platt talked with pride about how much he delegated, and how he used trips like these to pop into the local facilities, mingle with workers, and give them friendly reassurances that they were part of the big HP family. "I'm the glue that holds things together," Platt said. It was a popular message within HP, but it sounded ridiculous to Dr. Hasan. When he visited regional offices, he grabbed the complaint log, medical records, and other vital documents. He grilled local managers on what they were doing wrong and how they planned to fix it. That was how hard-charging executives built businesses in the 1990s. Thinking about Platt's approach, Dr. Hasan told himself, *If I'm just the glue, division managers will think that they're just the glue, too. Nothing will get done.* He went home and thought about selling Hewlett-Packard stock short, a way of betting that the price would drop.

By early 1998, a gold-rush mentality had taken hold in the rest of Silicon Valley. Startups such as Netscape Communications now had stock-market values in the billions of dollars, even though they hadn't yet turned a profit. Established high-tech companies such as Sun Microsystems and Intel were repositioning themselves as providing the essential building blocks for everyone else's Internet strategy. High-tech stocks were leaping as much as 10 percent a day, and venture capitalist John Doerr was about to make his famous pronouncement that Silicon Valley was enjoying "the greatest-ever legal creation of wealth in the history of the world." Everyone had a delicious piece of the action—except Hewlett-Packard.

Now Dick Hackborn's voice began to be heard again, in blunt, compelling terms that commanded other directors' respect. HP was missing the Internet, he argued. Its software developers hadn't grasped the importance of the World Wide Web; its computer strategy showed limited awareness of the Internet's impact, and the company's own Web site was feeble. He got no joy out of criticizing HP, but someone had to speak the truth. If people wanted to know how to do it right, Hackborn suggested, they should look seven hundred miles north, to the stunning example being set by Microsoft chairman and founder Bill Gates. For the past four years, Hackborn had been a Microsoft director while continuing to serve on the HP board. Hackborn had watched admiringly in 1995 as Gates reoriented his entire company around the Internet. That took guts, Hackborn believed. That was a performance worthy of Dave Packard: stubborn, controlling, and just plain right. Hackborn had always regarded Hewlett-Packard as the most important commitment in his life beyond his family. But with exasperation in his voice, he had started telling friends, "I certainly feel more effective on the Microsoft board."

Matters came to a head when HP's directors met to talk about the company's Internet strategy. On the second day of the board meeting, Hackborn and fellow director Jay Keyworth pressed Platt for examples of HP's best Internet initiatives in the works. The answers disappointed them. As Keyworth remembered it, Platt looked at several lower-ranking executives in the boardroom and said, "It's up to you guys to tell me."

More setbacks followed. HP's executive vice president in charge of computers and printers, Rick Belluzzo, announced in early 1998 that he was quitting to become CEO of a much smaller company, Silicon Graphics. In an obvious slap at Platt, Belluzzo told *The Wall Street Journal* that he saw the new job as a chance "to implement more change and to provide more leadership." In case anyone missed the point, Belluzzo told *Business-Week* a few months later: "I look at HP as being in maintenance mode. HP has got tremendous potential, people, technology, and a great brand, but there's something missing that would move the company to the next level."

Platt was stunned. "You could have knocked me over with a feather when Rick said he was leaving," he later remarked. He had promoted Belluzzo fast, giving him control of 80 percent of HP's businesses at age forty-four. Not only that, Platt had told directors that Belluzzo was the likely next CEO at some point. The two men hadn't been getting along especially well during Belluzzo's last few months at the company, and Platt was concerned that Belluzzo was "bringing a lot of anger into the office" because of personal tensions that had nothing to do with Hewlett-Packard. But Platt had believed all those issues were fixable.

Directors weren't happy about this turn of events. "Maybe Rick had what it took to be CEO of Hewlett-Packard, and maybe he didn't," one director later said. "But we shouldn't have found out about him leaving only when it was a fait accompli." Adding to the board's chagrin, Platt hadn't developed any other executives on his team to the point that they could be considered credible successors anytime soon. Especially indignant was Dick Hackborn, who had long regarded Belluzzo as a rising star. Back in the early 1990s, when Belluzzo lived in Boise, he was a frequent visitor to the shabby little office on Fairview Avenue. Belluzzo and Hackborn would go out for three-hour lunches at a Marie Callender's pie shop down the road, munching on French dip sandwiches and plotting ways to push HP to new heights. When Hackborn retired in 1993, he had offered Platt some friendly guidance about working with Belluzzo. "He's extremely good at driving change, but he needs support," Hackborn said. "If you disagree on something, let him know early and the two of you can work it out. Once you do that, he'll work miracles for you." Letting Belluzzo slip away, Hackborn believed, was a major loss.

All through 1998, Hewlett-Packard was mired in its own private slowdown, even as competitors enjoyed their biggest boom years ever. The company's sales advanced only 9 percent, one of HP's worst showings in history. Computer-stock investors gave up and switched their bets to two smaller, faster-growing rivals, Sun Microsystems and Dell Computer. Both those upstarts surpassed HP in stock-market valuation in 1998, even though they had less than half the revenue and far-shorter operating histories. Sun did it with an explosively fast growth rate and a brilliant Internet-oriented strategy, capped by the brash slogan "We put the dot in dot-com." Dell did it with a much smarter way to sell personal computers, getting rid of middlemen in favor of direct phone, catalog, and Web site links to its customers, which cut costs and improved customer satisfaction. HP couldn't figure out an effective response, and its stock barely budged in the midst of a legendary bull market. Wall Street analysts began portraying HP as a geezer, treating its sixty years of history as an outright liability. If they needed any encouragement, Sun's brash CEO, Scott McNealy, egged them on. "Sun was kind of in-your-face in public," Platt later recalled. "You competed on performance with them. If you fell very far behind, you were going to get your butt kicked around the block."

HP needed to get moving in a hurry, and Platt did his best to bark out tougher orders. At the start of a weekend managers' meeting in Monterey, California, in early 1998, he angrily pointed out that the company had fallen short of Wall Street's profit expectations for five quarters in a row. Platt asked all two hundred attendees to write down two things they planned to do differently by the following Monday. Platt reviewed their answers that evening and came out even angrier the next day. "You guys just don't get it, do you?" he snapped. "I expect more coherent plans from you moving forward." It was a brave outburst on his part, but it came too late to change things. Six years of nurturing the softer side of HP had left employees and managers unwilling to take any sudden steps until everyone had talked things over and decided as a group that they liked the new direction. "Terminal niceness" had set in. In that environment, Platt might as well have tried to shoo seagulls from the coastal rocks outside the conference center. He could create a momentary flutter, but he couldn't really change anything.

Anxious to find some way to revitalize the company, Platt seized on the idea of splitting Hewlett-Packard in two. From a personal standpoint, he was being run ragged by the demands of competing with Sun and Dell. In addition, he was expected to keep an eye on a dozen smaller markets—ranging from microchip design to life sciences—that mattered to the company's instrument business. Why not cleave off the 40,000 employees who constituted the instrument division and let them find their own way as part of a new, stand-alone company with its own chief executive? The remaining 85,000 HP employees would reassemble as part of a leaner outfit, tightly focused on computers and printers. Instead of being one big, slow-moving company, HP might turn into two nimbler, faster-paced outfits, each of which could excel in its own way. The more Platt thought about the idea, the more he liked it. "It made sense for so many reasons," he later said. He engaged management consultants at McKinsey & Company to work through the details, and they came back to him upbeat as well. Not only did the split have great long-term potential, it might provide an instant pop to HP's stock price. Investors were bound to see a comparison with AT&T, which had created a stock-market darling in 1996 by breaking off some of the oldest parts of the phone company and renaming them Lucent Technologies.

Add it all up, and Platt saw nothing but opportunity. Partway through 1998, he presented his idea to a generally receptive HP board. Some directors, like Bill Hewlett's son Walter, had been tinkering with their own thoughts about a possible spinoff. Others, like Dick Hackborn, Jay Keyworth, and Sam Ginn, a savvy telecom executive, saw the industrial logic behind the deal quite quickly. The most aggressive dissenter was Dave Packard's son, David Woodley Packard, who believed that the entire enterprise would suffer if the bulk of the company were separated from the sixty-year heritage of the instrument business. His indignation boiled over when told that the Hewlett-Packard name would stay with the computer and printer business, where it had great value in consumers' eyes. In board meetings, David Woodley Packard kept pointing to the instrument business and saying, "That's the real HP! That's where the name ought to stay." Unable to persuade anyone, David Woodley Packard decided to relinquish his directorship after twelve years of board service. No one made any effort to stop him.*

Although Platt didn't explicitly say so, his initial presentation of the spinoff plan appeared to envision having him stay on as chief executive of the slimmed-down Hewlett-Packard, while Ned Barnholt, head of the instrument business, would become CEO of the breakaway company. At a board meeting in January 1999 at the Garden Court Hotel in Palo Alto, however, directors decided that they had other plans. All the stagnation issues that had bothered them a year earlier had grown worse. The company had now missed Wall Street's profit expectations for nine consecutive quarters. Revenue in the first quarter of fiscal 1999 had grown just 1 percent. The company's stock-market performance had gone from troubling to pathetic. Director Jay Keyworth handed out a chart of recent share-price trends for twenty major high-tech companies. HP ranked dead last. Directors were openly asking: Do we have the right leadership at the top of HP?

Unwittingly, Lew Platt already had given his boardroom colleagues all the ammunition they needed to build a case against him. Shortly after

---

* Directors offered David Woodley Packard a retirement dinner in his honor, but he declined. As a farewell present, board members tracked down a $920 rare edition of a famous play that they thought David Woodley Packard might enjoy. It was Shakespeare's *Hamlet*.

Rick Belluzzo's departure, Platt had asked a well-known industrial psychologist, Richard Hagberg, to conduct in-depth personal assessments of HP's leadership team. "We used him to help members of the team, myself included, understand ourselves better and see if we could build a team that had better chemistry," Platt recalled. Hagberg threw himself into the project with enormous energy, canvassing top executives about what they thought of one another and administering elaborate personality tests. Pencils in hand, executives spent two hours marking "true" or "false" such statements as "I would never spend my money on a steam bath" and "If someone accidentally burned me with his cigarette, I would certainly mention it to him."

Platt participated in the full Hagberg review—and then let board members see the results. The spectacle saddened and slightly nauseated one of Platt's remaining supporters on the HP board. The profile, in one director's words, portrayed Platt as "an excellent manager, but not a great leader." Board members talked at length about the profile, which put into words some of their long-simmering concerns. There was a bluntness about the printed report that took the conversation beyond half-expressed qualms and into the realm of direct criticisms that demanded immediate attention. As those conversations played out in various settings, one board member recalls, "Some of the directors made Lew Platt start to doubt himself."

Finally, at the Garden Court board meeting, matters came to a head. Jack Brigham, HP's general counsel and secretary to the board at the time, recalled that longtime director John Fery, the chairman of Boise-Cascade, took Lew Platt aside and told him that it would be best if HP looked for a new chief executive to run the main company after the instrument business was spun off. "Everything was very politely expressed, but it was clear the other directors weren't sold on Lew," Brigham later said. As conversations continued, Brigham realized that the director most outspoken about Lew Platt's performance was Dick Hackborn.

Platt was jolted at first. He proposed that if other directors didn't want him staying on as chief executive, perhaps he could give up that title and remain simply as chairman. The head of HP's services business, forty-year-old Ann Livermore, might make a good new CEO, he suggested. But other directors weren't buying. They had soured on Platt's ability to set the company's strategic direction, and they believed that keeping him as chairman wouldn't fix that problem. Besides, while Livermore was seen as an executive with great potential, few directors thought she was ready to command the entire company.

Eventually, Platt acknowledged the board's will. "I could see pretty well by then what was going on," he later said. "Why fight it? I was going to be out of there in a year anyway, once the split was complete. So, I resolved, this would be a good time to make the transition." In early March 1999, HP announced that it would be splitting in two. Ned Barnholt indeed was tapped to be CEO of the instrument spin-off, ultimately renamed Agilent Technologies. Hewlett-Packard itself would look for a new chief executive, and for the first time ever, it would entertain candidates from other companies. Platt, in a press release, tried to make everything sound smooth and orderly. "I'm approaching my fifty-eighth birthday," he said, "so it's an appropriate time to look for a successor." Just as he hoped, Hewlett-Packard's stock jumped on the breakup news. It finished the day at $68.63, up $2.75 a share.

Now, directors' attention turned to their most exciting challenge of the 1990s—picking a radically different sort of leader for Hewlett-Packard. In a matter of days, a nationwide hunt could begin in earnest. But first, the HP board needed to do three things. It needed to hire an executive-search firm to beat the bushes for candidates and run the interview process. It needed to decide which three or four directors would sit on the search committee that would make most of the key decisions. And it needed to write up confidential job specifications, so that insiders all knew what type of person they were seeking.

Acting quickly, the HP directors hired Jeff Christian, head of Cleveland-based Christian & Timbers, to handle the search. They created a four-person search committee, chaired by Sam Ginn, head of the regular nominating committee. John Fery of Boise-Cascade would join him; his many years of big-company experience were seen as a boon. The two most important slots on the search committee would be filled by old-time rivals for the CEO job at the start of the decade: Lew Platt and Dick Hackborn. Platt asked to be on the committee, and other directors decided that was fine. He had come to terms with his own departure admirably well, and he seemed like the best person to do first-round interviews with candidates, checking out their basic grasp of HP's place in the world. Hackborn hadn't campaigned to be on the committee, but other directors implored him to join it. Of the fourteen board members, he had the deepest understanding of HP's strategic challenges and opportunities. Seven years earlier, Hackborn had shaped Hewlett-Packard's destiny by walking away from the CEO's job. Now he would chart the company's course a second time by steering someone else—most likely an outsider—into command.

The search was almost ready to begin. First, though, Jeff Christian and the four committee members needed to sketch out their dream candidate. Did they want someone from the computer industry, someone with all the traditional skills that had defined HP? For a few days that seemed like the right path. Then, almost in unison, everyone on the search panel started talking about a much bolder approach. "What about a great athlete?" Christian asked. All four directors on the search committee picked up on that notion.

Before long, Christian had a new set of specifications. Detailed computer-industry expertise wasn't quite so critical anymore. Instead, he was tasked to find "an incredible leader." He could look at people with a much wider assortment of backgrounds, as long as he found someone who understood large, complex organizations, who was a leading-edge thinker about new technology, and who could shore up HP's brand in the market-place. Find someone who can maintain the important aspects of the company's culture while creating a higher sense of urgency, Christian was told. Find someone who can drive the company higher and take advantage of the new opportunities with the Internet. It was an ambitious wish list, and Lew Platt had one more request. He wanted someone with star power: someone who could dazzle the world in ways that would make HP's rivals jealous.

"All other things being equal," Platt declared, "you'd like to find someone who is a bit more of a media personality. That's part of the game these days."

Chapter 3

GIVE ME A CHANCE!

In the mid-1990s, just as Hewlett-Packard was growing old and tired, the American public became transfixed by a belief that the high-tech boom was doing much more than cranking out faster and more powerful gadgets. Something called "The New Economy" was radically reshaping the most basic rules of business, pundits argued. Every time anyone bought a personal computer, used a cell phone, or logged onto the Internet, he or she was stepping into an awesome future in which a few strategic twists in the high-tech sector were about to redefine every aspect of business. Rapidly falling prices for computing power and phone service would usher consumers into a world of unimaginable plenty. Price inflation and scarcity would disappear for good. Mass adoption of Netscape's Internet browser and Hotmail's free e-mail service would foreshadow a new era in which the most brilliant tycoons succeeded by making their merchandise free. The interconnections that made e-mail and fax machines so appealing would somehow transform the roles of cars, farms, steel, and oil companies before long. *Wired* magazine editor Kevin Kelly declared in 1997 that network behavior would become "the entire economy."

For many of HP's leaders, such messages were as jarring as Times Square to an Amish farmer. Hewlett-Packard was a company of literal-minded engineers; it wasn't a hotbed of transformational euphoria. But as New Economy evangelists spread their gospel throughout the United States and the world, two profound changes occurred that Hewlett-Packard couldn't ignore. In the stock market, investors embraced even the zaniest New Economy theories as prophecies that were sure to come true. Old-fashioned yardsticks of profitability and balance-sheet stability were discarded as obsolete. Companies that "got" the New Economy were seen as awesome investments, no matter how high their stocks climbed. Companies that couldn't tell a compelling New Economy story about their own business were dismissed as dinosaurs. And as financial fates diverged so sharply, companies recast their leadership ranks. They promoted their best storytellers and advocates—regarding them as the natural leaders of this exuberant new age. Charismatic optimism mattered every bit as much as technical expertise—maybe even more so. The national role models were chief executives such as Steve Case at America Online and John Chambers at Cisco Systems: salesmen and marketers by training, who knew how to make their company's offerings seem irresistible.

If Carly Fiorina hadn't existed, the New Economy would have needed to invent her. She was one of the brightest faces in telecom, savvy, personable, and marvelously persuasive. Her business cards in the late 1990s identified her as a top executive at Lucent Technologies, maker of the CBX 500 Multiservice WAN switch and other highly technical products. But she didn't really sell phone switches. She sold panoramic stories of hope and progress. She was a striver in the best sense of the word, improving her own life year by year and sharing her ebullience with customers, colleagues, and bosses. Even Ludwig van Beethoven was put to work on her behalf. As she explained to one interviewer: "His music is passionate and tormented. You can hear him struggle and ultimately achieve what he's after."

Born in Austin, Texas, in 1954, Cara Carleton Sneed grew up in a family that saw the dramatic potential in almost everything. (The nickname "Carly" emerged in college; the surname Fiorina didn't take hold until her second marriage, in 1985.) Her mother, Madelon Juergens Sneed, was a portrait artist who sketched her daughter from age four onward. Her father, Joseph T. Sneed III, was a constitutional law scholar who dashed off to Ghana in the late 1960s to become one of the world's great experts on the Ghanaian constitution. His three children tagged along as part of a whirlwind series of travels that caused them to attend five different schools on three continents while growing up. "You learn to be pretty adaptive," Fiorina later said. "I was perennially the outsider, but I got to the point where it didn't scare me anymore."

Business was slow to beckon. At Stanford University, Carly Fiorina majored in medieval history. Her favorite class, taught by a rambunctious young professor just two years out of graduate school, involved reading hundreds of pages a week of religious writings from the Middle Ages— and then distilling those tracts into two-page, single-spaced papers. "It rendered all the fat out of a body of ideas, boiling it down to the very essence of its meaning," Fiorina later said. Her direct knowledge of Aquinas, Bacon, and Abelard would come in handy only very intermittently in the rest of her life, but the process of distillation proved invaluable. Later on, Fiorina would establish herself as one of corporate America's leading sloganeers, coining memorable phrases by the hour.

Nudged by her father to become a lawyer, Fiorina spent one semester at UCLA Law School. "It left me cold," she later said. "I had a blinding headache every day." Before long, she dropped out and drifted for a year or two. She worked as a receptionist at a small real-estate firm; she taught English in Italy; she made a disappointing first marriage. In 1978, she enrolled in business school at the University of Maryland, still not sure where she was headed.

Two years later, she got a job as a management trainee at AT&T. Her first assignment was to sell long-distance service and phone equipment to Native American tribes. It was a tough, unglamorous task, and her next few assignments weren't any easier. But she was determined enough to succeed that she stayed up until 3 A.M. some nights, drafting weekly budgets at her kitchen table. By the early 1990s, Fiorina was a vice president at AT&T, with her own fan club. "Carly was professional and elegant," public-relations manager Kathy Fitzgerald recalled. "Her clothes were at the high end of style: a very form-fitting black top, a very stylish skirt. She wasn't flirtatious, but she had an enticing personality. It was just incredible to have a female executive who was that attractive, that young, that effective . . . and that smart."

Customers liked her, too, especially when Fiorina stepped in to mend problems that weren't of her creation. In the early 1990s, Ameritech executive Bob Knowling was in charge of downtown phone service for Chicago. He grew furious at AT&T for a series of multihour phone-switch outages and decided to "raise holy hell with Carly," knowing that she was three levels up the chain of command at AT&T. She vowed to get the problems fixed fast, telling him, "Something is wrong in the relationship when this is the first call that I get from such an important client like you." Knowling was flattered—and disarmed. The next day, Fiorina flew out to Chicago, heard him out in more detail, and made rapid changes in the way AT&T handled the Ameritech account. From that point onward, AT&T came through for him. As Knowling later put it, "Carly had done some incredible magic."

In September 1995, Fiorina began the project that ultimately made her famous: taking Lucent Technologies public. The 120,000-employee phone-equipment business was being spun off from AT&T. A handful of top executives needed to prepare financial documents and then storm across Europe and the United States to drum up investors' excitement in the new stock. Other people on the team wanted to position the spin-off as a sturdy heir to 119 years of AT&T tradition. That's wrong, Fiorina argued. The only hope was to reinvent it as something new, she believed. By naming the company Lucent, she wanted to evoke the light of sunrise, of victory, and of visionary leadership. She argued for weeks with lawyers about how to define the company's basic business in official documents, until they capitulated and did it her way. Lucent wasn't an old-line phone-equipment maker anymore; it was the pioneering company in a new industry: communications networks. The difference sounded arcane, but it was crucial. Now she and two older colleagues, Lucent chairman Henry Schacht and president Rich McGinn, had a New Economy story that they could tell to the world.

Fiorina, Schacht, and McGinn began a multicity road show in March 1996, seeking to raise $2.7 billion from investors. When they started, there was a genuine risk that they might fail. But as the three executives traveled from city to city, the crowds kept growing. In London, portfolio managers packed one of the city's elegant, seventeenth-century guildhalls to hear the Lucent story. By the time the road show reached Zurich, there wasn't enough room to seat everyone. The constant presence of crowds was feeding on itself, pulling in stragglers and passersby throughout the Swiss city's financial district. A few days later, the team darted into Boston for what originally was intended to be a small, informal breakfast. Not anymore. Hundreds of men and women managing money for Fidelity, Putnam, Colonial, and other financial firms swarmed into the Boston Harbor Hotel. All of them demanded a chance to squeeze into the breakfast room, too.

"We had a good story, and we told it perfectly," Lucent investment banker Jeff Williams later recalled. "Give Carly all the credit for making it happen." In her most ingenious move, she championed a brash logo that became Lucent's rallying symbol: a hastily painted red circle with white streaks where the paint ran dry. It was meant to convey the raw energy of projects so new and bold that people didn't have time to fill in the gaps. AT&T never would have chosen such a symbol. That was the point: Lucent had remade itself as the company of tomorrow.

Onstage, Fiorina enchanted the crowds. Years later somber investment specialists still remember the bright red dress she wore on the day Lucent went public. They remember her smile, her gestures, and especially the way she invited people to step into her intoxicatingly appealing version of the future. She wove numbers effectively into her remarks, talking about $100 billion of growth that awaited Lucent in its key markets, a tally so vast that she believed it made her industry more alluring than the Internet. But the full power of her remarks came at the very end, when she let go of everything except her own faith. Her final three words in New York—"Watch us now!"—brought some investors to their feet.

Not only did Fiorina sparkle; she created an atmosphere of wickedly good fun that became contagious. On a dare one time, she began humming a giddy 1960s pop tune—"Up, Up and Away (My Beautiful Balloon)"—in the midst of a colleague's presentation to investors. He grimaced. Fiorina had just finished her own short speech and now was sitting four feet away from him, onstage. She was wrecking his concentration. But within a few months, the colleague, Lucent controller Jim Lusk, was quoting some of Fiorina's favorite slogans, such as "Dream an audacious future for yourself." He had every right to be ebullient. The Lucent road show had been a spectacular success. Investment bankers had raised an unexpectedly hefty $3 billion, and Lucent's stock was soaring in its public trading debut. It would finish 1996 up 92 percent.

The better Lucent fared, the bolder Fiorina got. A few months after Lucent went public, she told the Newark *Star-Ledger* that the breakup from AT&T was "like splitting the atom. It's releasing a whole lot of energy." Old-timers in the telecom industry watched her in action and grumbled that she was "driving beyond her headlights." She reminded them of a motorist doing 90 mph on a twisty highway at night when limited visibility justified only 60 mph. To her boosters, this ability to operate right on the dividing line between gutsy and outrageous was part of her allure. "There were people who resented her success," investment banker Jeff Williams recalled, "but she charmed the resentment right out of them."

How could Fiorina pull it off? Usually, people who sustain such showmanship have an enormous inner sense of drama, seeing themselves as the central character in a never-ending struggle between good and evil. Fiorina could keep her bravado under tight control when she needed to, but during a midcareer master's program at MIT in 1989, a few classmates got an unforgettable glimpse into her psyche. In an elective course, business students were reading *Antigone* as a way to spur a class debate about life's toughest choices. Most classmates regarded the famous Sophocles play as an unbearable tragedy, in which the title character is driven to her death because she will not relinquish her beliefs before an unjust king. Their comments dwelt on the lost opportunities for compromise. Not Fiorina. She said Antigone's courage inspired her. "Carly related to that play to an extraordinary degree," classmate Dan Hesse later recalled. "She felt it was almost autobiographical, this story of someone carrying the responsibility of the world on her shoulders. I used to tease her about it. I nicknamed her Antigone."

As a Lucent executive, Fiorina brought that passion to everyday commerce and made it seem heroic, too. As her career kept advancing, she became one of Lucent's most visible public speakers, addressing crowds on topics such as "The Communications Revolution." In-house speechwriters crafted much of her message, and while she liked most of their work, in her rewrites she slashed away the last traces of timidity. She didn't visit faraway cities to say, "I'd like to think that access to new information will become ubiquitous." Instead, she recast the text so that she could evoke all the majesty and simplicity of a preacher's Sunday sermon: "A century ago, the telephone began to transform the world. It changed our concepts of time and distance. . . ."

If she had come of age a generation earlier, Fiorina might have felt enormous pressure—as a woman—to tone down all traits that made her stand out. But her career took off just as doors began to open for women at big companies. In parts of AT&T and Lucent, old-fashioned men still plastered their office walls with *Rocky* movie posters. They were the Bell Heads, people she once referred to as having "twenty-inch necks and pea-sized brains." Top executives, however, wanted to transform both those companies into fresher, more open-minded places. At several key stages of her career, Fiorina benefited greatly from mentors such as Lucent chairman Henry Schacht and AT&T network systems chief Bill Marx, both of whom labored to clear a path for a talented young woman. As Schacht frequently told associates, "If you aren't promoting women and minorities into very top management, you aren't making use of the full talent pool in America."

In the treacherous world of workplace interplay between men and women, Fiorina coped with indignities early on, before redefining the rules her way as a top executive at Lucent. During her first months at AT&T, an older colleague invited her to a "business meeting" at the Boardroom, a strip club in Washington, D.C. She regarded it as a hazing ritual and an attempt to prove that she wasn't tough enough to succeed in a man's world. Determined not to be intimidated, Fiorina hailed a cab and headed to the strip club. "I was clutching my briefcase like a badge of honor," Fiorina later recalled, "telling myself: 'I am a businesswoman. I am. I am.'" Once inside, she talked shop with a half-dozen AT&T managers and clients, trying not to seem either outraged or amused by what was going on around her. When other patrons tried to coax one of the waitresses to stand on the table and undress, the woman demurred. She looked at Fiorina, sitting calmly in a navy blue business suit, and said: "Not while the lady is here."

That story inspired other women at AT&T. Just by her no-nonsense carriage, Fiorina could evoke better conduct in a rough crowd.

Later, as more women made it into management ranks, Fiorina lightened up. In the mid-1990s, she became known as the best-dressed woman at Lucent, with a clothes closet so vast that her husband mischievously offered to take visitors on a tour. When a colleague's teenage daughter stopped by the office one day, the girl asked Fiorina for advice about what kind of dress to wear to the high-school prom. Fiorina put on her most serious face and declared, "Two words of advice. Expensive and decisive! That's my philosophy." For months afterward, that edict became a surefire argument winner in one New Jersey home: "But Mom, just remember what Carly said. Expensive and decisive!"

Finally, as Fiorina grew truly powerful, she confronted the most disruptive parts of the old-boy network and crushed them. In the late 1990s, Fiorina had risen to be president of Lucent's global service provider business, overseeing the company's largest and fastest-growing business, with $20 billion a year in revenue. She grew concerned that a new acquisition, Ascend Communications, was bringing a frat-house culture into Lucent. So a few hours before a giant talk to 2,000 Lucent and Ascend sales representatives, she prepared a surprise involving three rolled-up athletic socks, borrowed from her husband that morning. She stepped out onstage in a loose-fitting pantsuit and started her talk gently, saying that she realized the two companies had somewhat different cultures. Then she began to get blunter—and earthier. "We at Lucent think you guys are a bunch of cowboys who don't understand carrier-grade quality," she said. "You probably think we're a bunch of wusses. Well, I think it's important that we really get to know each other." With that, she set aside her suit jacket. Now everyone in the audience could see an unmistakable bulge in her pants, just where a virile man might protrude. The bulge—produced by those three athletic socks—was shockingly big. As people gasped, she delivered her closing line: "Our balls are as big as anyone's!"

The meeting collapsed into chaos at that point. People howled, shrieked, and gasped. Five minutes later, they still were sputtering in disbelief. And over the next year, the macho Ascend culture disintegrated. Sales representatives who learned to do things the Lucent way stayed. Those who couldn't adjust left.

While Fiorina was becoming a swashbuckling figure in the telecom industry, the rest of American business took a bit longer to acknowledge this remarkable new presence. But a single magazine article in 1998 changed that forever. *Fortune* magazine writer Patricia Sellers decided to rank the fifty most powerful women in business. Rather than populate her list with women running toy and cosmetics companies, Sellers hunted for leaders at world-class enterprises, whose life stories would show that women could excel at serious jobs anywhere. Lucent was a natural place to look. Its stock was soaring; it was an avatar of the New Economy, and one of its executive vice presidents, Pat Russo, was female. Sellers called Lucent to schedule a Russo interview and started chatting with the company's press chief, Kathy Fitzgerald. "We'll get you set up with Pat," Fitzgerald said. "But you ought to meet someone else, too." It was Carly Fiorina.

Before long, Sellers was sitting in a Lucent conference room, listening to Fiorina's life story. What Sellers heard defied all the stereotypes—and had her spellbound. Fiorina talked candidly about her bumpy experiences right after college, confiding that when she dropped out of law school, her father told her: "I'm very concerned, and I don't think you're going to amount to anything." One of her best business ideas, the Lucent logo, came into being partly because the design was reminiscent of her mother's abstract paintings, Fiorina added. When the interview was over, Sellers knew Fiorina would rank among the top women on her list. The only question was which Lucent executive to highlight more: Russo had the fancier title, but Fiorina had the better story. Wanting an expert's opinion, *Fortune* called Lawrence Babbio, a plainspoken executive at Bell Atlantic who knew Lucent extremely well. "I'm not going to pick between Pat and Carly," Babbio said. "But let me tell you this. I don't care what other forty-nine people are on your list. If Carly Fiorina doesn't come out on the front cover, then I'm going to cancel every *Fortune* subscription at Bell Atlantic, because I've just determined that you people don't know what you're talking about!"

That clinched it. When the October 12, 1998, issue of *Fortune* reached its 800,000 subscribers, everyone knew that Carly Fiorina was "The Most Powerful Woman in American Business." Her face was right there on the cover, projecting confidence and optimism. As Sellers wrote, "She's at the center of the ongoing technology revolution that's changing how we live and work."

For Fiorina, the sudden recognition was a shock, a thrill, and a danger. "I had stopped thinking of myself as a woman in business," she later said. Now, gender was about to become a bigger part of her public identity, whether she liked that or not. She would be celebrated as a feminist hero by some; she also would be typecast by millions of people who hadn't even met her. The sudden fame could alienate her from Lucent colleagues and other women. Still, she was a celebrity now. There wasn't any turning back.

Fiorina's ultimate boss, Lucent chairman Henry Schacht, congratulated her right away about the *Fortune* cover. Then he spoke his mind about executive recruiters, who were sure to bombard her with exciting job offers at other companies. His advice was coolly pragmatic; both of them knew that the era of lifetime loyalty to a single company was long past. "Look, you've got to make up your own mind," Schacht said. "It's not disloyal to think about other alternatives. If we can't keep you fully challenged, then shame on us. But you owe it to yourself—and to our company—not to get distracted by the wrong kinds of offers. If it becomes known that you're considering offers, the headhunters will descend on you and you'll never be able to shoo them away. Decide very clearly in your mind what kind of job offer you would pay attention to. Whatever your goal is, don't talk to people about anything less."

Over the next seven months, Fiorina ignored dozens of recruiters' pitches. She tossed their message slips in the garbage. When an unfamiliar recruiter named Jeff Christian left word in March 1999 that he had something urgent in mind, Fiorina snubbed him, too. He called three more times and couldn't get past her secretary. Finally, on his fifth attempt, Christian shrewdly called her office in the evening, after all the nonexecutives had gone home. As she picked up her phone, Fiorina heard a breathless, excited man's voice. "Hi, this is Jeff Christian. Don't hang up. I'm calling about Hewlett-Packard."

Fiorina paused. She savored his opening line for a moment. Then she said, "Well! You've got my attention."

A few days later, Fiorina and Christian met for lunch at the Hilton Hotel in Short Hills, New Jersey. The restaurant was largely empty, and most of the other guests were elderly women with blue-rinsed hair. That was fine. If anyone at Lucent saw Fiorina lunching with a recruiter, gossip would travel fast. In this first meeting, Christian wanted to know about Fiorina's career challenges and triumphs. He would learn about her business philosophy that way; he also could tell how powerfully the chance to run Hewlett-Packard was tugging at her. Whenever candidates abandoned their corner-office reserve and began telling rich, dramatic stories from the heart, Christian knew something magical was starting to happen. Partway through the meal, he realized Fiorina had crossed that threshold.

"What struck me," Christian later said, "was that in her career, she

constantly had been sent into troubled situations. And at every juncture except one (a Lucent-Philips joint venture to make telephone handsets) she
had been able to fix things. She had a methodology. She would go into an
area and spend a lot of time listening at first. She was a big believer that organizations already contained a lot of the right ideas. People just didn't feel
they had the authority to get them done. She listens to customers. And
then she shares the things that people should stop doing, the things they
should focus harder on doing, and the new directions they should try."

For Fiorina, the meeting also let her tell a favorite story of personal
courage. In her early thirties, working in Washington, she had pursued a
government contract for AT&T that everyone thought she would lose.
Partway through the procurement cycle, she learned that details of her bid
were being leaked to competitors. "That's wrong," she declared. "It needs
to be stopped, and we should go to court if necessary." Other AT&T executives shivered at the idea of a high-profile suit. But she pressed on and
won a boardroom audience with AT&T chairman Jim Olson. He asked her
to write out a plan of action for the phone company. Grabbing a yellow
pad, she did so on the spot. He took her suggestions, read them out loud,
and asked other AT&T leaders what they thought. It was a nail-biting moment for Fiorina; if her ideas got hooted down, her peers and bosses
wouldn't forget. But she believed in her approach, and so did everyone else
in the room. After three years and a dizzying number of court appearances,
Fiorina and AT&T were fully vindicated. "It was one of the great forma-
tive experiences of my life," she later said. From it she took away a lifelong
lesson: Stand tall. Stand alone if you have to. Always know that you can
win a fight if you are right.

After that first meeting, Christian and HP's four directors needed to assess Fiorina's chances. The honest answer was: No one knew for sure.
Christian had listed one hundred candidates at the start, with plans to
tighten the search's focus before long to about a dozen serious contenders
and then ultimately to four finalists. Fiorina acknowledged that she had one
potentially serious disadvantage: She didn't know the computer industry
nearly as well as other contenders who had worked in that field for decades.
Still, she was an interesting long shot, certainly worth moving from the list
of one hundred to a much narrower list of serious contenders. Would she
go any farther? That depended on what the rest of the field looked like.

In the first six weeks of the search, Christian conveyed a lot more bad
news than good to the HP search committee. The long bull market had
flooded many prime candidates with enormous paper profits on their stock

options, all of which would be forfeited in the event of a job switch. "We talked to people who had $350 million or more on the line," Christian later recalled. HP wanted to recruit top talent, but there was no way it could match such forgone windfalls with nine-digit signing bonuses. Even more disturbing was that some executives at other tech companies said they would consider the job only if they could obliterate what they regarded as HP's asphyxiating corporate culture. "I'd probably fire twenty thousand people," one such candidate said. "I'd ask the entire board of directors to resign. I might keep some of them, but I'd want the option to get rid of anyone. And I'd scrap the HP Way. It sucks. There's no other way to describe it. It just plain sucks." At that rate, Hewlett-Packard might as well call in corporate raider Carl Icahn and ask him to dismember the company.

Two people with inside connections to Hewlett-Packard shot up their hands and asked to be considered, too, but neither attracted unanimous support on the search committee. One was Ann Livermore, the head of HP's services business, who had Platt's backing. She remained on the contenders' list through the entire search, but except for Platt, most other directors believed they would be better off looking outside. Meanwhile, Hackborn's longtime protégé, Rick Belluzzo, signaled from his new job at Silicon Graphics that he wanted another shot at HP's top position. Hackborn wished Belluzzo good luck but said he wouldn't play an active role for or against Belluzzo's candidacy. Other directors would have to decide. As it happened, the circumstances of Belluzzo's departure a year earlier had left enough bruised feelings that no other director was eager to champion his cause.

By late spring, HP had compiled its first pass at a finalists' list. Three of the top contenders came from major Silicon Valley companies: Ray Lane, chief operating officer of Oracle Systems; Ed Zander, president of Sun Microsystems; and Paul Otellini, an executive vice president at Intel. Joining them was Carly Fiorina, the outsider. All four had excellent jobs already, with prospects of rising to the top simply by staying where they were. They could afford to be coy, testing HP to see how much it wanted to woo them. From this point on, the candidates would be keenly attuned to their standing in the race. If any of them thought they were slipping, they would quickly call it quits.

Otellini dropped out first. He had met with Platt and Hackborn, both of whom saw him as a rising star likely to play a big role in the technology sector in a few years. He understood the industry intimately, with twenty-five years of experience at Intel, including responsibility for launching the

Pentium microprocessor. But Platt couldn't get an accurate reading of his interest level and Hackborn had some doubts about Otellini's plan to revive Hewlett-Packard's PC business. Before other search-committee members could weigh in, Otellini let everyone know he would rather stay at Intel and make his career there.*

Lane stayed in the running much longer, but the courtship never really clicked. During interviews, he talked mostly about ways to fix HP's enterprise-computing business, an area he knew extremely well from his days at IBM and Booz Allen Hamilton before arriving at business-software maker Oracle in 1992. Lane couldn't get excited about printers and PCs, however, and it didn't take long for directors to sense his apathy. Anxious to keep up appearances of a multicandidate search, directors asked him to take the Hagberg personality test. Lane reluctantly complied, only to tell himself partway through the exam: "This is the stupidest thing I've ever done. I want to be back at Oracle."

The two most intriguing candidates, by far, were Zander and Fiorina. As Scott McNealy's right-hand man at Sun, Zander had been pummeling Hewlett-Packard in the marketplace for years. Now, in the privacy of a job interview, he was able to dissect HP's flaws with chilling accuracy. "I told them HP wasn't firing on all cylinders," Zander later recalled. "They needed hungry, aggressive, very focused people in their sales force. They didn't have that. They were lethargic." Zander had the classic credentials for success at Hewlett-Packard: an electrical engineering degree and an MBA. If directors really wanted to stay within the computer industry and turn over the reins to a savvy, tough competitor, Zander was the logical choice. But Zander's blunt remedies were hard for directors to stomach. Also, he had been intensely loyal to McNealy for more than a decade. It would take an extraordinary effort to pry him away from Sun, and Platt in particular couldn't bring himself to plead for McNealy's deputy to save the company. HP's slim chances evaporated completely when Zander was left waiting for half an hour at one breakfast appointment because of a schedule mix-up. Eventually even Hackborn realized that the Sun executive was unpoachable.

Meanwhile, Fiorina was off to a very good start. Everything clicked in her opening interview with Platt, who already knew her slightly from routine HP-Lucent business dealings. *She's smart; she can learn,* Platt told him-

* Staying at Intel worked out well for him; in 2002 Otellini was promoted to president of the giant semiconductor company.

self after their conversation. He talked candidly to her about Hewlett-Packard's fading fortunes, saying that the company lacked strategic vision and a sense of urgency. He asked what she would do with the HP Way, and her answer was refreshingly thoughtful and restrained. She didn't say it sucked. She didn't declare war on employees or directors. She simply said, "I'd use it to change the culture in the way that you think it needs to be changed."

Sam Ginn met with her next, and it didn't take long for the two telecom veterans to connect. He appreciated Fiorina's climb up the phone-company ladder, particularly her stint in AT&T's management development program. "It's an excellent program," he later said. "I did it myself when I was at AT&T." In two meetings with Fiorina, he focused on letting her know how much Hewlett-Packard was ailing. "We've got real work to do here," he said. In his view, the HP Way had become perverted into something the founders never intended. "Personal employee satisfaction is trumping almost any business decision," he explained. She talked about what she had done to light a fire under people at Lucent, which resonated with Ginn. Soon afterward, when he was golfing in Vail, Colorado, Ginn ran into Lucent's CEO, Rich McGinn, and discreetly asked what he thought about Fiorina. "She's excellent," the Lucent chief replied, not sure why Ginn was so curious.

Fiorina started to feel swept up in something exciting, too. She had admired Hewlett-Packard enormously earlier in her career. In fact, when she was starting the Lucent launch, she had benchmarked HP's performance in the mid-1990s as a goal for Lucent to emulate. Now, she could tell, "this was a company that was losing relevance. It just didn't seem to be on the map anymore. It was on a downward trajectory when everyone else was on an upward trajectory." Even so, hadn't she spent much of her career stepping into troubled situations and fixing them? If there was ever a challenge worth doing, this was it.

What's more, Fiorina thought she saw an opening that no one else did. She had bought Dave Packard's 1995 autobiography, *The HP Way,* years earlier and had recently picked it up again. Eventually she would read it six times. As she thought about the can-do spirit that inspired everyone at Hewlett-Packard in the early years, she believed she could help rescue the company by going back into its history and pulling out lost strengths that could guide a modern transformation.

"Give me a chance!" Fiorina told Sam Ginn, in the middle of their second interview. "I can make this stuff work!" They were sitting just outside a fried-chicken kiosk in the San Jose International Airport. Harried passengers were walking past them all the time, unaware that the fate of one of America's biggest companies was being played out by two people nibbling on chicken and sipping sodas from paper cups. Ginn loved her eagerness. She was pouring her energy into the search, even agreeing to take the nine hundred–question Hagberg personality test. (Zander refused.) When her results came back, they were splendid. According to the test, Fiorina was a strategic visionary who could create excitement and buy-in with customers and her management team, while also being able to follow up with tactical goals to make sure that good things really happened. All the character references that Fiorina submitted checked out perfectly. Her old boss Bill Marx said that HP's challenges sounded very similar to those she had handled masterfully already at the phone company. Christian briefly tried phoning around the telecom industry to see what other people thought. One former AT&T executive denounced Fiorina with a vehemence that startled Christian, in essence calling her a charlatan. Christian dismissed him as a jealous man, frustrated that he wasn't being considered for the job.

Fiorina decided to give a talk in mid-June at San Francisco's Commonwealth Club about her favorite topic, "The Communications Revolution." People who knew only about her Lucent job got a fine overview of industry trends. Delicately slipped into the speech, however, were comments that could be read as a road map of what she hoped to do at Hewlett-Packard. She started one part of her narrative in 1996, when Lucent, against the odds, was trying to make it as an independent company. She described it as a company with a proud heritage, a turbulent identity, and gleeful competitors predicting it would fail. "Business as unusual was the tune our company was going to have to dance to," she said. "That was clearly going to be an up-tempo, creative, interpretive piece, not a stately promenade. Jazz, not classical. We've loved those rhythms, and so have our investors." A handful of HP managers who knew that Fiorina was a contender for the top job at their company got hold of a bootleg transcript of her talk. They photocopied it, passed it along to a few friends, and built up intense hopes that Carly Fiorina would come rescue them.

What did Dick Hackborn think? He was the one director who hadn't fully signaled his preference yet, and that meant that his voice would likely determine Hewlett-Packard's next CEO. He and Fiorina had lunched together in New York earlier in the search, but that was just a get-acquainted session. She was coy about her interest then; he wasn't nearly ready to decide anything either. Now both were prepared for a much more serious conversation. They met for a four-hour lunch at the Chicago O'Hare Hilton, a reasonable halfway location for both of them. Once again, Fiorina ended up in a strange joint that only a spy could love. This time it was the Gaslight Club, an imitation speakeasy where the waitresses wore vampy fishnet stockings. The two business leaders hardly noticed. Within minutes, they were talking about Hewlett-Packard more bluntly—and more affectionately—than either had expected.

Fiorina started by voicing bewilderment about Lew Platt's latest move. In the midst of the search, he had announced that he would be giving HP's main divisions even more autonomy than before. Each division chief would now become CEO of his or her own business unit. As Fiorina saw it, the company urgently needed more centralized guidance, not less. "If you're going to keep this company together, there has to be real value to the portfolio," she argued. "And if there's going to be value to the portfolio there has to be a unifying strategy and focus. We can't have four CEOs doing their own thing. If the board really thinks this is the direction the company needs to move, then I'm not the person for the job." Hackborn heartily agreed. Platt's move didn't make sense to him either. And Hackborn liked the decisiveness of a job candidate who could draw lines and say, in effect, "I can't work here if you're making these mistakes." He had done so himself many times in his own career, with great success.

A few minutes later, Hackborn began taking Fiorina through some of the key business challenges that needed to be fixed. The PC division was acting as if Dell didn't exist. HP's sales force was tripping all over itself, sometimes pressuring customers to abandon one division's reliable HP products in a misguided attempt to sell another division's offerings that weren't well suited to the customer's needs. "We're in danger of losing all the things that made this a great company," Hackborn said. He talked about how frustrated he was with Hewlett-Packard's eroding growth rate. The company was losing stature in its industries. Sun's inroads bothered him. IBM's greater success irked him. Even the fact that smaller printer companies, such as Lexmark, could make inroads against HP's enormous lead in the inkjet and LaserJet businesses annoyed him.

Fiorina picked up Hackborn's themes and refined them. She talked about what had worked well for her at Lucent in building an industry-leading sales force. She offered some advice about splitting HP and Agilent, so that the greatest energies of the company didn't get yanked out by the spin-off company. AT&T had been weakened in unexpected ways by the

Lucent separation, and she wanted to make sure that those problems didn't occur with Hewlett-Packard.

Mostly, Fiorina listened. She had come to the lunch regarding Hackborn as the Yoda figure of HP: the seldom-seen but all-knowing elder figure of supreme respect. She had discerned already that other board members would be extremely mindful of Hackborn's conclusions. Ultimately, she saw him as the crucial decision-maker in the search, so she wanted his insights on everything: How strong or weak was the management team she might inherit? What was each board member like? What about the four representatives of the Hewlett and Packard families who were serving as directors? How involved were they? Hackborn's answers reassured her. Most of HP's top executives were solid, and some had the potential to be stars. The family members were nice people but not deeply interested in the business. Some of the other directors were world-class business leaders who could help a new CEO who was willing to work closely with them on big strategy issues. To his surprise, Hackborn noted, none of the other candidates had bothered asking about something as basic as the makeup of HP's board. Fiorina was the first. That was a very good sign.

Several hours into the meeting, Fiorina began speculating about who should be chairman if she became CEO. She didn't want to consolidate all the top titles in her own hands right away; she would need some wise-uncle support in the background for at least the first year if she made the move to Hewlett-Packard. She knew Platt had hoped to remain as chairman for a while, and she thought he could help referee the split between HP and Agilent. But before she got more than a few sentences into that prospect, she could tell that Hackborn didn't like that idea. As she was learning, Hackborn and Platt didn't really get along. Right at that moment, an idea popped into her mind. Looking at Hackborn, other people might see a wrinkled retiree with sunken eyes and white hair. She saw something different: the best mentor she could ask for. He could be her special counselor, a role that she had welcomed repeatedly in her career. And so, rather than get tangled up in another Platt conversation, she looked at Hackborn and said: "Well, actually, Dick, I think you ought to be chairman."

The idea startled Hackborn at first. He hadn't thought about the chairmanship for a long time. In recent years, he had been seeking to wind down his boardroom commitments to Hewlett-Packard and walk away from what had become a bad situation, but the more he and Fiorina talked about having him become chairman, the more he warmed up to the idea. As their meeting came to an end, Fiorina told Hackborn, "Think about it." She headed toward her plane, feeling more confident that if she were offered the chance to be HP's next CEO, she could handle the job. She felt especially good about working with Hackborn.

"I've got him hooked!" Fiorina told herself as she flew back to New Jersey. She was right. Soon after that O'Hare get-together, Hackborn briefed the entire Hewlett-Packard board on his recent chat with Fiorina. "I could see he was dazzled by her," HP director Pattie Dunn later recalled. "They had hit it off. He was really excited about her vision for the company. She had a feel for the company's strengths and weaknesses. It corresponded with his feel." Hackborn expressed mild concern about Fiorina's lack of a technical background, but that didn't seem to be a top-priority worry to him. If he became chairman, he said, he could be her mentor. Besides, she struck him as a remarkably quick learner who would probably acclimate to HP quite quickly. "We may be getting one of the top two or three CEOs of our generation," Hackborn declared. "She could be the next Jack Welch."

For the rest of the HP board, which was already caught up in Fiorina fever, the notion of having the new chief executive elevate Dick Hackborn to the chairman's job was absolutely exhilarating. "It shows she's passed the IQ test," director Jay Keyworth quipped. Other directors had been worrying that if Hackborn quit the HP board out of frustration, they would be denied their smartest thinker. As Pattie Dunn later put it: "The nice thing about picking Carly for CEO was that it saved Dick Hackborn for HP. That can't be overestimated."

In New Jersey, Fiorina began telling her most trusted confidants that she felt it was her destiny to take command at Hewlett-Packard. It would be a chance for her to help one of the world's great technology companies find its way again. It would be a chance for her to return to northern California, where she had spent part of her childhood and gone to college. Her father, federal judge Joseph Sneed, was living in San Francisco. Her mother, Madelon Sneed, had died of cancer shortly before the HP search began. But at one point her mother had asked Fiorina if there was any chance she might be returning to California. It was easy for Fiorina to believe that the Hewlett-Packard job would have suited her late mother's wishes perfectly. On Thursday, July 15, 1999, Fiorina signed the contract that made her HP's next chief executive. The next day, she told everyone at Lucent that she was leaving. She said all the right things in her farewell note—talking about the HP job as a "once-in-a-lifetime opportunity," while saying how much she would miss the people of Lucent and what a privilege it had been to work there. She closed by saying: "I will carry you in my heart always and be cheering you on."

With that, it was off to California for good. On Saturday evening, she finally met HP's full board of directors for the first time. She had spoken to board members once before on speakerphone, but the selection process had been handled strictly by the four directors on the nominating committee. Now it was time to shake hands, hug, and congratulate one another.

Fiorina had also spent two hours earlier that day meeting alone with Ann Livermore, the HP services-division boss, who appeared stunned not to have been picked as CEO. By all accounts, their meeting went well. "She's going to need me to help her navigate the company," Livermore told a friend a few days later. "And if she's as great as she seems, I have an incredible amount that I could learn."

The next day, Sunday, July 18, resembled the final anxious bits of fussing and preparation that precede a wedding—or a coronation. Fiorina arrived at HP's headquarters late in the morning and spent the rest of the day meeting with press advisers and then joining a dozen of HP's senior executives for a get-acquainted dinner on the patio outside the executive-office wing. "None of us know you," the head of HP's inkjet division, Antonio Perez, blurted out. "Why don't you tell us something about yourself and what you intend for the company." Well aware that every word of her answer would be deconstructed for months, Fiorina parried the question nimbly. "Before we do that, I think Lew ought to tell you why the board has decided to have me here." Platt rose to the occasion, providing a little history about the search process and telling everyone that he and all the other directors were very enthusiastic about their choice.

The next day, Monday, July 19, it was time to tell the world. No one knew how Carly Fiorina's selection would be received, but Hewlett-Packard by tradition tried to present all of its major corporate news in smooth and calming tones. That was in keeping with the company's low-key, engineer-driven culture. New products were launched on time; production deadlines were met; new leadership teams were installed according to plan. Until the moment that the press conference began, it was still possible to believe that the Fiorina era would begin in a fashion not too dissimilar from the start of the Young era or the Platt era.

Then the journalists' questions started pouring in. "How does it feel to be the most powerful woman in America?" "What does this say about the glass ceiling for women?" "Can Carly appear on *Oprah*?" "Can Carly appear on *60 Minutes*?" All of a sudden, Hewlett-Packard had a celebrity CEO. And no one inside the company had any idea how to cope.

Chapter 4

RULES OF THE GARAGE

A t first, television viewers saw only the darkened outline of a small garage. Then the lilting sounds of a shepherd's folk tune could be heard. The garage's red roof brightened as if caught by sunrise. An unseen female narrator started to speak, in a strong, confident voice that commanded instant attention.

"This is the workshop of radicals," Carly Fiorina declared. "This is the garage where two young men with five hundred dollars in venture capital invented an industry." Hewlett-Packard's new chief executive was launching the company's first corporate brand campaign in nearly a decade. For a few seconds, viewers were transported back to the 1930s. Grainy, black-and-white footage introduced Dave Packard and Bill Hewlett, puttering in the garage where HP was born. They were jaunty young men, still shy of their thirtieth birthdays. Packard held up one of the company's first products, the boxy gray audio oscillator. In the voice-over narrative, Fiorina propelled the story along. "The idea was simple," she declared. "Invent something useful—or it doesn't leave the garage. It was so simple, it was radical." As she spoke, the camera returned to the brightly lit contemporary garage. The building was about to be visited by a person casting a modest shadow on its double doors. And now the commercial abruptly revealed Fiorina herself, in an intense close-up, delivering the best lines of the entire ad.

"The company of Bill Hewlett and Dave Packard is being reinvented," she declared. "The original start-up will act like one again. Watch!" In the ad's final image, Fiorina, in a black pantsuit, nestled against the creamy white garage door, smiling and self-assured.

When that ad campaign became public in the autumn of 1999, it mesmerized HP employees. At last, the grand old company of Silicon Valley was standing tall again. With passion and bravado, Hewlett-Packard was telling its story to the world. "I had tears in my eyes watching the video," employee Val Stinson wrote in an e-mail to headquarters. "I actually began to feel the pride again, that I hadn't realized I had lost, about working for

HP. Thanks, Carly!" Hundreds of other employees around the world fired off e-mails to Fiorina, echoing Stinson's jubilant words. "In my twenty-five years at HP, this is the most exciting branding I've seen!" a British employee wrote. Engineers said they felt inspired to do better work. Sales representatives said they felt emboldened to attack the competition harder than ever. "I felt like my team just won the Super Bowl," one employee wrote.

In the most stunning testimonial of all, a fifteen-year veteran of the company wrote to say that the $100 million marketing campaign associated with the garage commercial had restored his faith in Hewlett-Packard, just as he had been on the brink of defecting to an HP competitor. Watching a company video introducing the commercial, "I was surprised to notice chills take over my body," he wrote. "I felt a strange mixture of enthusiasm for the future and shame for my cynical muttering expressed just moments before. After watching the video, I put away the offer sheet that would lead to my departure. I remembered what it felt like to be an HP employee so many years before. And I wondered: Is it possible once more?"

Carly Fiorina had barely unpacked her boxes, and already she was enchanting Hewlett-Packard employees. Given a chance to get her staging just right, she could inspire people in a way that rivaled the charismatic pull of Dave Packard or Bill Hewlett. She combined the aspirational rhetoric of the New Economy with a keen eye for HP's long-neglected historical strengths. She was ready to take a proud, insular company on an exciting new journey, modeled on what she had helped accomplish at Lucent. In her big public speeches and video broadcasts to the workforce, Fiorina was every bit as dazzling as the HP search committee had hoped. She was so persuasive that employees joked that she could run for president—and then wondered whether that was a whimsical comment or a prophecy.

Soon after Fiorina arrived at Hewlett-Packard, she got a congratulatory letter jointly signed by Bill and Hillary Clinton. "They said: 'Carly, we are delighted for you; we can't wait to see you here at the White House,'" recalled Gary Fazzino, HP's head of government affairs. Eventually, Fiorina and the president met for fifty minutes. As they talked about her principles of leadership and her life story, Clinton paid rapt attention. Afterward, Fiorina told her staff: "He's very charming. I can see why he got elected twice." Later that day she visited Capitol Hill, where twenty-two senators scurried to meet her. The senators lingered for ninety minutes, eager to know her views on trade, education, and the Patent Office. Fiorina probably could have discussed her favorite medieval philosophers and cap-tivated the senators, too. Fazzino, who had guided HP executives through Washington since the days of Dave Packard, had never seen any of his bosses display that sort of star power.

Could Fiorina make that early burst of excitement add up to anything? That was the hard part. After reviving the HP brand, she wanted to central-ize control of the company and assemble an Internet strategy. She also wanted to revitalize the sales force, trim costs, and create an overall sense of urgency for employees. If she wasn't careful, her to-do list could stretch so far that it would become utterly unmanageable. All that she had to guide her was a belief that if she could undo the past few years of HP mistakes, the company's great enduring strengths would come through. "I had this mental image of buildings wrapped in layers and layers of gauze bandages," she later said. "The sound was muffled. The light was muffled. The din and bright lights of the real world were so filtered. Part of my job was to take the bandages off."

For all the early cheering, there was a lot she didn't yet know about Hewlett-Packard, and the moment she unclipped her microphone, her clout dwindled. Everything about this new job was vastly bigger than any-thing she had attempted at Lucent. For all her natural ebullience, she was largely at the mercy of the global economy and the complex legacies she inherited. Most of all, she had to reckon with the uncertain loyalties of employees on five continents who might endorse change until they real-ized that some of their favorite practices would be swept aside.

Adding to the drama—and danger—of her new job, Fiorina had en-tered a company packed with people whose personalities were exactly the opposite of hers. Insiders familiar with the famous Myers-Briggs personal-ity scale quickly sized up Fiorina as an ENFP: an extroverted, intuitive, feeling, and perceiving person. Industrial psychologists call such people energizers or champions. "They have great influence because of their ex-traordinary impact on others," one expert wrote. By contrast, HP employ-ees typically were regarded as ISTJs: introverted, sensing, thinking, and judging persons. Such people are organized and methodical; they are the "guardians" who heed well-established experts in their field but resist new approaches that don't make sense to them. Like it or not, the interaction of Fiorina's zeal and HP's innate caution amounted to an epic daredevil sci-ence experiment. Could one charismatic outsider make good on her prom-ises to change an entire company of eighty-five thousand people? Or if times got tough, would an army of traditionalists decide that Fiorina's agenda was just a short, crazy folly—and perhaps try to flush her out of the company entirely?

At first, Hewlett-Packard employees just wanted to marvel at this astonishing new presence in their lives. Women at the company wondered whether Fiorina had any children. (She didn't, but she was close to a three-year-old granddaughter by her husband's first marriage.) Sailing enthusiasts wanted to know the name of her fifty-two-foot boat. *(Alchemy.)* And gossipy sorts wondered whether she took a hairdresser with her on business trips. (She said she didn't.)

Whenever Fiorina spoke—even on the most routine matters—she put to work a unique vocabulary, full of zesty phrases never heard at Hewlett-Packard before. Out of admiration or mischief, aides created underground dictionaries to help people master Carly-speak. "I'm jazzed about that!" Fiorina regularly told people, when she was excited about a new project. She urged people to be "ambidextrous," when she wanted them to jump back and forth among her priorities. Managers who didn't appreciate her rapid deadlines got their clocks reset to Carly Time with the admonition: "Faster is better than slower. Always, always, always!"

Above all, pragmatism ruled. In her lexicon, "perfect enough" was a high compliment. It meant that people could stop fussing over every last detail in favor of charging into the marketplace with something that could beat the competition if it was launched with enough speed and excitement. Longtime HP executives took awhile to absorb this shocking new message. But after a while they decided they liked it. Even Webb McKinney, the bookish fifty-three-year-old in charge of personal-computer sales, eventually went hell-bent for sales growth with a system that worked in the United States but wasn't yet refined enough to operate well in Europe. Details could wait for later. In the meantime, McKinney decided that what he had was perfect enough.

Unlike Lew Platt, Fiorina thrived on being the center of attention. "When you're starting a revolution, the first thing you do is seize control of the airwaves," she told one aide. Fiorina posted her speeches on the company Web site. She traveled from city to city, meeting employees in an updated version of the founders' old coffee talks. She stepped up HP's security services, mindful of the risks faced by any high-profile woman in America. As mail and speaking invitations poured in, she hired three assistants to handle her scheduling and paperwork. HP's chief executive wasn't an obscure figure anymore. An in-house publication started a column called "Travels with Carly" that provided gossip-column fodder about the boss, and she indulged it. As Fiorina told *Forbes* magazine in the autumn of 1999, "Leadership is a performance."

Fiorina's pay package flabbergasted HP old-timers when it was publicly disclosed a few months after she joined the company. She got $1 million in base salary, $65 million in restricted HP stock, $36,000 in mortgage assistance, and $187,000 in moving expenses. When she left Lucent, her base pay had been just $350,000. But she had walked away from $70 million in Lucent options, and her lawyer argued that she deserved a dollar-for-dollar offset in her new job. "That's more money than I made in my entire career," Platt later said. His astonishment spoke for a whole generation of HP employees who had seen the company spend cautiously as it filled almost all vacancies by promoting from within. For other directors, the hefty signing package was the price of landing a star. In the hothouse financial climate of 1999, any company wanting to recruit a great new CEO could expect to pay that much. Only when Fiorina's lawyer badgered Hewlett-Packard to move her yacht through the Panama Canal did her new employers balk. "Just sell the boat," HP director Sam Ginn said. Ultimately, she did.

Fiorina rattled employees a second time when she decided to rebuild HP's fleet of corporate aircraft. Dave Packard and Bill Hewlett had been early enthusiasts of private planes, believing they made sense for a company with operations scattered around the world. (They also had used their jets to haul an occasional moose carcass back to Silicon Valley after a hunting trip to Idaho or Western Canada.) During the John Young era, the company owned an elegant Gulfstream III. But Lew Platt felt it was ostentatious for anyone, even the boss, to use corporate aircraft when a coach seat on United or American would suffice. So Platt had greatly shrunk HP's air force in early 1999 as a cost-cutting move. Many employees came to regard his spartan values as their own. Unaware how much it would irk the workforce, Fiorina decided to reintroduce top executives to the joys of private-jet travel. Within a few months of her arrival, Hewlett-Packard had acquired two Gulfstream IV jets for $28 million apiece.

Minor controversies aside, Fiorina carefully followed the newcomer's creed that had served her well for more than a decade. She hunted for good ideas half-buried in the bureaucracy while identifying inane practices that could be stopped right away. "Send me the Ten Stupidest Things We Do," she told an employee group at the end of one speech. "I'll read it." Soon after taking office, she announced that the nine-hundred-question psychological profiles wouldn't be used nearly so much; she had found them "bizarre." She declared war on brand clutter, pointing out that HP's profusion of minor brand names—Chai, Tape Alert, Vectra, and the like—was confusing customers and weakening what should be the best brand name of all: Hewlett-Packard.

Everything Fiorina did pointed her toward the original Addison Avenue garage as a rallying point for her new agenda. "I knew we had to use the culture to recapture the culture," she later said. "We had to go back to the roots of the place." As Fiorina toured Hewlett-Packard, she found mid-level marketing executives who had been pounding the table for more than a year, pleading with their bosses to make wiser use of HP's heritage. One of these managers, Bojana Fazarinc, had helped prepare a twenty-minute video for a cable-television show, packed with testimonials about the company that Bill and Dave built. On that video, Steve Jobs, the irascible founder of Apple Computer, shared warm memories of being a twelve-year-old in 1967, scrounging for electronics parts, and calling Bill Hewlett for help. Hewlett chatted with the boy for twenty minutes on the phone, gave him all the parts he wanted, and later arranged for him to get a summer job at HP. The warm gestures made a big impression on Jobs, who declared on the video: "Bill and Dave had an essential faith in people. They believed that people were noble. If you gave them the right tools, they would get the job done."

Fazarinc's video languished within Hewlett-Packard for months, but the moment Fiorina saw the first rough attempts to document HP's history, she knew she had struck gold. A few weeks into her new job, Fiorina summoned executives from a cutting-edge ad agency in San Francisco, Goodby Silverstein & Partners, to discuss ways of repositioning Hewlett-Packard to the world. She wanted an ad campaign that went beyond promoting specific HP computers and printers; it ought to create excitement and admiration around the entire Hewlett-Packard brand. High-tech marketers nationwide had watched with envy a few years earlier as IBM, the biggest and most bureaucratic company in the computer industry, successfully redefined itself as a friendly, Internet-savvy outfit. If IBM and its ad agency could pull off such a transformation, surely Hewlett-Packard could reclaim its good name, too.

At Goodby, creative manager Steven Simpson sat down with a copy of Dave Packard's autobiography, *The HP Way,* so that he could better understand the company's early history. Gradually, Simpson drafted a manifesto that he called "Rules of the Garage." They were ten maxims of the instrument age: exactly the sort of principles that guided the men who built the early oscillators, volt meters, and atomic clocks of the 1930s, 1940s, and 1950s. "Keep the tools unlocked; work whenever," Simpson wrote. "Perform more than you promised. . . . If the person at the next bench sees what you're working on and doesn't say 'Wow!' start over." He printed the rules in simple white letters, arranged them as an overlay in front of a photograph of the original garage on Addison Avenue, and then sent his initial working draft to the company for review.

Fiorina loved the concept, but both she and Susan Bowick, the company's head of human resources, decided that the draft rules didn't capture HP's current direction. "Carly and I started faxing stuff back and forth," Bowick later recalled. "We just basically said, 'This is what we want to go with.' It was pretty different from what the ad agency produced." By the time Fiorina and Bowick were done, the allusions to next-bench engineers and topflight performance had disappeared. Newly coined rules had taken their place, notably "The customer defines a job well done" and "Invent different ways of working."

More rejiggering lay ahead. Goodby and HP executives wanted to showcase the Addison Avenue garage as the centerpiece of HP's new television commercials, but getting access to the famous site was problematic. Dave Packard's old house had changed hands multiple times, finally becoming a Palo Alto investor's rental property. The garage in back was being leased for one hundred dollars a month by florist Michael McHugh, who stored his pushcart inside and cursed at a family of mice nibbling on his carnations. Hewlett-Packard had turned its back on the humble garage for so long that it couldn't reassert an overriding claim to the space. "We didn't even ask," one HP employee later remembered. "We were in such a hurry." Instead, the ad team picked out a back corner of HP's corporate campus and hurriedly erected an ersatz garage.

The lawn in front of the little building was made to look like a rutted driveway. Sports-utility vehicles rumbled back and forth until they wore down a hundred-foot stretch of grass. Ad-agency camera crews started shooting a concept video and realized they hadn't thought about who would narrate the ad. An anonymous actor was one possibility, but ad-agency president Rich Silverstein had a better idea. Carly Fiorina herself could be the narrator. The ad needed a voice of the future, and she personified that. "I really want this," Silverstein told HP managers. Fiorina was wary at first, knowing that Hewlett-Packard ought to be the star of the ad, not herself. But ad-agency executives and her own employees coaxed her into an on-camera role.

"Employees were asking me, in a way, 'How committed are you to this place?'" Fiorina later explained. "Think about it. I'm an outsider. They don't know me. They were asking: 'How much are you willing to risk for this place? Is it life's work or is it just a fling?'" Starring in the ad, she believed, would convince HP employees that she really cared about the company.

By crafting the garage commercial the way she did, Fiorina was seizing control of HP's heritage and turning it into a legend. The black-and-white footage from the 1930s was genuine, shared freely by the Packard family. But as Fiorina stood in front of the faux garage, the birthplace of Hewlett-Packard was being transformed into something akin to Abe Lincoln's log cabin. Reality and imagination now blurred together in the interests of creating the most persuasive symbols possible. Fiorina's intentions were admirable: She wanted Hewlett-Packard to be a famous marketplace leader that inspired its employees to do great work, rather than a worn-out technology company known only for its amiability. If that transformation could be aided by taking a few liberties with HP's history, everyone involved in the "Rules of the Garage" project cheered her on and in fact nudged her that way. The garage didn't need to be on Addison Avenue anymore. The rules didn't need to be literal precepts from Dave Packard's writings. As the company's chief mythmaker, Fiorina now possessed extraordinary powers. It was up to her to use them wisely.

Just as the new ad campaign was about to be launched, one of Fiorina's secretaries got an intriguing phone call. It was from Bill Hewlett's second wife, Rosemary, who wanted to know if Fiorina would like to meet her husband for lunch at his home in the foothills a few miles west of the company's headquarters. The only possible answer was: "I'd be thrilled." Fiorina had been thinking a lot about the founders during the "Rules of the Garage" campaign. During some travels to HP's German facilities, she had come across posters of a young Bill Hewlett rappelling off the side of a mountain. He was movie-star handsome then, with a delightful smile that reminded friends of a naughty little boy. Fiorina knew that the modern-day Hewlett was in his late eighties and very frail, but she wanted to reassure him that the company was in good hands.

On November 5, 1999, Carly Fiorina and Bill Hewlett met briefly for the only time in their lives. It was a warm, sunny day, and Hewlett was sitting in a wheelchair on the patio behind his house in Los Altos Hills, looking out on the swimming pool. A series of strokes had incapacitated him greatly. He couldn't walk. He couldn't dress or feed himself. He could squeeze out a few words a day, but only with great effort. A full-time nurse tended to him. Aware that her husband couldn't be much of a host, Rosemary Hewlett had invited four of his longtime friends to join the luncheon: HP retirees Alan Bagley, Edwin van Bronkhorst, and Bob Boniface along with Hewlett Foundation trustee Arjay Miller. The visit, clearly, would be defined by what Fiorina could make of it.

Fiorina did her best. "It's a great honor to meet you," she told Hewlett. She walked around the table, close to his wheelchair, and crouched down so he could hear her better. "I've been seeing all these pictures of you," she said. "And I want you to know, you were a hell of a good-looking guy!" Hewlett just stared. Fiorina thought she saw a flicker of amusement in his eyes, but that was all. She promised to keep HP strong as a technical leader in its fields and to maintain the highest regard for what she called the company's "shining soul." She mentioned that she had been to the garage where the company started. She hoped that at least a little of her message was getting through. And then Hewlett muttered something. The visitors strained to comprehend. They picked up only one word: "Here." Hewlett spoke again. This time his male nurse translated. "Bill said, 'Get me out of here!' " the nurse explained.

In years to come, Bill Hewlett's five-word command would be told and retold throughout Silicon Valley, eventually turning into a rallying cry for Fiorina's foes. Immediately after his comment, Hewlett was bundled up and carried to a nearby van for his daily drive to gaze at the nearby Pacific coastline. What exactly he meant by "Get me out of here" will always be a mystery. The three guests who remember the comment most clearly—Fiorina, Miller, and Bagley—all are loath to hazard a guess. "I couldn't claim to read Bill's mind," Bagley later said. "We know that he liked to take his ride every day. It was the only thing in his life that he still could enjoy. But we also know that Bill never put up with much b.s. About all we really know is that he was uncomfortable being there."

Fiorina hardly had time to brood about it. A few minutes later, she was lunching indoors with the other guests, who showered her with questions about her agenda at Hewlett-Packard. "I notice you've been promoting females," Bagley mischievously remarked. "Do you have plans to hire any males?" Before Fiorina could answer, another of the elderly guests, retired Stanford Business School dean Arjay Miller, interjected: "Only if they're qualified!"

At the end of the luncheon, Miller turned to Fiorina and said, "I think the philosophy that you're bringing to this is just right. Make the changes that have to be made and get in front of the customer. I'm an old business-school professor, and I give you an A-plus."

Because Carly Fiorina poured so much energy into reviving Hewlett-Packard's brand, some people viewed her as just a saleswoman or marketer at heart. No so. More than anything, Fiorina regarded herself as a high-level strategist, charting companies' destinies. She loved to tackle the landmark questions for which a single yes/no decision might have billion-dollar consequences for years to come. Was it time to revamp the entire organizational structure? Replace top executives? Slash costs? Change the basic business mix? Other executives might get vertigo in such settings or become blusterers who tried to do too much too abruptly. Fiorina stayed calm, focused, and decisive. This was her comfort zone.

As early as her MIT fellowship year in 1988–89, classmates pegged Fiorina as a big-picture thinker who commanded authority *because* she skipped the details. "Carly had an outstanding intellect, with an abundance of strategic clarity," recalled Nigel Taylorson, a British banker in the program. He loved the way she summarized complex issues. Then one morning, Taylorson stumbled into class after a long evening at a local pub with Fiorina and a few other classmates. Their group hadn't prepared one bit, yet Fiorina got the class discussion off to a roaring start. Suddenly, Taylorson saw a pattern. "Her main secret was her confidence," he later observed. "She may not have had a clue about the subject, but she addressed it with such confidence that you would never know. Her technique in these situations was to get into the discussion very early, when it was still in the preliminary generalization stage. The professors never noticed that as the discussion became more detailed, she quieted down considerably."

A crucial step in Fiorina's strategic evolution occurred in August 1997, when she got her first chance to wield boardroom power. She became a director of Kellogg, the venerable cereal company, joining the likes of future Defense Secretary Donald Rumsfeld, former Time Incorporated chairman Richard Munro, and former Ford Motor Company president Harold Polling. Most newcomers would have been intimidated by such powerful elders. Not Fiorina. "It took her thirty seconds to have an impact," Polling later remembered. The problems at Kellogg seemed so glaringly obvious to her. Earnings were slumping, upstart rivals like General Mills were cutting into Kellogg's market share, and the cereal maker lacked the willpower to do much about it. "She'd look at the strategic plan and say: 'That's not quick enough,'" Munro later recalled. "She'd say, 'You can do twice as well as that. And it shouldn't take you six months to get there.'"

Within two years of Fiorina's arrival, Kellogg was a changed company. She helped pick a new and younger CEO, Carlos Gutierrez, who closed surplus factories, took aim at General Mills with new products, and shook up the company's leadership team. Kellogg wasn't as cozy anymore, but it was a lot more efficient, and it was winning back investors' respect. People who knew the company credited Fiorina with spurring much of that transformation. She became one of the first people whom Gutierrez turned to when testing new ideas before announcing them. "I knew she believed in me," he later said. "But I knew she would challenge me, too." Just before announcing a massive staff shakeup, Gutierrez asked Fiorina what she thought. Her three-word reply—"Right. Clean sweep!"—encouraged Gutierrez to charge ahead.

At Hewlett-Packard, Fiorina stormed into action with a new strategic agenda as well. In August 1999, she gathered a dozen top lieutenants for a three-day off-site meeting at the Seascape resort, fifty miles south of HP headquarters, to explain the new order. She wasn't planning to fire any of them or to replace them with Lucent cronies. All the same, she knocked people out of their comfort zone before they had finished pouring their morning coffee. "None of you will be in exactly the same jobs in a few months," Fiorina told a roomful of startled executives. "I'm not prepared to tell you what the new jobs will be, but I'm quite certain they will be different."

Operating managers were shocked. For the previous few years, Platt had been granting them extraordinary autonomy. Over the next three days, Fiorina informed them the headquarters perspective was about to matter a lot more and that Hewlett-Packard would adopt more unified strategy in which the printing, computing, and services businesses would be closely yoked together. Debra Dunn, who was about to become vice president for strategy and corporate operations, looked around the room and saw several managers with stunned looks on their faces, signaling "Man, my world is just getting blown up here!" Inkjet-printing chief Antonio Perez challenged Fiorina so directly that she took him aside at break time for a private chat. When he came back, he was much quieter. Either Fiorina had won him over or he had decided further argument would be pointless.

Despite all the tension, Fiorina's fans believed that she made an overwhelming case for greater centralization. On the final day of the Seascape meeting, the new CEO stood at an easel and listed all the problems that HP executives themselves had said needed fixing. "We aren't growing fast enough," she wrote. "We aren't profitable enough." The company's businesses had great potential to help one another, she asserted, but that wasn't happening. "We're leaving diamonds on the floor," she declared. Without explicitly pointing fingers at anyone, she was telling executives it was time for a change. People who resisted wouldn't be regarded as good team members.

In early 2000, Fiorina carried out a sweeping reorganization that made good on her promise to redefine everyone's jobs. The company didn't need a myriad of unconnected divisions anymore. That approach was driving customers crazy. In particular, major customers such as Ford Motor and Boeing were grumbling that Hewlett-Packard pestered them with dozens of separate sales teams, each pushing a narrow line of products, rather than addressing their total needs in one unified conversation. It was time for HP to stop dissipating its market impact and creating wasteful duplication that way.

To fix these problems, Fiorina decided to borrow a page from her Lucent playbook. Instead of letting each division handle its own research, manufacturing, sales, and marketing, she would reorganize Hewlett-Packard into quadrants. Two vast sales and marketing groups—known as the front end—would take command of customer relationships. One group would talk to mass-market consumers; the other would focus on the Fords and Boeings of the world. Meanwhile, manufacturing and research for all of HP's products would be separated and redefined as the "back end." That would be split in two as well, with printing and imaging making up one half and the entire range of computer initiatives—from PCs to servers to services—grouped in the other half.

Fiorina's ideas looked great on a white board, but some top executives shuddered. "I was a deer caught in the headlights when she described the front and back end," the longtime head of laser printing, Carolyn Ticknor, remarked in mid-2000. Ticknor was used to having full profit responsibility for her business. In a new job as head of printing and imaging's back end, she had more responsibility but less control over her business, which was jarring. Before long, it emerged that HP's accounting systems couldn't precisely allocate costs between the front end and back end. As a result, some salespeople raced to beat their quotas, only to saddle HP with what ultimately turned out to be unprofitable new orders. After two years of insisting that the front-end/back-end system would work in its original format, Fiorina eventually switched to a hybrid model that let executives regain more product-line responsibility. She was right that HP needed to show a better face to its customers. She was wrong in thinking she could retool a vast company from top to bottom in a matter of months without creating unwanted new snarls.

Fiorina was running into the hardest challenge of all in remaking Hewlett-Packard, the inevitable tug-of-war between a new CEO and some ninety thousand tradition-minded employees. Midlevel managers and rank-and-file employees didn't openly attack her new ideas. They just meandered around them. In big public forums, Fiorina laid out her agenda crisply and starkly, appearing to win managers' wholehearted support. But in the next few days, managers huddled privately to decide whether they really liked everything they heard. They softened her goals slightly, adjusted the timetables, made a few commonsense exceptions—and by the time they were finished, essentially gutted whatever Fiorina was trying to achieve. Resistance was so subtle and pervasive that she couldn't accomplish anything by getting angry. There was no obvious opponent. It was just the system.

One of Fiorina's favorite consultants, organizational-change expert Dan Plunkett, reassured her that she was on the right path. "HP has all the attributes of a very well-developed bureaucracy," he remarked. It could leave a lesser CEO feeling like a frightened mouse lost in a maze. All the same, Plunkett believed that Fiorina was right on the big issues and so persuasive and determined in person that over time she would prevail.

Fiorina also had the ability to change HP's gene pool, month by month, simply by altering the kinds of people who were hired, and the kinds of people who were let go. All through the Platt years, HP had an astonishingly low employee turnover of barely 5 percent a year. The company was inbred and proud of it. Once Fiorina took charge, that rate doubled, particularly among the company's top three hundred executives. Fresh faces from Motorola, Xerox, and Netscape came in. The hybridization of the HP workforce was happening so gradually and imperceptibly that it never made headlines, but over time, it could become Fiorina's greatest ally in her efforts to reshape the company to her tastes.

In early 2001, Fiorina got to fill her first big vacancy: chief of the print and imaging business. Carolyn Ticknor was on her way out, in what was officially described as a retirement. Antonio Perez, the former inkjet boss, had left the company, too, believing he could do better as chief executive of a French maker of smart cards. (He lasted a year there.) But within the printer group's executive ranks, Fiorina had already spotted her kind of executive. He was Vyomesh Joshi, an engineer by training but an enthusiastic, hungry evangelist by temperament. He had worked at Hewlett-Packard since 1980, and somehow bureaucratic caution hadn't ever infected him. He had won Fiorina's respect in 2000 by championing two risky but exciting projects, digital cameras and a more aggressive role in the sub-$100 printer market. Neither expansion would help profits right away, but both had the potential to accelerate the growth rate of printing and imaging dramatically over the next few years. What's more, unlike his predecessors, Joshi had made peace with the front-end/back-end experiment. The new structure reminded him of a boyhood visit to an ascetic temple in India. Pilgrims there achieved spiritual strength by surrendering material possessions, he observed. Perhaps HP executives could become stronger by letting go of old divisional controls, too.

When Fiorina called to offer Joshi the best promotion in his twenty-one years at HP, she didn't encumber him with any weighty speeches about his new responsibilities and the burdens of running the company's most profitable businesses. Instead, she flooded him with optimism. He could do the rest. "I'll always remember what Carly told me in that phone call," Joshi later remarked. "She said, 'I'm so excited! VJ, we've got a chance to make history together.' "

Fiorina tried to bring that same unquenchable optimism to the creation of an effective Internet strategy for Hewlett-Packard. In this case, however, her timing was wretched. Internet mania reached its peak during her first year on the job, causing almost every big, established company to act a little wild in an effort to seem with the times. HP put on its party clothes just as the fun was about to stop. Marketers came up with something called e-speak, billed as a way to help companies communicate better in the Internet age. Designers produced a wired prototype of a community of the future called CoolTown. Meanwhile, HP computer executive Ann Livermore went all out to win a big order in early 2000 from Amazon.com, the online merchant that for a brief time was seen as the most brilliant enterprise in America.

Mindful of the challenges that any new chief executive faces, Fiorina sought advice from someone else in a similar position, Novell CEO Eric

Schmidt. He was a former Sun executive who had been recruited into Novell with much fanfare in 1997. Over lunch, Schmidt wryly recounted his ups and downs. He had zoomed into Novell in a chauffeured Hummer, part of an opening-day ceremony that resembled a coronation. But initial flattery from employees, analysts, and the media proved deceiving. At some point, Schmidt cautioned, "You will have an 'Oh, shit!' day, when you realize that the problems are much deeper than you thought." From that moment on, he said, you are at most ninety days away from announcing bad quarterly results. What happens next will be your true test as a CEO.

Fiorina listened attentively, but for most of 2000, there wasn't any reason to worry. HP stock had climbed as much as 40 percent since her arrival date. The company's revenue was growing at 15 percent a year, nearly double her predecessor's pace. Profits appeared strong. "We're moving up and some of our competitors are moving down," she told HP managers at a leadership meeting in June 2000. She was ready to jab at Scott McNealy, the Sun Microsystems executive who had bedeviled Lew Platt for years. "He can't stop talking about HP," Fiorina said at the leadership meeting. "At their analysts' meeting in December, he actually spent four precious minutes of analysts' time running a videotape which was basically a spoof of me. It had a garage; it had a blond woman, and in the course of this video a wrecking ball came, wrecked the garage, and knocked it on top of the woman's head." Did that disturb Fiorina? Not at all.

"I find it unbelievably flattering," she declared. Not only had Fiorina taken control of HP's airwaves; she regarded herself as jamming everyone else's broadcasting towers.

Best of all, even her most straitlaced lieutenants were getting into the mood. The company's chief of computer systems, Duane Zitzner, was a ten-year HP veteran who readily betrayed his origins as a math major from a tiny Wisconsin farm town. His scuffed shoes, his worried expressions, and his never-ending attention to details made him the periodic butt of jokes. But he was a relentless worker and a master at squeezing down production costs. All through the spring and summer of 2000, Fiorina worked closely with Zitzner to oversee the development of the new Superdome computer. The machine was supposed to be the workhorse of HP's enterprise computing group, and they both decided it was time to launch it with showmanship. So the company booked the main ballroom at New York's Regent Hotel in September 2000, invited hundreds of journalists and analysts, and set up the high-tech industry's version of a rock concert. Throbbing music opened the event. A dry-ice machine added an otherworldly quality. Rollers propelled the thousand-pound computer across the stage.

Out bounded Zitzner, who hailed Superdome as "one damn spank server." His sudden foray into ghetto slang brought howls of laughter from the crowd—but Zitzner didn't mind. Neither did Fiorina. At least he was trying.

Chapter 5

INSIDE THE BOARDROOM

When Carly Fiorina took the leadership baton from Lew Platt, everyone wanted to portray the handoff as smooth and amiable. Just after Fiorina arrived at the company in July 1999, she and Platt sat on a patio outside the company's Palo Alto headquarters and swapped achingly polite compliments about each other, to be shared in a broadcast to all employees. "You have done a wonderful job of leading this company," Fiorina told her predecessor. "I'll look forward to your coaching and support in the months ahead." Platt glanced down modestly and replied, "You can be assured that you will have my full support. Anything I can help you with during the transition, I'll be there."

Two months later, however, at Hewlett-Packard's September board meeting, it was clear that Lew Platt's mood had soured. He was about to cede the chairman's job to his old rival, Dick Hackborn, and as a practical matter, Platt was becoming irrelevant. Fiorina wasn't seeking out his advice. Days would go by without the two of them having any contact. Platt had organized a trip to Asia so that Fiorina could meet some of HP's key business partners there. In those meetings, once pleasantries were exchanged, Fiorina didn't defer to him at all. She took command of the conversation, sketching out ambitious plans for Hewlett-Packard's expansion in each particular company. The hosts thought she was incredible, but Platt thought she was promising too much. It was time to speak his mind.

Exercising his power as a longtime director, Platt asked for a few minutes to address the board without Fiorina in the room. This would be an "executive session," without the usual board aides or HP insiders watching the proceedings. It would be a chance for raw, blunt talk among directors only. Fiorina picked up her papers and headed out the door. She would wait in her office until the directors invited her back.

"She doesn't want to take any advice from me," Platt said, after Fiorina left the room. He went through the details of their Asia trip together, stop by stop. No matter what the hosts asked, Fiorina had an answer. That galled Platt, who believed that she was going beyond the bounds of her technical knowledge. Even worse in his eyes, Fiorina was promising growth in every market. Asian executives were delighted, but Platt wasn't sure that all her claims would come true. He had built his career around the time-honored virtues of underpromising and overdelivering. She was a New Economy leader who propelled people into the future with audacious goals. The more that audiences embraced Fiorina's rhetoric, the more Platt's stomach churned with anxiety that she was undermining Hewlett-Packard's credibility. As he spoke, other directors sensed he was having second thoughts about HP's new chief executive. In fact, Platt seemed to be wondering if the company had made a mistake.

Platt wasn't done yet. Someone needed to step in and coach Fiorina more aggressively, he contended. He had been willing to play that role, but evidently she didn't want him, and the board didn't want him either. So be it. Someone had to take that role, and he doubted that Dick Hackborn— the incoming chairman—could do it. Someone needed to punch through Fiorina's damnable certainty that she was right all the time. As Platt put it: "Every now and then, everybody who has any credibility says, 'Gee, I just don't know about that. Let me check into it and I'll get back to you.' Anybody who answers every question is suspect as far as I'm concerned, particularly after they've been on the job for a month."

Directors winced. Platt was clearly an angry man. He was venting frustrations that weren't just about Fiorina; they were about a new generation's way of doing business and about his place in HP history. He had tried so hard for thirty-three years to do everything right for Hewlett-Packard, and now there wasn't going to be any applause when he left the stage. For a moment, no one knew how to respond. They looked at Hackborn, waiting for his reaction. He sat silently, wishing that Platt hadn't embarked on such a hasty performance review of his successor. The board's role was to help Fiorina succeed in her new job. If something was bothering Platt, why couldn't he have found a safer channel for his concerns, instead of disrupting the board meeting so publicly with his worries?

Finally, independent director Sam Ginn weighed in. "Hey, guys," he said. "Can I remind you of something? What the hell did we hire her for in the first place?"

And with that, the board found its voice. Directors reminded themselves of all the stagnation and feebleness that had led them to look outside for a new CEO just a few months earlier. Hewlett-Packard had lost its verve. It was an aging Cadillac in the slow lane, being passed by zippy young rivals that were the equivalents of BMWs, Porsches, and Miatas.

Carly Fiorina was the cure. She was bringing HP youth, passion, and optimism. If her leadership style wasn't exactly to Lew Platt's taste . . . well, that was probably all for the best. All the progressive-faction leaders on the board—Dick Hackborn, Jay Keyworth, Pattie Dunn, Phil Condit and others—began to speak up now, rallying to Fiorina's defense. One or two of the old-time directors, who were about to retire or move to the Agilent board, thought Platt might have a point. But it wasn't their boardroom anymore. Control was moving into the hands of modernists who saw the world the same way that Carly Fiorina did. Everyone in the boardroom wanted to weigh in and be part of this redefining moment. In the rush to do so, directors lost track of time. By one tally, they spent two hours in their closed-door executive session.

All the while, Fiorina waited in her office, watching the minutes tick by. Nobody was coming to get her. Platt wasn't just sharing a few brief words. This was turning into a marathon session, in which the rest of the directors, quite literally, were talking about her behind her back. Finally, Dick Hackborn came into her office. Fiorina was sitting on a small sofa, with her feet tucked under her. She knew she was steeling herself for a long period of being tested.

Hackborn sat down next to her. He explained that Platt thought she was moving too fast. She pressed him for details, and he took her through Platt's concerns, one by one. Fiorina disputed some of them, but mostly she just listened. Hackborn "was just tremendously empathetic," Fiorina later said. "I remember us sitting very close together on a couch. And the physical presence was comforting." From the moment she had arrived at Hewlett-Packard, she had sensed that Platt's standing would be a very sensitive issue. But she felt she couldn't let it slow her down. Hewlett-Packard needed to be shocked into wakefulness as soon as possible, and she required full boardroom authority to do it.

Once Fiorina had taken stock of Platt's concerns, it was time to fight back. "Dick, this board cannot have me on probation," she said. "We made a deal. We're in this together. We know what it's going to take. We have to proceed. We can't, we *can't* get cold feet now."

Hackborn quickly reassured her. "No, that isn't what this is about," he said. He let her know that he believed Platt's concerns were out of line. He made it clear that other directors were firmly on her side and in favor of change.

An invisible line had just been crossed. The Hewlett-Packard board wasn't seeing itself any longer as a force of restraint, reinforcing time-honored ways of doing things and championing prudence. The board was becoming a war council, pushing for change as fast as the rest of the organization could tolerate it. Interpersonal conflict wasn't automatically horrifying anymore: a sign that someone had stepped too far. In the new era, the old guard's sputtered protests could be construed as good news. If the traditionalists were angry, it meant that fresh ideas were starting to take hold. Directors had started moving toward this new worldview in early 1999 when they guided Lew Platt to the door. That was invigorating, and there would be a lot more to come.

The boardroom was about to become the command center of a worldwide battle to redefine Hewlett-Packard. Creating shareholder value would be the directors' stated goal. There would be an implicit sense that the right way to achieve this would be to make Hewlett-Packard into more of a world-class leader. Fiorina and her directors believed the company ought to be the biggest and most successful competitor in more of its markets. It ought to speed up growth and get costs under control. Ultimately, the company should stand tall in the public eye. As much as those goals overlapped, they carried with them a conviction that Hewlett-Packard ought to serve shareholders by getting bigger and stronger. Strategies that involved taking apart the company—such as a second, Agilent-style spin-off—never were going to be anyone's first choice. The company might need to undertake sizable layoffs if times got tough. But as board members prepared for bold departures from the past, their natural preference was for strategic makeovers that could lead to giant acquisitions.

At the most fundamental level, directors' subservience to the wishes of Dave Packard and Bill Hewlett was coming to an end. Back in 1957, when the company went public, the patriarchs created what is commonly known as a "founders' board." They invited their old college professor Fred Terman and a few other trusted friends and community elders to join the board. That worked wonderfully as long as Packard and Hewlett called the shots. The founders wanted a little friendly advice in the boardroom and some help extending their business networks into new areas. Informal slots were created for "a finance man," "a medical man," and "a scientist" to round out the board. As HP became much bigger, the people picked for these directorships became far more prominent. But the founders didn't expect anyone else in the boardroom to steer the entire enterprise in new directions, let alone overrule them. It was their company.

As old men, Dave Packard and Bill Hewlett had preserved their grip on the board—so that it could last even beyond the grave. They enlisted their oldest sons as HP directors in 1987 and followed with a daughter and a son-in-law in 1993. The publicly stated reason was that the Packard and Hewlett families and their foundations owned as much as one-third of the company's stock and ought to have proportionate boardroom representation. That bland statement concealed deeper fears, however. People close to the founding families say that Dave Packard in particular worried that HP might become a takeover target someday. Corporate raiders had stalked some of America's most venerable businesses. The best defense against a takeover, of course, was a well-run business. As a last resort, the founders believed, packing the boardroom with family members might ward off the barbarians.

Hewlett-Packard never became a takeover target, but all through the 1990s, the four heirs' presence on the board became an awkward and occasionally annoying fact of life for everyone else. Dave Packard's son, David Woodley Packard, was a hard-to-please iconoclast who sometimes brought up the narrowest of issues. He complained repeatedly, for instance, that the printer division's type fonts didn't handle certain two-letter combinations as well as they should. The letters *fi* shouldn't be formed separately, he said. They should be printed as one unified unit, known as a ligature, with the upper curve of the *f* merging into the dot of the *i*. Aesthetically, he had a point; as a practical matter, it struck everyone else as a bizarre way to squander boardroom time. Some employees at the Boise printing division began voting their HP shares against him when he stood for renomination as a director, just because the ligature orations irritated them so much.

In all these disputes, David Woodley Packard's erudition never was in doubt. He had earned a Ph.D. in classics at Harvard in 1968 by taking all the words ever written by the ancient Roman poet and philosopher Livy and entering them into a searchable database, back in the days when such a project required sixty-five thousand punched cards and eleven miles of magnetic tape. He could decode the software programs burned into a microchip, rewrite them into a different application, and squeeze his version back onto a different chip. He was the intellectual equal of his famous father. But, in the words of one insider, "He just didn't have the business gene."

Bill Hewlett's son-in-law Jean-Paul Gimon was another family member who couldn't find a natural home on the board. He was a successful French banker, managing Credit Lyonnais's operations in North America. He had married Bill Hewlett's oldest daughter, Eleanor, and made his home in Greenwich, Connecticut. When Gimon joined the board in 1993, he had hoped to be valued as someone bringing a European perspective to the boardroom of what was now a truly multinational company, but his noticeable French accent and his less-than-direct connection to Bill Hewlett doomed him to be seen forever as nothing more than "the son-in-law." In the words of HP director Sam Ginn, "He was an empty suit. I mean, he came to the meetings, but his questions were very often not even related in a way that you could understand what he was asking."

Two other family members fared better in the boardroom, in part because they were diligent, quiet, and didn't make waves. One of Dave Packard's daughters, Susan Packard Orr, joined the board in 1993 and served at length on the compensation committee, ultimately becoming its chair. She had overseen the contract negotiations with Carly Fiorina in July 1999, steering that sometimes-contentious process to a successful resolution. Orr had earned an MBA from Stanford in 1970 and ran her own business in Palo Alto providing computer technology to nonprofit enterprises. As another HP director put it, "She's not a strategist, but she brought a lot of other strengths to the board."

Bill Hewlett's oldest son, Walter, was seen as the most reliable of the bunch. He had been a physics major at Harvard and was a gifted runner, finishing the 1964 Boston Marathon in the fastest time ever posted until then by a nineteen-year-old. He was blessed with his father's good looks, friendly grin, and peaceful disposition, but there was a hesitancy about him that friends found either endearing or a bit poignant. Walter Hewlett drifted a bit in his twenties and thirties, getting separate master's degrees in engineering and operations research, and then training briefly to be a concert organist. As much as he liked music, he found he got unbearably nervous before concerts. Ultimately, he decided he was "stretching in a direction I was not meant to stretch." He opted instead for a doctorate in music at Stanford, later forming a research center that brought modern database technology to the humanities. In that job, he wrote many lines of computer code himself.

When Walter Hewlett joined the HP board in 1987, he told the San Jose *Mercury News* that he would be invisible at first, adding, "My role on the board for at least two years is to listen." He stayed mum for a while, but over time he established plenty of his own grassroots connections with HP's operating units. He visited the printer division in Boise frequently and became friends with Dick Hackborn. He took apart HP laptop computers with a screwdriver so that he could see how all the components fit together. He and David Woodley Packard became known as the only directors who could write computer programs capable of running on a Unix operating system. Subdued by nature, Walter Hewlett didn't speak much at board meetings. But he was a thoughtful steward for the HP Way and a knowledgeable contributor on technical issues. "He was a good board member," Lew Platt later said. "He seemed to have a well-developed sense of what you ought to talk about and what you shouldn't."

In the mid-1990s, Platt suggested that all the second-generation family members take a three-day course on directors' responsibilites, so they could contribute more to the company's governance. Only Walter Hewlett went at first. A year later, Susan Packard Orr followed. Platt's request came at a sensitive time when some directors felt they were doing a lot to accommodate the founding families' desires. To help Dave Packard cope with his deafness, for example, a court stenographer had entered the boardroom in the early 1990s to produce on-screen transcripts for the chairman emeritus. Fellow director emeritus Bill Hewlett sometimes glanced at the stenographer's screen, too. As Bill Hewlett got older and frailer, other directors remember his son Walter sitting beside him, explaining anything that seemed puzzling.

Given all the business upheavals at most other big companies during the 1990s, it is astonishing that the founders'-board era lasted as long as it did at Hewlett-Packard. During that decade, the founding families' four-seat representation on the board did become an increasing source of friction. By the late 1990s, the founding families' combined stakes in Hewlett-Packard dropped below 20 percent, reflecting the patriarchs' many gifts of HP stock to worthy causes and some portfolio diversification by Bill Hewlett's largest foundation. Yet the family members still clung to four of the fourteen board seats, giving them 29 percent of the directorships. Near the end of his time in office, Platt circulated a confidential questionnaire to all the directors, asking them if the families were overrepresented. Most of the nonfamily directors said yes.

Dick Hackborn, in a 1997 interview, called the fourteen-member board too big for effective strategic discussions. He also said it was too meager in big-business or computer-industry expertise to be really valuable in helping the company's chief executive steer the enterprise. "It's a board in transition," Hackborn said. "The time is rapidly approaching when the board is going to have to get more involved."

With the Agilent spin-off, all the pent-up pressures for boardroom change at HP finally burst into the open. It was decided that both Hewlett-Packard and Agilent would be reconstituted with smaller boards, making it easier for directors to take decisive action. Most directors were asked which board they would rather join. Two directors with close ties to the civic-minded nonprofit world—David Lawrence of the Kaiser Permanente health plan and Thomas Everhart, the former president of Caltech—opted for Agilent. "The medical man" and "the scientist" had left the HP board.

Meanwhile, plans were made to pare back the founding families' representation to just one directorship at each company. At first, that reduction seemed to be happening almost of its own accord. David Woodley Packard stormed off the HP board shortly before Carly Fiorina's arrival, because of his deep unhappiness with the decision to break Hewlett-Packard into two companies. Walter Hewlett, who liked the spin-off idea, told everyone he would leave the HP board and cast his lot with Agilent. Other directors saw this as a fine opportunity to squeeze Jean-Paul Gimon out of the picture and leave Susan Packard Orr as the only family member on the HP board. Gimon was appalled at the notion that he wouldn't be nominated for another term. He protested to fellow director Sam Ginn, who ran the nominating committee, and to Dick Hackborn, but the other directors wouldn't budge. Finally Gimon took his case to Walter Hewlett, who proposed a fateful compromise. As Walter Hewlett later recalled, "I said, 'Look, if you're not going to keep Jean-Paul, you really ought to have a Hewlett or someone representing Hewlett interests.' And they said, 'OK, Walter, you can be on the HP board.' So I ended up being on both boards."

The net effect was to reassemble the HP board into a leaner, bolder group that was eager to help Carly Fiorina redefine Hewlett-Packard in the most ambitious ways. Starting in January 2000, the company's boardroom seated just ten directors, instead of the old fourteen. Lew Platt vanished, with Dick Hackborn taking over as chairman. Of the other six nonfamily directors, three were high-powered corporate leaders in their own right, who knew how to map out new strategies and then look for the acquisitions or partnerships that could make them come true. Sam Ginn, a lifelong telecom executive, was the first to arrive, attending his first HP board meeting in 1996, a few days after Dave Packard's death. Ginn had combined his AirTouch cell-phone business in 1999 with Vodafone PLC of Britain in a $56 billion deal. Phil Condit joined the board in 1998; he was chairman of Boeing and the architect of the aerospace industry's biggest merger ever. Patricia Dunn also joined in 1998; as chair of Barclays Global Investors, she ran a money-management powerhouse in San Francisco with

$800 billion in assets.★ All three of them were itching for a chance to help strengthen the company.

"When is the last time we created a new market for HP?" Ginn kept asking. The company was good at improving existing product lines, he acknowledged. But it needed to unleash the creativity and innovation necessary to produce the next printer business. He supported efforts to make HP's existing businesses more profitable, but he hammered away at the notion that Hewlett-Packard ought to be doing more than fine-tuning what it already had; it should be looking for ways to augment its position in markets that it could dominate. That might involve acquisitions; it might not. Either way, Ginn was encouraging the company to take bolder steps.

Condit was every bit as adamant. "Literally ever since I joined the board," he said in April 2002, "the primary focus has been long-term strategy." He freely shared lessons from his own experience at Boeing, most notably his decision in 1997 to buy archrival McDonnell Douglas, which had a much stronger defense-contract business and a much weaker commercial-aviation line. Fusing the two companies together had its bumpy moments, but it ultimately produced a bigger, stronger business.

Fiorina could feel good about the rest of her board too. Jay Keyworth, a former presidential science adviser in the Reagan administration, had served on the HP board since 1986; he had a strong sense of the company's heritage and generally aligned himself with Dick Hackborn on strategic issues. Bob Wayman, the chief financial officer of Hewlett-Packard, had been on the board since 1993; she regarded him as a strong member of her management team. The final seat would be hers to fill; John Fery, the retired chairman of Boise-Cascade, had reached age seventy and was ready to step down. Wanting an entrepreneurial, New Economy perspective, Fiorina picked Bob Knowling as her tenth director. He was the CEO of Covad Communications, a fast-growing provider of high-speed Internet access. It didn't hurt that she and Knowling had worked together for years in the telecom industry, going all the way back to the days when he was running the downtown-Chicago phone hubs for Illinois Bell and she was managing his account at AT&T. They knew how to get along just fine.

★ Dunn succeeded Paul Miller, a renowned Philadelphia investment manager who had been the board's "finance man." In her first months on the board, Dunn impressed colleagues with her keen knowledge of the ways that Wall Street trends might make a difference for Hewlett-Packard. It was a new world. There was no reason anymore that the "finance man" needed to be a man.

Before Fiorina joined Hewlett-Packard, one of her best mentors, Lucent chairman Henry Schacht, had offered some useful advice. "Pay attention to your chemistry with the board," he said. "No detail is too small. When you hold board dinners, think about how the place cards ought to be arranged, so that the right people are talking to one another." Fiorina took that principle to heart when it came time to compose directors' photographs for Hewlett-Packard's 1999 annual report, the first one issued during her tenure. Instead of posing everyone in dark suits standing in a row, she opted for a much more casual approach, with male directors wearing open-neck shirts and women wearing slacks, all standing in clusters of three. In her own cluster, Fiorina invited Dick Hackborn and Walter Hewlett to stand beside her. Hackborn was an obvious choice; he was about to take charge as chairman. She didn't know Hewlett nearly as well, but his selection wasn't random. Regardless of what had happened to the son-in-law, the new CEO of Hewlett-Packard wanted everyone to know she was proud to stand next to a real Hewlett.

The new board's mission was about to be charted by Chairman Hackborn and CEO Fiorina, working in tandem. There was an odd-couple charm to their interplay. He was an introvert in his midsixties, an electrical engineer by training who had joined Hewlett-Packard nearly forty years earlier, in the twilight of the vacuum-tube age. She was a much younger crowd-pleaser who enjoyed talking about the exciting times that lay ahead in the "digital renaissance." Yet for all their obvious differences, Hackborn and Fiorina harmonized perfectly in the boardroom. They both were big-picture pragmatists, looking for something new and bold that worked. They were loyal to their friends, loyal to their company, and—serious rebels at heart—eager to shake up the status quo.

By accepting Hackborn as her expert guide to the customs and lore of Hewlett-Packard, Fiorina unwittingly bought into his shortcomings as well. While Hackborn knew HP's senior executives extremely well, he hadn't lived in the Palo Alto area since 1977. He wasn't intensely attuned to the likes and dislikes of lower-level employees at headquarters, let alone the tastes of HP's powerful retirees and alumni who populated Silicon Valley. What's more, Hackborn in his prime had been known for a desire to create an apparent business crisis every now and then just to stir up people on his team and get them working in more decisive ways. Managers in Boise periodically were told to double revenue or speed up delivery dates, instead of languidly enjoying 15 percent annual growth. Hackborn's penchant for disruption worked perfectly in a company in which too many people played it safe and someone had to make things exciting. But with Fiorina eager to foment change as well, the two rebels had the potential to goad each other ever deeper into the danger zone.

Still, the mentor/protégée relationship suited both of them. Hackborn already had provided Fiorina with a crash course on the printer business, distilling twenty years of expertise into a few hours of facts, judgments, and aphorisms. Now he shared pointers about working effectively within the HP culture. Quiz the divisional controllers if you need straight answers to tough questions, he counseled; they know everything. Get people to trust you by trusting them first. Underpromise and overdeliver. She soaked up all the advice she could get. Only when Hackborn got too immersed in the details—wanting to see drafts of a minor press release before it was issued—did she push back. Fiorina needed a few wise words on the biggest issues; she didn't want undue meddling in her daily routine.

Hackborn began making his mark in the boardroom in early 2000 with two deceptively modest changes in directors' routine. The HP board typically scheduled six major meetings a year, on the third Thursday and Friday of odd-numbered months. In the Platt years, just about all of Thursday had been burned up by committee meetings, as small groups of directors took turns reviewing the pension plan, internal audit reports, and other details. There was hardly any time available to focus on bigger issues. Instead of scheduling committee meetings one after another, Hackborn decided they should all meet concurrently, early on Thursday. That would create a big new window of time on Thursday from 4 P.M. through the dinner hour, during which the entire board could debate top-level strategy.

Hackborn also introduced a high-powered directors' Web site with secure passwords that only board members could access. He used that as a way to disseminate briefing materials ahead of time so that directors could arrive at meetings sharp and well informed. Colleagues could see the change right away. "Nobody could get away with sitting back and just listening and nodding," Pattie Dunn later remarked. "This became an activist, engaged board." For years, Hackborn had wanted to bring the Hewlett-Packard board to life. Now his moment had arrived. He had big plans for Thursday's new strategy discussions—and so did Fiorina.

"Right at the beginning of Carly's tenure, the agenda was clear," recalled Larry Sonsini, a powerful Palo Alto attorney who counseled the Hewlett-Packard board during both the Platt and Fiorina years. "There were strategic issues that had to be addressed. Who is the real competition?

Who do we need to face off against?" Once directors settled on the right targets, they began talking about the best ways to improve Hewlett-Packard's position. Among the most exciting options was the chance to undertake a giant acquisition—something that Dave Packard and Bill Hewlett hadn't ever felt comfortable pursuing.

For a few months in late 1999 and early 2000, HP's directors toyed with ways of radically accelerating the printer group's push into photography and digital imaging. Among the boldest ideas under consideration: buying Eastman Kodak—a deal that probably would have cost Hewlett-Packard $30 billion or more. After modest deliberation, however, directors decided that wasn't the way they wanted to go. Anyone buying Kodak would acquire not just its operating assets, but also various environmental, pension, and employee-health-care obligations, dimming the allure of the combination. Besides, as Fiorina later noted, "The thinking was that their business was changing into a digital business. We felt we could own a digital business without them."

Instead, the board decided, the printer business should expand by internal growth or perhaps by some much smaller, carefully targeted acquisitions. Ultimately, the company did just that, negotiating in 2001 to spend $882 million to acquire Indigo N.V., a Dutch-Israeli company that made commercial-grade printers suitable for cranking out mail-order catalogs, labels, business flyers, and the like. Hewlett-Packard had owned 13 percent of Indigo for some time, and the two companies worked well together.

The Indigo initiative did produce a jaw-dropping moment in the early stages of negotiations. At a board meeting in Napa Valley, California, Walter Hewlett startled his colleagues by telling them that he had purchased some Indigo stock for his own account. "I thought of it as being independent of HP," Hewlett later said. "When it became clear that HP had a direct interest in this, that put me in a sort of—almost a conflict situation. I dropped that stock like a hot potato. If I had believed that HP was going to make an investment in Indigo, I would not have bought the stock myself."

Directors were speechless. With the HP board now scouting actively for acquisition candidates, directors would be privy to an extraordinary amount of sensitive, potentially market-moving information. They needed to keep that information strictly confidential. The company's general counsel, Ann Baskins, was especially mindful that directors not do anything in their personal stock trading that could be viewed as a conflict of interest by anyone. When Hewlett dumped his Indigo stock, he ended up with a slight loss on the investment, so no one could accuse him of having made money in the stock market inappropriately. But the whole episode unsettled some of Hewlett's fellow directors. Naïve as his mistake may have been, there wasn't any room in HP's boardroom either for naïveté or mistakes.

Walter Hewlett became even more isolated in early 2001 when the only other founding-family member remaining on the board, Susan Packard Orr, announced that she would be stepping down. She told fellow directors that she had too many obligations in her life and wanted to reduce her commitments. She chaired the Packard Foundation, which at that time had more than $10 billion in assets; she was a Stanford trustee; and she was deeply immersed in a campaign to upgrade the Lucile Packard Children's Hospital, named after her late mother. But board members who knew her well sensed that her departure reflected more than just a crowded calendar. As Orr became prominent in philanthropic circles, it was harder for her to jump back and forth between the worlds of making money and giving it away. She felt urgently needed in the eleemosynary world; she felt almost superfluous on the HP board. In private conversations with two different directors, she remarked, "I have no idea why my father wanted me on the board." Fiorina, Hackborn, Ginn, and Hewlett urged her to stay. She had been a popular and admired director. But she was adamant, and in April 2001 she stepped off the board. That left Walter Hewlett as the last family representative.

All the while, the board's hunt for the big strategic fix continued. Once the Kodak proposition perished in early 2000, directors focused much more intently on HP's opportunities and challenges in the computer industry. Surveying all the segments in which Hewlett-Packard competed, it was easy to draw up a long list of segment-by-segment rivals. Dell Computer and to some extent Compaq Computer were the companies to beat in the personal-computer business. Sun Microsystems was the archrival in servers, workstations, and other business-class computers. EMC and Network Appliance were attracting attention for their success in the market for data-storage devices. The computer-services and -outsourcing industry was highly fragmented and full of interesting rivals, ranging from Electronic Data Systems (EDS) to the Big Five auditing and consulting companies.

In terms of across-the-board competition, however, only one name really mattered: IBM. The ninety-year-old giant of the computer industry had stumbled a bit in the early 1990s. Then, under the leadership of CEO Lou Gerstner—recruited in 1993 from outside the computer industry, too—IBM had roared back into prominence. It was a major force in markets ranging from semiconductors and memory devices to laptop computers, servers, storage systems, and computer services. Most important, IBM used its industry-leading position in computer services to build up deep, wide, and intensely profitable relationships with its biggest customers. "Nobody ever got fired for buying from IBM" had been folk wisdom in the computer industry since the 1960s. It had become true once more in 2000. If Hewlett-Packard really wanted to aim high in its strategic makeover, it ought to find ways to confront IBM much more effectively than ever before. Get that right, and all the smaller competitors would be left trembling.

Hewlett-Packard on its own had little hope of catching IBM anytime in the foreseeable future. IBM in mid-2000 had a stock-market value of about $200 billion and was on its way to posting annual revenue of $88 billion. HP's market capitalization and revenue were barely half those amounts. But the right acquisition could bring Hewlett-Packard much closer. Carrying out a major acquisition also would shake off a longstanding bit of defeatism that was limiting HP's ability to keep pace with other giant companies. The folklore within Hewlett-Packard was that the Palo Alto company just wasn't any good at making acquisitions pay off. The familiar litany of disappointing deals included the 1989 purchase of Apollo Computer for $476 million and the 1997 acquisition of VeriFone, an electronic payments company, for $1.18 billion. After those investments backfired, many HP managers had decided that acquisitions of all kinds were jinxed. Now, Fiorina, Hackborn, and the rest of the HP directors were in a position where they could try to prove otherwise.

In September 2000, Fiorina thought she saw the winning opportunity. She and the HP directors had identified computer services as a fast-growing, relatively high-profit-margin business in which Hewlett-Packard wasn't nearly as big as it ought to be. Within HP, Ann Livermore, head of the business customer organization, was trying to expand this area contract by contract. But Livermore and Fiorina both liked the idea of leaping into the top ranks by acquiring a major computer-services company. They looked briefly at EDS, before deciding that its business mix wasn't optimal. A better prospect, they believed, was the consulting division of PricewaterhouseCoopers, one of the Big Five accounting firms, which had diversified heavily into computer services. Some 31,500 PwC consultants had built up a thriving business helping big companies install, upgrade, and manage their computer systems. By contrast, HP's services division had just 6,000 consultants. PwC officials set an asking price of $17 billion or $18 billion, which Fiorina and the HP board thought might be steep. But it wasn't preposterous, and they looked forward to closed-door negotiations that might clinch winning terms for everyone.

To Fiorina's intense chagrin, the *Sunday Times* of London broke news of the PwC talks in its September 10, 2000, edition. When stock trading resumed the next day, HP shares fell 3 percent, amid investor jitters that the acquisition would hurt the company's short-term earnings. When Hewlett-Packard executives tried to persuade investors that the deal made sense, they found that industry chatter had turned so strongly against them that there wasn't much hope of making headway. When they tried to refocus the negotiations on a lower acquisition price, they ran into serious resistance from PwC executives.

Even bigger obstacles arose when HP negotiators got an up-close look at everything that would be involved in trying to close the deal. PricewaterhouseCoopers wasn't a single unified enterprise throughout the world; it was an ad hoc alliance of about twenty-five partnerships and limited-liability corporations in each of its major markets. PwC partners in Britain, the United States, and Germany had indicated they wanted to do a deal with Hewlett-Packard. But other partners hadn't been fully consulted, and they didn't like the terms being proposed to them. They wanted more money. If Hewlett-Packard didn't agree, it wouldn't have any presence in certain countries. If it did capitulate, partners at other PwC offices would likely hold out for more money, too. And because the partners who owned the largest stakes in PricewaterhouseCoopers happened also to be the star consultants whose continued hard work was most essential to the deal, Hewlett-Packard was about to be stuck in the awkward position of writing giant checks to PwC executives who might suddenly feel no real need to report to work the next day. "The farther we got into it, the more we realized that it was a hairy deal to do," remarked Marty Korman, an attorney at Wilson Sonsini who was advising Hewlett-Packard.

In mid-November 2000, Fiorina finally walked away from the PricewaterhouseCoopers deal. In a conference call with major investors, she said it just wasn't possible to price the deal in a way that would help Hewlett-Packard's own stock and also make it likely that most key consultants would stay. Accepting blame for the misstep, she told investors: "In hindsight, I let the PwC opportunity linger for too long." By then, it was clear that the cooling of Internet mania was slaking big companies' desire to rush to spend millions of dollars on computer consultants. The revitalized Hewlett-Packard board could defend each step of the PwC engagement and disengagement as the wisest possible choice at the time. After more than a year of strategic pondering, however, Fiorina and her directors hadn't accomplished anything concrete in their hunt for a decisive strategic breakthrough. They had talked a lot. They had given Fiorina leeway to overhaul a lot of HP's regular operations. Everything else was just in the planning stages.

After the PwC setback, it was time to regroup. Director Jay Keyworth had wondered at one point whether Hewlett-Packard could outfox the competition by buying Apple Computer and trying to bring some of that company's cleverest technology to a much wider market. That idea had flickered on and off in the HP boardroom for years, going back to the days when David Woodley Packard—a big Apple enthusiast—was a director, but it never found much support. As much as board members admired Apple's innovativeness, they all believed its business had been through so many bumpy stretches that it would be an exercise in constant frustration to try to revive that company. As one director archly put it, "It would be like marrying someone with leukemia."

There were other acquisition prospects as well. Compaq Computer had been behaving for more than a year like a company that might want to be acquired. In late 1999, Fiorina had met Compaq's new chief executive, Michael Capellas, at a Washington technology conference. When Capellas started their conversation by observing, "Everyone thinks you're going to buy us," Fiorina shot back: "Well, how would you feel about that?" At that point, Capellas did everything but plead for confirmation of his own rumor. "It depends on the price," he said. Fiorina and the HP board weren't in a hurry to do anything with that prospect, but it was interesting to know.

In September 2000, Dick Hackborn stepped down as chairman of Hewlett-Packard, slightly ahead of schedule, but agreed to remain a director. He had planned to serve a full year as chairman, but decided by September that Fiorina was seasoned enough to take on all the company's leadership titles. "I think he just hated the procedural stuff," Fiorina later remarked. As far back as the John Young era, Hackborn had never liked setting agendas, reviewing the minutes, or performing other administrative chores. He preferred to keep operating behind the scenes as the board's top strategist, a prospect that Fiorina found reassuring. So in the first few months of 2001, Hackborn, Fiorina, and Keyworth surveyed a computer industry that was rapidly going from boom to bust. They needed to figure out Hewlett-Packard's next move.

Expanding HP's services business remained a nice goal, but it wasn't the top priority anymore. The most urgent problems involved Hewlett-Packard's enterprise-computing division, which sold powerful machines for $10,000, $50,000, or even $1 million to business customers needing to manage their data and Web sites. Hewlett-Packard had built up a sturdy business based on the Unix operating system and its own microprocessor designs, known as PA-RISC. But that particular corner of the market was stagnant at best. The most appealing growth prospects at the time involved cheaper, standardized designs built around Microsoft's Windows NT operating system. Rivals such as Dell Computer and Compaq Computer were building—and selling—NT servers at a brisk rate. Hewlett-Packard had been trying to make inroads in this area for years, but its strategic focus had been erratic and its market penetration disappointing. The storage business looked like another growth sector that was eluding HP. To stay competitive in enterprise computing would require serious research-and-development outlays, and those costs couldn't be responsibly financed unless the enterprise-computing business got a lot stronger in a hurry.

Fiorina needed a small commando team to help her and the board analyze the situation. She wanted a candid assessment of where Hewlett-Packard really stood. But she also wanted to avoid distracting or demoralizing key executives within HP's computer operations. "They had enough on their plates," Fiorina later said. "Once you start this kind of conversation, it gets pretty all-consuming. It can distract people from what they have to do."

Back in her Lucent days, Fiorina had worked closely with a handful of strategy consultants at McKinsey & Company. She liked their work. They were smart, thorough, and discreet. What's more, one of the McKinsey consultants whom she knew best, New York–based Michael Patsalos-Fox, was shrewd enough in the early months of 2001 to send her small, unsolicited packages with his thoughts on HP's competitive positioning. The initial McKinsey analysis wasn't flattering, but it wasn't horribly insulting either. It was exactly the sort of conversation starter likely to elicit a reply. Sure enough, in April 2001, Fiorina called Patsalos-Fox with a request that he take a more serious look at Hewlett-Packard.

"I'm troubled by our position in the enterprise-computing market," Fiorina said. She was choosing her words delicately. It was becoming clearer by the month that Hewlett-Packard was pointing the wrong way: relying too much on the slow-growth Unix market segment and not making a name for itself in the more appealing Linux and Windows NT pieces of the server business. "The big question was: 'How do we regain momentum in the server business?'" Fiorina wondered. "We had already sunk an incremental $700 million into R&D on the server side. We were feeling tremendous strain because of the economic slowdown."

Patsalos-Fox and two McKinsey colleagues, Steve Coley and Robert Uhlaner, came back a few weeks later with a sobering analysis. They had culled through the whole spectrum of Hewlett-Packard's main computing operations and couldn't find much of anything that amounted to clear growth engines for the future. The company had been either too stingy or too ineffective in the previous few years as it spent money in an attempt to build up its computer operations. Dell Computer was widening the gap in the personal-computer market. Hewlett-Packard was only beginning to capitalize on opportunities in the data-storage business. Fiorina had articulated a strategy that involved getting stronger in services, storage, and Windows NT servers. Saying it was one thing; making it happen was another.

Keep looking, Fiorina said. Start to think about what this means for the stock price. The McKinsey partners came back later in the spring of 2001 to say that, based on their analysis of the company's position at the time, they couldn't see much reason for HP stock to be trading above $30 a share. At that time, shares were changing hands at about $33. The implication was obvious. If Fiorina wanted to get the stock moving upward again, she needed to do something drastically different from merely continuing the status quo. In such settings, chief executives have been known to blame Wall Street, the press, or the messenger bearing bad news, in a frantic effort to insist that everything is fine at their company and someone else is at fault. But Fiorina digested the news pretty calmly. She asked the McKinsey consultants to regroup and think about what options Hewlett-Packard might have to get things right again. "I want to know the answer here," Fiorina said. She set only two constraints on the McKinsey team's efforts. Look for strategic moves that fit in with HP's already-stated strategies on enterprise computing, she said.

"And don't sell the company."

Chapter 6

THE BILLIONAIRES' LEGACY

One of the most acclaimed books of the early 1990s was *Father, Son & Co.*, a two-generation tale of the men who built IBM. In the early chapters, the strong-willed father, Thomas Watson, Sr., towered over everyone. His son, Tom Junior, struggled to find his own way as a young man, eventually becoming an air force pilot in World War II. Only in a series of hair-raising combat adventures did the son learn the true nature of leadership, gaining the skills that would later help him drive IBM to greater heights than his father could imagine. That candid, emotion-filled account of a business dynasty apppeared on the best-seller lists for more than three months. Among the people who bought the book was Walter Hewlett. "It's one of my favorite books," he later remarked. "The relationship between father and son was very interesting to me, because I had a strong father."

It's easy to see why Walter Hewlett found the Watsons' saga so instructive. Bill Hewlett at times demanded the impossible from his children, explaining circular equations to Walter when his son was in second grade and getting exasperated when the little boy didn't catch on. On family ski vacations, Bill Hewlett was the fastest one down the slopes and had little sympathy for people who couldn't keep up. One time, when his oldest child, Eleanor, strained to match her father's pace, she lost her balance and tumbled into the snow headfirst, with her skis flailing helplessly in the air above her. Bill Hewlett took one look at his daughter's predicament, decided she wasn't seriously hurt—and skied on. She could extricate herself.

Bill Hewlett could be an extraordinarily attentive and loving father as well. When his children were young, he snuck into the Hewlett-Packard workshop at odd hours to make kites, blocks, and swing sets for them, believing he could craft something more delightful than any toy store offered. When the children got older, he took them for all-day mountain hikes near Lake Tahoe, packing enormous picnic lunches and pointing out wildflowers along the way. He loved to show off his knowledge, but he admired children who could outwit him every now and then. His daughter

Eleanor formed "The Society to Prove Papa Wrong," taking him to task if children asked him the length of the Mississippi River and his off-the-cuff answer was six miles too short.

That mixture of tough-mindedness and good cheer showed in the way Bill Hewlett cleared certain paths—and closed off others—as his five children reached adulthood. In contrast to many successful executives, he never encouraged the next generation to enter the business. At some level, he (and Dave Packard) must have foreseen unbearable pressures on any offspring who tried to make their way up the HP ladder. Being modestly successful would never suffice. If the children didn't surpass their fathers' accomplishments, they would be seen as failures by business associates, by the media—and ultimately by themselves. In that case, it was wisest to steer them away from a career choice that could only disappoint. In the words of one top HP executive who came to know the founding families well: "Dave and Bill never felt that their successors should be their own progeny. They were such good businessmen. I think they felt that just wasn't the right path."

When twenty-six-year-old Walter Hewlett spent the summer of 1970 in production control at a Hewlett-Packard facility in West Germany, his father told him, "You can work for HP, but I want you to understand that if you do, you're going to be treated like everybody else. There's no special consideration." Even though Walter Hewlett enjoyed the work, he never rejoined the employee ranks. When the children weren't in earshot, Bill Hewlett was even blunter. He frowned when his middle son, Jim, lined up a one-year tour of duty in the early 1970s as a computer-systems engineer at HP's Cupertino, California, facilities. "I'm not in favor of this in any way," Bill Hewlett told a Cupertino research executive. "I want you to be twice as tough on him as anybody else." Jim Hewlett by all accounts did an excellent job as a computer programmer. At the end of the year, he also walked away from HP, never to return.

All the same, Bill Hewlett invited his children into the other great arena of his public life: philanthropy. As early as the 1950s, he realized that Hewlett-Packard's business success might make him an extremely wealthy man. He was worth $150 million by the mid-1960s and more than $1 billion by 1986. Beyond a certain point, he believed, it wasn't really his money. He told his children that he felt very lucky to have created a company in such a fast-growing industry. "We were sitting on the nose cone of a rocket, and we didn't even know it," Bill Hewlett once remarked. He planned to leave his children a small slice of his wealth, but not too much, for fear it would lead them astray. Instead, Bill Hewlett and his first wife, Flora, set up a foundation in 1966 that over time would become the main holder of his fortune. He intended to become a philanthropist in his later years, championing conservation, education, the arts, and many other worthy causes. When Bill Hewlett became unable to carry on, Walter and the other children could help channel the Hewlett fortune toward the public interest.

"I was a placeholder at first," Walter Hewlett recalled. When the William and Flora Hewlett Foundation was created in December 1966, twenty-two-year-old Walter Hewlett joined his parents as the entity's third trustee. His main duty at the beginning was to provide an extra signature when needed. "But it was clear to me," Walter Hewlett later said, "that eventually the foundation would have some major assets, and that I would have a role to play."

Sure enough, by the end of 2000, the Hewlett Foundation was shepherding $3.9 billion, making it the twelfth largest foundation in the United States. Gravely ill Bill Hewlett wasn't able to attend meetings anymore; he was merely the chairman emeritus. Taking over his responsibilities as chairman was Walter Hewlett, now a silver-haired man in his midfifties. The handoff during the course of the 1990s was so smooth that foundation directors can't remember a moment when they suddenly realized that Bill Hewlett had stepped back and Walter Hewlett had taken command. Meeting by meeting, though, that transfer gradually happened. Bill Hewlett's role at the foundation gradually diminished. His oldest son calmly stepped forward, leading board meetings and setting policy. Deprived of his father's support for a shot at leading Hewlett-Packard, Walter Hewlett was graced with a second chance at the Hewlett Foundation. He made the most of it.

For all of the Hewletts and Packards, in fact, philanthropic obligations at the end of the founders' lives suddenly vaulted the children into new positions of prominence. As octogenarians in the 1990s, Dave Packard and Bill Hewlett controlled two of the largest fortunes ever amassed to date in the United States: as much as $9 billion apiece of company stock. Most of that wealth was headed into family foundations that would become bigger than their Rockefeller, Mellon, or Getty counterparts. Someone needed to decide how all that money should be spent. The details of grant-making could be delegated to dozens of hired program officers, but final authority, it was decided, ought to rest at least partly in the hands of the founders' children. Nobody knew better than Eleanor, Walter, Jim, Mary, and Bill Jr.

what it meant to be a Hewlett. Nobody knew better than David Woodley, Nancy, Susan, and Julie what it meant to be a Packard.

Would the children get it right? At first, some of them were unnerved by the enormous responsibility placed in their hands. They had been raised to live genteel lives on a much smaller scale. They drove Volvos and Hondas. They lived in nice but hardly ostentatious homes. By and large, they were shy, somewhat bookish people who flinched from public attention. Commenting in 1998 on his late father's wealth, David Woodley Packard remarked: "I wish he'd started spending the money sooner. I wish he hadn't left four kids to struggle with it."

Over time, though, the siblings in both families rallied. They drafted lists of their parents' values, including integrity, belief in individual leadership, and a willingness to think big. They vowed to be guided by the same principles. The Packards in particular sought expert advice, prompting David Rockefeller and Warren Buffett to share pointers about the stewardship of family fortunes. Ultimately, the siblings took heart from the fact that they were Packards. They were Hewletts. They were born to lead, and if they tried hard and conscientiously, there was a good chance they could carry on their parents' greatness. Susan Packard Orr, the most focused of the Packard children, began talking about the notion that her family's foundation could serve as a model for other public-spirited tycoons and their children.

If the Hewletts and Packards were starting to sound a bit like Old Money aristocrats, it wasn't an accident. They were becoming Silicon Valley's version of the Lowells, the Cabots, the Astors, or the Harrimans. They spoke out discreetly but with great impact on community issues. Throughout Silicon Valley, practically every museum, theater, or music gruop started its fund-raising drives with an appeal to the Hewlett or Packard foundation. Veneration reached its peak on the Stanford University campus, where administrators—with good reason—regarded the founding families as their greatest benefactors. "The Hewletts and the Packards are right behind Leland and Jane Stanford in terms of having an impact on the university through their philanthropy," the university's vice president for development, John Ford, said in 1998. By one tally, Bill Hewlett and Dave Packard each gave more than $300 million to Stanford while they were alive, and far more through their estates and foundations after their death.

The great irony, of course, was that Silicon Valley professed to be all about new money, new companies, and new ideas. Most of the time, that was true. Everyone else was still scratching for a lucky break, but the Hewletts and Packards had moved beyond that. They had earned billions by arriving in Silicon Valley before everyone else, building a great company, and making the most of its opportunities. They could take wealth for granted and think about how best to deploy it in ways that would serve humanity.

The founding families' new role came about so quickly—yet so smoothly—that no one ever stopped to think about the consequences. In the first year or two of Carly Fiorina's tenure at Hewlett-Packard, everyone took for granted that the families, the foundations, and the company all nestled together seamlessly. It had been that way for decades. With the founders out of the picture, however, and their children largely swept off the HP board, the old dynamic no longer applied. The foundations were becoming independent foci of power. As long as Hewlett-Packard stock performed well, the foundations and the families were likely to remain loyal, passive investors. They would cheer quietly, raise sufficient cash every year by selling a sliver of their holdings, and try to spend the money wisely. But if HP's share price ever stumbled, the foundations and the families would be tugged in disturbing new directions. Would they sit still and watch the economic value of Dave Packard's and Bill Hewlett's lifework erode? Or would the foundations publicly rebuke HP management and agitate for a different course? No one knew. No one in power at Hewlett-Packard or the foundations even imagined asking those questions.

On January 12, 2001, Bill Hewlett died at age eighty-seven. Hewlett-Packard saluted his life by publishing sixteen pages of photos and employee testimonials about the "huggable cohort with the twinkle in his eye." The montage started with a page from HP's first ledger in 1939, featuring a handwritten entry for W. R. Hewlett's monthly salary of $50. Employees shared dozens of stories about a powerful man's humility, including the time Bill Hewlett put himself to work on the Mountain View, California, assembly line for a few minutes in the 1970s. He was HP's chief executive then, but at heart he was still an engineer who wanted to know how a new drill press worked—and he was comfortable sitting in for a factory worker to find out. Other pages listed Hewlett's many honors, including the National Medal of Science, awarded by President Reagan in 1985. The tribute finished with a photo of Bill Hewlett in a wheelchair at a Stanford reception in 1996 flanked by Dave Packard on one side and Microsoft founder Bill Gates on the other. In that shot, Gates is leaning forward at an almost impossible angle, craning to hear every word that the elderly HP founders had to offer.

The fullest tribute to Bill Hewlett came eight days after his death, in a memorial service at Stanford. One of his longtime hunting buddies, Arjay Miller, the former dean of the Stanford Business School, recounted warm memories of singing songs at night around a campfire. Herant Katchadourian, a director of the Hewlett Foundation, praised the HP founder for being unaffected by an immense fortune and being "immune to the corrosive effects of money." Walter Hewlett spoke last, sharing stories of his father's love of music and his endless curiosity about everything from the life of John Adams to the Spanish conquest of Peru. "I feel so very fortunate to have had him for a dad," Walter Hewlett said.

All told, more than a thousand people packed Stanford's Memorial Church to pay their respects. Swarms of employees and former executives from Hewlett-Packard attended, including Lew Platt, who sat with Ned Barnholt, the CEO of Agilent. Carly Fiorina appeared as well, listening to the tributes with an expression of admiration and outright awe on her face. She handed out programs before the service, a gesture that was viewed as either gracious or presumptuous, depending on what people already thought of her. But for all the Hewlett-Packard faces in the audience, keen observers couldn't help notice that no company executive had been invited to speak. By contrast, three of the five speakers had ties to the Hewlett Foundation. In life, Bill Hewlett had been a businessman above all. In death, his family and friends were reclaiming him as a father and a philanthropist.

The only memorial-service speaker who talked at length about Hewlett-Packard was Dave Packard's son, David Woodley Packard. He was wonderfully droll at times, sharing letters that his mother had written in 1938, in which she wondered whether Dave and Bill's little venture in the garage would amount to anything. He also sketched the first outlines of what would soon become a feisty defense of the old ways. "It's hard for me to believe that . . . HP doesn't even make instruments anymore," David Woodley Packard said at one point. Near the end of his remarks, he read letters that HP employees had sent after his own father died in 1996. Several of them saluted the founders as immortal—and delicately implied that all the executives who came afterward were just passing through. "As much as I know intellectually that I work for a Fortune Fifty company," one employee wrote, "my heart always felt, still feels, like I work for Bill and Dave."

The five Hewlett children closed the service by singing one of their father's favorite hymns, "Our God, Our Help in Ages Past." Then, in the next few months, they began the fresh challenge of sorting out their late father's estate. When Bill Hewlett died, he had already steered a major part of his assets into the foundation, but his estate still controlled 112 million shares of Hewlett-Packard, valued then at about $3.4 billion. Almost all that wealth was destined for the Hewlett Foundation. Until his will cleared probate, that stock would be held in the Hewlett Trust, jointly administered by Walter Hewlett and seventy-four-year-old Edwin van Bronkhorst, who had been HP's chief financial officer in the 1970s and early 1980s. As a practical matter, Walter Hewlett would be in charge of the trust, as well as chairing the family foundation.

By the time of Bill Hewlett's death, the Hewlett Foundation had grown to forty-seven employees, making more than five hundred grants a year in a wide range of areas. The foundation bankrolled twelve programs to promote responsible fatherhood in blighted areas, as well as nine initiatives to promote journalists' coverage of environmental issues. It set aside $450,000 to help Stanford researchers catalog and analyze Martin Luther King's papers. It took chances with some of its grants, supporting not just well-established arts groups such as the Boston and San Francisco symphonies but also some scrappy experimental theater groups in Berkeley and Santa Cruz, California. In one of its best-known initiatives, the foundation awarded $5.5 million to MIT to put all of the university's course materials online, free of charge, so that indigent students around the globe could tap into the Internet and get a taste of a top-tier American education.

Three family members—Walter Hewlett, older sister Eleanor Hewlett Gimon, and younger sister Mary Hewlett Jaffe—sat on the foundation's ten-member board. The siblings didn't micromanage philanthropic work. Daily decisions were left in the hands of the foundation's president, Paul Brest, a former dean of the Stanford Law School. But Bill Hewlett's love of nature, shared by his daughter Mary, inspired the foundation to channel more than $20 million a year to protect the land. Latin America became a full-fledged program area, too, reflecting the interests of both Bill and Walter Hewlett. In a far-reaching gesture, Walter Hewlett created the separate $100 million Flora Family Foundation, so that twenty-one family members, including Bill Hewlett's twelve grandchildren, could initiate modest grants of their choosing, without distorting the mission of the big foundation. Other directors applauded. As one of them put it: "Someday those grandchildren will take their aunts' and uncles' places on the big foundation. We want them to learn to be informed philanthropists as early as possible."

Joining the Hewletts at every board meeting was a prized visitor from Boise: Dick Hackborn. The mastermind of Hewlett-Packard's printer business was best known to the wider world in 2000 as Carly Fiorina's mentor. Hackborn was quietly playing exactly the same role for Walter Hewlett by serving on the Hewlett Foundation's board. "Dick had a very pragmatic sense of how to get things done," Hewlett Foundation officer David Lorey recalled. "He didn't speak very much at board meetings, but when he did, everyone listened to him. Dick also seemed quite comfortable talking about what Bill Hewlett might have done in a situation. Walter hardly ever made reference to his father. At least once a board meeting, Dick would lean back and say, 'You know, here's what your dad thought about that.'"

Dick Hackborn had known Bill Hewlett very well, not just as a boss but also as a worried older man pouring out his concerns to a younger confidant. Both of Bill Hewlett's heart attacks—in the late 1970s and late 1980s—had occurred at remote Idaho ski resorts. Each time, Dick Hackborn was one of the first HP executives to reach Bill Hewlett's bedside. The two men talked for hours during Hewlett's recovery period, often touching on topics that might have been off-limits otherwise. At the end of those conversations, Dick Hackborn knew much more than just Bill Hewlett's views on the calculator business: He knew what the patriarch thought about life. So when Dick Hackborn announced that he was retiring from Hewlett-Packard in 1993, Bill Hewlett recruited him ardently for the foundation board, refusing to take no for an answer. "I want someone who really knows business—particularly the HP style of business," Bill Hewlett explained. "The family needs that."

In the foundation boardroom, Dick Hackborn helped graft the best of the HP Way into a philanthropic setting. Foundation managers realized how important it was to trust their grant recipients, much as Dave and Bill had trusted their employees. "We aren't doing the work; the grantees are doing it," Walter Hewlett later explained. "We don't have the expertise; they do." Much like Hewlett-Packard, the Hewlett Foundation also steadfastly resisted the temptation to revel in its own importance. Operating costs were held to 6 percent of each year's grants, and people kept looking for ways to trim that figure. In their eyes, the ideal foundation kept its staff small and its processes simple. It was time to be the R&D of charity, funding daring new programs that might have a great impact in years ahead. Just as with the classic Hewlett-Packard, the Hewlett Foundation was all about "making a contribution."

One of the foundation's gutsiest initiatives grew out of Bill Hewlett's identity as a peacemaker who loved to solve problems. From the early 1980s onward, the foundation looked for ways to improve dispute mediation around the world. Hardly anyone else in the philanthropic world could imagine building an entire grant-making category around this notion, so the Hewlett Foundation pioneered the field of "conflict resolution." It bankrolled efforts along the Rio Grande to sort out water-rights disputes between the United States and Mexico. It supported everyone from Alaskan tribal chiefs (who got an $80,000 grant to improve their negotiating skills) to the Council on Foreign Relations. Over time, a classic Hewlett Foundation formula took shape, with five basic elements: Narrow the battleground to the smallest number of issues possible; search for common ground on everything else; gather reliable information that both sides can trust; set up talks in private, without public intrusion or posturing; and even when formal talks go badly, look for back-channel forms of communication, treating everything as confidential because premature publicity could be deadly.

At that stage, Walter Hewlett could be justifiably proud of the Hewlett Foundation's ability to stop fights. There wasn't any reason yet for him to consider what would happen if he and the foundation ever decided to *start* a fight.

For Hewlett-Packard's other founding family, Dave Packard's death in 1996 wasn't just a tragedy—it was a convulsive event that led to complications worthy of Tolstoy. Dave Packard was such an inspiring and overpowering character that he couldn't prepare the world for his absence—and to a large extent, he didn't try. Having initiated a magnificent philanthropic agenda, he left only partial instructions for his children about how to carry on. As a result, the four Packard children had to pick their way through a psychological and strategic minefield before they could fully assert themselves as second-generation leaders. Their ability to prevail speaks to the family's strength of character. Their disagreements along the way added excitement to the process and ultimately meant that family leadership would end up in unexpected new hands.

All his life, Dave Packard had been a humble man in the everyday details of life—but breathtakingly audacious when it came to major projects. In his final few appearances at HP events, when everyone knew that he was a multibillionaire, the elderly founder drove up in a clunky Oldsmobile station wagon that was at least five years old. Employees wondered why one of the world's richest men would favor such a shabby car. Finally one had the nerve to ask him. "If you fold down the backseats, it has the largest flatbed area of any car I've found," Packard patiently explained. "That way, when I go to the garden-supply store, I can take home more plants and bulbs."

Dave Packard's charitable work started squarely in the "humble" side of his life. He, his wife, Lucile, and his children sat around the kitchen table in the 1960s and decided how much money to give to the arts, the schools, the local hospital, and other causes. Dave Packard brought the checkbook, Lucile Packard brought the ideas, and everyone passed grant requests across the table. Officially, these were the earliest meetings of the David and Lucile Packard Foundation. But the meetings were so informal, and the amount of money so modest, that it was easiest to think of the Packards as running a "kitchen-table" foundation. The most spirited discussions came when Dave Packard wanted to write checks to the Hoover Institution, a hotbed of conservative thought on the Stanford campus. He cherished its way of thinking, which his more-liberal daughters thought was dreadful.

By the early 1980s, Dave Packard's philanthropy was barreling into the "audacious" category. Two of his daughters, Julie Packard Stephens and Nancy Packard Burnett, had trained as marine biologists, and they conveyed their enthusiasm about the sea to their father. Soon this retiree in his seventies was talking constantly about the oceans as the last great frontier. He set out to build the best aquarium in the world in Monterey, California, with a preeminent marine research center attached. The project initially was budgeted at $30 million. Everything turned out to be more expensive than planned, so Dave Packard wrote more checks. Costs spiraled higher, and he wrote even more checks. Eventually he spent more than $50 million to create the Monterey Bay Aquarium Research Institute, and he loved every cent of it. Not only did he visit the facility constantly but he took command of an exhibit explaining the tides, and he built miniature replicas of the earth and the moon himself.

On the Stanford campus $40 million of Packard money, starting in 1986, paid for the construction of a state-of-the-art children's hospital.

That was Lucile Packard's project. She cared enormously about sick children, going back to her college days in the 1930s, when she was an active volunteer in a children's convalescent home. Until that point, Dave Packard out of modesty had refused to let Stanford name any buildings after the Packards, even though he was a prolific donor. But when Lucile Packard fell ill with what would prove to be terminal cancer, Lawrence Crowley, a director of the still-unfinished hospital, visited her bedside to show her the latest plans for what would be the Lucile Packard Children's Hospital. She protested. Couldn't the facility be named after the entire Packard family? "No," said Dave Packard, who was standing at her bedside. "This is your project. I'm not going to agree to anything other than that."

As long as Dave Packard was alive, his four children could watch in awe as he stormed from project to project. They all sat on the board of the Packard Foundation, which had become big enough by the early 1990s to employ more than a dozen program officers in downtown Los Altos, California, about a ten-minute drive from the Packard home. The siblings got plenty of chances to oversee people making $20,000 grants, but the really big elements of Packard philanthropy still came directly from Dave Packard's head, heart, and checkbook. He picked the foundation's key grant-making areas to match his interests, ranging from population, the environment, and science to education, children, and the arts. If he saw something that merited a $20 million check, it was more likely to come from his own huge holdings of HP stock than from the foundation's noticeably smaller portfolio.

"We asked Father if he would consider transferring some of his stock to the foundation gradually while he was still alive," Susan Packard Orr recalled in a 1998 interview. "We wanted the benefit of his input in building up the foundation." Dave Packard did steer about $2 billion of HP stock into the foundation in the last decade of his life. As substantial as that number seemed, it was less than one-third of his wealth. He went to the grave with $4.8 billion of HP shares to his name. Allowing for various bequests to relatives, more than 90 percent of that stock would come roaring into the foundation's hands once his will cleared probate. It would be up to the next generation to sort things out.

"We were caught a little unaware" by how much money was involved, recalled Dean Morton, a longtime foundation trustee and retired HP executive. Federal law requires foundations to give away at least 5 percent of their assets each year or lose much of their tax-exempt status. The Packard Foundation would have a grace period of a year or two, but before long it would need to start giving away $400 million or more each year. In the past, program officers had doled out modest amounts to historically black colleges, the Sierra Club, and other worthy groups, but the foundation was about to be vaulted into a whole new league. It would need to disburse more than a million dollars a day.

A million dollars a day. That concept both thrilled and terrified the Packard children. Dave Packard's middle daughter, Susan Packard Orr, felt the responsibility most keenly, as the foundation's new chair. Low-key and methodical, she was seen by her father as the sibling best able to rally everyone around a common goal. "I'm not bringing any big ideas," she conceded in a 1998 interview. Unlike her father—who could give away $40 million in an instant and be confident that his gift would better the world—she wasn't yet comfortable operating on such a scale. The other siblings weren't either. "It's stressful," David Woodley Packard remarked after his father's death. "Most families end up screwing up. We've got a great opportunity to do something good. I just hope it all works out."

Dave Packard did leave his children one attempt at a road map: an eight-page letter that he titled: "Some Random Thoughts About the Packard Foundation." He had written the letter in the late 1980s while recovering from back surgery, and he updated it only slightly afterward, despite repeated pleadings from family advisers. In his writings, he urged his children to keep the foundation heavily concentrated in HP stock. "Disregard entirely" the usual Wall Street advice to diversify, he thundered. Short-term profits or losses in the stock market shouldn't govern anyone's thinking about whether to stay in HP stock. Instead, he wrote, foundation trustees should think about "the impact on the company, on employees, and on the communities in which HP operates."

Dave Packard also told his children to regard global overpopulation as the foundation's top priority. If the current growth rate of 2 percent a year continued for long, he warned, it would mean "utter chaos for humanity. . . . The highest priority of our foundation must be to do what can be done to get the worldwide population growth back to [an appropriate level]. We must support abortion and every other policy that will help."

The full letter was vintage Dave Packard: adamant, tightly reasoned, and overpowering. As the four children came to terms with their new responsibilities, however, they made the first of several brave decisions. Population initiatives would indeed remain a very important part of the foundation's work, fitting into the "big four" priorities of environment, population, science, and education. But the Packard Foundation wouldn't be turned upside down to become a tool of the most severe Malthusians. Times had changed. The specter of a planet ruined by too many hungry mouths seemed a lot less worrisome a decade after Dave Packard wrote his letter, thanks largely to an abrupt drop in China's birth rate. And so, with the greatest respect possible for their late father, the children started to chart their own course.

Susan Packard Orr set the new tone, arranging more than a year of strategy and planning meetings after her father's death. She was the only Packard sibling with an MBA (Stanford 1970). One of her father's friends had teased her about the degree, saying, "I don't know if you will ever be able to use it, but at least it will help you understand your husband's career." For once, the men of Dave Packard's generation weren't sufficiently farsighted. Over time, Susan Orr and her colleagues put together a winning game plan that involved hiring more program officers, raising the average grant size, and recruiting a new chief executive who was well versed in the running of big organizations. The foundation hired Richard Schlosberg, former publisher of the *Los Angeles Times*, as the foundation's CEO, succeeding Colburn Wilbur, an admired pioneer who had been with the foundation almost since its kitchen-table beginnings. Susan Orr might not champion big ideas herself, but she was creating a framework in which other people's big ideas could emerge and thrive.

Soon a Big Idea worthy of Dave Packard took shape. In 1997, foundation program officers brought word that key stretches of the California coastline might be sold to developers. The land could be saved as wilderness, but it might cost as much as $42 million to do it. Did the Packard Foundation want to step in? "Yes!" was the definitive answer from Nancy Packard Burnett and Julie Packard Stephens. The Packards had always been keen conservationists, and the two Packard sisters knew some of the coastal stretches themselves from their own nature hikes. Together with Packard Foundation adviser Michael Mantell, the sisters and Julie's husband, Robert Stephens, drafted plans for the foundation to put up half the purchase price and line up other private donors for the rest. A year later, the deal was done. A six-mile stretch of coastline north of Santa Cruz, known as the old Coast Dairies land, would be turned over to the state of California and left wild forever.

The Packard sisters and Robert Stephens celebrated with a hike and a picnic on the land, pointing out plants by their Latin names and admiring the sunset against the Pacific Ocean. One of the best views on earth would stay that way. It wouldn't ever be cluttered by service stations and condos; it would always be the quiet home of *Salix lasiolepis* and *Festuca rubra*.

"It was a spectacular time for us," foundation director Dean Morton recalled years later. "We had this really wonderful push in conservation. We were able to make these enormous land purchases. It was one of the most enduring things we could do." All told, the Packard Foundation committed to spending $175 million over five years to purchase more than a quarter million acres of endangered wilderness in California. Acquisitions stretched from the Pacific coastline to the mountain country near Lake Tahoe. Historians called it the biggest such push by a single family in nearly a century. It evoked comparisons to the early 1900s, when the Rockefeller family deeded much of its western land holdings to the federal government, creating such public treasures as the Grand Teton National Park.

Soon afterward, Susan Packard Orr found her own Big Idea. The Lucile Packard Children's Hospital had been admitting patients since 1991, but almost from the start, the facility's enormous potential was jeopardized by a series of high-level campus quarrels. As the Packards saw it, Stanford's powerful medical school was treating the hospital like an unwanted stepchild. Instead of recruiting brilliant pediatric surgeons to practice exclusively at the children's hospital, the medical school was relying on its own adult-focused surgeons to handle pediatric cases. Care was adequate, but in the closely watched rankings of America's best children's hospitals, the Packard Hospital wasn't even in the top ten. Dave Packard had seethed about such slights in the last few years of his life, but his outbursts didn't accomplish much. Medical-school officials had their own priorities, and the angrier Dave Packard got, the more his adversaries let him know that he wasn't the beacon guiding their lives. At one point, the medical school went for more than a year with only an interim chairman to run its pediatrics department.

Someone needed to strike a more soothing tone. In the late 1990s, Susan Packard Orr rose to the occasion. She became friends with Harvey Cohen, the hospital's new chief of staff and the medical school's chairman of pediatrics. She gave $10 million of her own money to the hospital and arranged for the Packard Foundation to contribute a further $100 million to a new, smaller foundation that would benefit the hospital exclusively. When Dr. Cohen needed to recruit star doctors or major donors, she came along to add a certain gravitas to his pitches. People who heard her on such occasions remember three magic sentences: "Mother was deeply committed to improving children's care. As was Father. I'm no less committed." In her soft-spoken, earnest way, Susan Orr was conveying more than sixty years of Packard dedication to the well-being of sick children. "We want this to be one of the very best children's hospitals in America," she explained. She hoped that the Packard Hospital could rival world-famous institutions in Boston and Philadelphia.

Wealthy donors and renowned doctors at other hospitals melted, one after another, when they heard her story. Helping Susan Packard Orr meant a chance to partake in greatness. Even more than that, it began to seem almost wicked to say no. The Packards had done so much already. Wasn't it time for other people to contribute too? Sure enough, into the hospital came a new chief of tissue surgery, recruited from New York University. In came a new stem-cell expert, wooed from Yale. In came a celebrated pediatric heart surgeon, lured from the University of California, San Francisco. With these star doctors building up centers of excellence, the Packard Hospital at last had a chance to rise into the top ranks of children's hospitals. "That's the hunger," explained Stephen Peeps, head of the Packard Hospital's foundation. "That's where Susan is carrying her mother's torch. She wants with every ounce of her body to accomplish that."

Only David Woodley Packard, the oldest of the four siblings, had trouble finding his footing in the new Packard Foundation. He was bursting with philanthropic ideas, many of them brilliant. His deep interest in classic films led him to become one of America's greatest film preservationists, working closely with the Library of Congress to save treasures from the silent-movie era. He appreciated antiquity in all its forms, and he helped finance important archaeological digs off the coast of Turkey. He championed many of the same conservative positions that his father did, making his own donations to the Hoover Institution and pushing for back-to-basics initiatives in primary education. That meant encouraging school vouchers and new curricula based on phonics instead of the "whole language" method.

All those preferences put him at odds with his sisters and others at the foundation who were more liberal. They preferred to stay out of grade schools and help universities instead. And while everyone admired David Woodley Packard's interest in the classics, no one truly shared it. To some extent, it was possible to operate as two foundations under one roof, with most money spent along the guidelines developed by Susan Packard Orr and a much smaller slice at David Woodley Packard's disposal. But that was a clumsy compromise, and it could work only if deep down, the siblings wanted to stay together. They didn't. People who saw the family in action believed the sisters found their brother overbearing. In turn, he chafed at their insistence that everything be carefully planned out and highly structured. "I'm suspicious about too much process," he declared in 1998. "I'd rather do the best we can, without huge committees and 'facilitators.'"

In the summer of 1999, the siblings finally parted company, as politely as possible. The Packard Foundation handed over 14 million shares of Hewlett-Packard and $75 million to a separate entity controlled by David Woodley Packard, the Packard Humanities Institute. The total award of $1.5 billion gave him, at last, a decently funded foundation of his own. He could run it in whatever way he wanted. His offices in Los Altos were just across the courtyard from the main foundation, and Susan Packard Orr continued to serve on the board of his foundation so that contact would not cease. If David Woodley Packard wanted to promote school vouchers or the translation of ancient Islamic manuscripts, no one was going to stop him.

To most casual observers, David Woodley Packard remained the apparent leader of the next generation of Packards. He was the only son, the oldest child—and the only sibling who regularly made public appearances. In the late 1980s, he had bought an old movie theater in downtown Palo Alto and spent more than $5 million on an immaculate restoration. On weekends, David Woodley Packard might appear on stage at his Stanford Theatre just before the screening of a Cary Grant classic to share a few words about the movie's significance and perhaps even allude to the latest goings-on at "my father's company." He was both erudite and sentimental, and his best one-liners were every bit as good as the movies he showed. He once told an interviewer that he had ignored film for decades, regarding it as "degraded popular culture," but then changed his mind entirely after seeing *Meet Me in St. Louis* at a Judy Garland festival in the mid-1970s. A zealous cinemaphile, he contended that scholars a thousand years from now would regard the films of the 1930s and 1940s as America's answer to the classics of ancient Greece.

As much fun as it was to step into David Woodley Packard's theater for a few hours, it wasn't the nerve center of Packard family thinking. Wealth and power remained concentrated at the big foundation, where his sisters and their advisers controlled eight times the assets of David Woodley Packard's PHI. And thanks to the high-tech stock boom in the final years of the Clinton administration, the Packard Foundation appeared to be growing richer and more powerful all the time. The value of its Hewlett-Packard stock topped $10 billion in early 1999. Every time HP stock inched ahead another dollar, the foundation's assets (before a two-for-one stock split) climbed a further $109 million. In mid-2000, the foundation's assets crested at $18 billion. King Midas had come to Los Altos.

"The mood at the time was just: 'Go! Go! Go!'" recalled Dick Schlosberg, the Packard Foundation's new chief executive. He hired nearly a hundred staffers in eighteen months, doubling the foundation's payroll. Program officers got green lights to try the most audacious things. The science program each year awarded twenty-four "genius grants" of $625,000 apiece, spread over five years, to promising young scientists. The population program targeted eight countries on three continents, ranging from Nigeria to the Philippines. Just when staffers thought they were pushing the limits of what one foundation could do, Schlosberg informed them that HP stock had climbed enough that everyone's budget could stretch another 15 percent. Did staffers have any more good ideas? The once-alarming goal of giving away $1 million a day became visible only in the rearview mirror; Packard Foundation officials were disbursing nearly *$2 million a day*—and loving it. Only Microsoft founder Bill Gates could do anything comparable.

All that gusto was based on one crucial assumption: that HP's stock price would remain strong. If the Packard Foundation ultimately wanted to give away 5 percent of its assets every year, its precise outlays were intensely dependent on investors' perceptions of Hewlett-Packard, as reflected in the stock's trading levels at any particular moment. The final frenzy of New Economy excitement had done great things for HP stock, but it was a very short-lived rush. As that mania waned in late 2000, Dick Schlosberg found himself obliged to reach for the brake instead of the gas pedal. With Hewlett-Packard stock in retreat, Schlosberg redrew the foundation's budgets for 2001 and 2002, pinching them slightly tighter. When HP stock slipped further, he trimmed the budgets a second time. The situation wasn't grim yet; there was still a lot of money to spend. But now there was reason to be anxious about HP's ability to withstand a decided change in the economic climate.

As much as Packard Foundation leaders worried about the ups and downs of HP stock, their counterparts at the Hewlett Foundation thought they could take a more detached view. Back in the 1980s, Bill Hewlett had told his foundation's investment officers that it was all right to diversify their holdings. In fact, he encouraged it, nudged along by foundation director Arjay Miller. The Hewletts set a long-term target of having just 15 to 20 percent of the foundation's assets in HP stock, in the belief that this would let them keep some ties to the company while greatly abating their portfolio risk. They would miss out on Hewlett-Packard's best boom years, but they wouldn't be hurt nearly so much by periodic downturns in the high-tech sector.

Everything was precisely calibrated within the Hewlett foundation— and then Bill Hewlett died in January 2001. Suddenly assets were about to double. The new holdings consisted almost entirely of HP and Agilent stock. As a result, the Hewlett Foundation was about to have an uncomfortably large economic interest in HP stock. Everyone at the foundation— starting with Walter Hewlett—would have to worry a lot more about Hewlett-Packard's prospects.

Chapter 7

THREE QUESTIONS

Throughout the winter of 2001, the New Economy was coming unstuck. Evidence of its waning appeal arrived every time Web surfers clicked onto the stock pages of Bloomberg, Yahoo Finance, and other online services. Suddenly, it wasn't fun anymore to track the share prices of Hewlett-Packard, Sun, Amazon, or Cisco. Tiny versions of HWP, SUNW, AMZN, LU, or CSCO weren't lighting up green anymore, as they did when fresh buyers kept propelling shares to new highs. A nasty shade of red dominated the screens instead: the color of stop signs and teachers' ink, now used to portray slumping stock prices. In a supreme irony, the New Economy's collapse was being chronicled most vividly on the Internet itself.

Hewlett-Packard, which had traded as high as a split-adjusted $68 a share in the summer of 2000, skidded to $30 in December. The stock rallied briefly to $38 early in the new year and then came in for further pounding. The rest of the high-tech sector fared every bit as badly. Share prices for Cisco and Sun crashed 70 percent or more. Carly Fiorina's old employer Lucent faltered amid concern that it had extended billions of dollars of trade credit to upstart telecom companies that wouldn't be able to repay those obligations. Many of the dot-com upstarts were obliterated entirely. All these companies were caught in an epic redefining of public attitudes toward the information age. Consumers scaled back their once-rabid appetites for electronic commerce and the latest PCs, cell phones, and handheld devices. Corporate customers stopped buying servers, enterprise software, and data networks as if their lives depended on it. Everyone still liked what technology could do for them, but they weren't in the midst of a blind, unthinking spending spree anymore.

On Wall Street, where perceptions meant everything, the news of customers' change of heart quickly translated into brutal markdowns in stock-market valuations. Companies that defined the New Economy had been lofted to such wild heights that the slightest suggestion of flaws in their prospects led investors to reach for the panic button. Chief executives tried to fight this trend for many months. They told Wall Street that any tech-sector downturn was likely to be mild, that their companies were well positioned for a slowdown, and that in the long run, their superior business practices would help them outlast weaker rivals if the shakeout got ugly. Everything sounded reassuring. But at a certain point, investors stopped listening. The high-tech industry was being buffeted by forces much bigger than anything a chief executive could understand, let alone control. The best hope of avoiding further portfolio losses was to pay attention to the marketplace—and to cover one's ears anytime a high-tech CEO spoke.

Among the poor performers was Compaq Computer, the Houston maker of personal computers, which had aggressively diversified in the late 1990s by acquiring Tandem Computers for $3 billion and Digital Equipment for $8.5 billion. Efforts to integrate both those companies into Compaq were going badly. So investors had two reasons to loathe Compaq: Its PC business was slumping and its acquisition strategy didn't appear to be working. Compaq's stock had begun to weaken in early 1999 and kept sliding for the next two years. By March 31, 2001, it was changing hands at just $20 a share, down more than 60 percent from its all-time high.

Compaq directors had seen enough. As early as the summer of 2000, they had encouraged their company's chief executive, Michael Capellas, to explore some sort of alliance or partnership with another computer company. "We wanted to be the next IBM," Capellas later recalled. Compaq's own product lineup had far too many gaps to make that a realistic dream, so Capellas brought a stack of charts into the boardroom, with green bars showing the relative strengths of Compaq, Dell, Sun, EMC, and a half-dozen other companies—including Hewlett-Packard. Amid all the pairings on his easel, he later recalled, the alignment between Compaq and Hewlett-Packard was "intuitively obvious." At that stage, HP had an appreciably larger market capitalization, meaning that if the two companies did combine forces, Compaq almost certainly would be swallowed up as the weaker outfit. But directors didn't flinch. In early 2001, they authorized their CEO to start a dialogue with Carly Fiorina. Licensing some of HP's Unix architecture was a safe starting point. If the chemistry seemed good, the talks could get much more serious.

Fiorina chatted with other chief executives so often that the first call or two from Capellas didn't stand out. Gradually, however, she began to notice that he was calling more often and staying on the phone longer than was necessary just to sort out a Unix-licensing deal. Something might be afoot, she realized. She mentioned the talks to several directors, including

Dick Hackborn. He had been intrigued by Compaq for some time and encouraged her to keep talking. Flirting with such a big acquisition prospect was radically different from anything Dave Packard and Bill Hewlett ever had done. Even so, Fiorina, Hackborn, and fellow director Jay Keyworth persuaded themselves that this was something Bill and Dave would have welcomed.

When HP's operating results started to deteriorate in the autumn of 2000, Carly Fiorina responded with good-natured jauntiness. In a conference-call briefing for Wall Street analysts on November 13, she reported that per-share earnings for the latest quarter would be about 10 percent below expectations. Fiorina blamed a variety of annoying but easily fixable missteps during the quarter. Sales commissions had puffed up needlessly, bad-debt expense wasn't managed tightly enough, and too much revenue came from selling products with unusually thin profit margins. By implication, there wasn't anything wrong with HP's core. Given a little time, all the profit-sapping irritants could be swept away. "We recognize we have let you down," Fiorina told the analysts, "but we hope you won't forget all the good things going on at HP. We will learn from this shortfall."

In internal briefings a few days later, Fiorina was outright defiant. "We hit a speed bump—a big speed bump—this quarter," she told employees. "But does it mean: 'Gee, this is too hard'? No way. In blackjack, you double down when you have an increased probability of winning. And we're going to double down." She informed employees and analysts that she was raising her growth targets for the company in fiscal 2001. Revenue would climb 17 percent, she declared, instead of the 15 percent that analysts forecast. Her cockiness reached its peak in an interview with *BusinessWeek*, in which she declared: "When you sail, you don't get there in a straight line. You adjust your course to fit the times and the current conditions. . . . We think we see where the market is going and that we're perfectly positioned." In the privacy of the HP boardroom, she criticized her old boss at Lucent, Rich McGinn, for making unrealistic promises to Wall Street. She vowed not to make that mistake.

On January 11, 2001, a chastened Fiorina conceded that Hewlett-Packard was stumbling and that she hadn't really understood the big picture at all. In a conference call to update Wall Street analysts, she said that when she saw HP's sales reports for December, "frankly, it was like somebody turned the lights out." Revenue in the current quarter wouldn't grow anywhere near 17 percent, she warned. The company would be lucky to achieve 5 percent growth. Improvement anytime soon was unlikely. She had sailed into a storm. She had doubled down and drawn a very poor card. Whatever the metaphor—and Fiorina had a million of them—she was facing the first serious crisis of her time at Hewlett-Packard. The "Oh, shit!" quarter that Eric Schmidt had predicted eighteen months earlier had finally arrived.

The first person to feel the heat was Bob Wayman, HP's longtime chief financial officer. "It's unacceptable that we got surprised this way," Fiorina told him. Her credibility on Wall Street depended on the reliability of the numbers provided to her by Wayman, who filtered and processed the raw data emerging from HP's operating units. "You can't make the same mistake twice," Fiorina warned. When she walked through the executive wing that housed Wayman's office, she sometimes snapped her fingers and mouthed a single word: "Exact!" Then she moved on.

Wayman got the message. For much of 2000, Hewlett-Packard's internal accounting had been in transition, amid attempts to provide better geographic breakdowns of profitability. "We had less clarity than we needed," he later recalled. He had watched patiently as divisional managers tried to get the hang of the new system, amid a general belief that HP's growth was accelerating. Now, Wayman declared that some of those refinements were too ambitious, and others just needed to be done right. It was time to get honest about how the business was faring. He made life hellish for a bunch of divisional treasurers and controllers. But he established an accurate—and chilling—picture of HP's true performance.

When Fiorina spoke to reporters at the giant CeBit technology fair in Hannover, Germany, on March 21, all her old jauntiness was gone. She had stopped claiming to be perfectly positioned about anything. "I'm not optimistic about recovery in the second half of this year," she said. "It is a bit like navigating through the fog."

As the high-tech downturn worsened, Fiorina attracted some of the harshest rebukes from Wall Street. By and large, she was sorting out HP's changed circumstances just as diligently as John Chambers at Cisco and Scott McNealy at Sun were dealing with their troubles. But Fiorina was vulnerable for three reasons that had nothing to do with her immediate job performance. As the shortest-tenured CEO of the bunch, she couldn't remind people of all the good things that had happened earlier in her watch. As the lone woman in command at such a giant corporation, she couldn't blend into the background in Silicon Valley. And as a charismatic leader who came to Hewlett-Packard with an implicit promise of better days to come, she became a tempting target of scorn when things got worse.

Within Hewlett-Packard, Fiorina was struggling for control as well. From the day she arrived, she had believed that HP's payroll was bloated, to the point that judicious cutbacks would make the company more productive and more competitive. Hewlett-Packard had 6,000 people in marketing, for example, while similar-size competitors thrived with a third that number. HP managers on average supervised just 6.3 people, whereas the industry average was 8.3. But whenever Fiorina tried to trim marginal jobs—even in areas where everyone agreed that Hewlett-Packard was haphazardly run—not much happened. In face-to-face meetings, lower-level managers told her they agreed with everything she was saying and would get on the project right away. Then weeks went by. Months passed. Nothing happened. She was at risk of being marooned by the same problems that had beset Lew Platt at the end of his tenure: bureaucracy, lethargy, and a company-wide belief that the HP Way entitled every employee to second-guess the boss.

In a visit to HP's Mexico City facilities in early March 2001, Fiorina tried to get employees properly frightened about hard times. After briefly congratulating them on a strong showing in 2000, she warned them: "If you're not growing as fast as the markets you're in, you're dying. This is not an optional journey. This is a journey about survival." Some employees took such messages at face value, but others held firm to their beliefs that Hewlett-Packard could make its way through tough times more gently. They noticed that as HP's business slump deepened, Fiorina vowed less often to preserve the company's "shining soul"—and when she did use that phrase, it wasn't persuasive. Her new messages were all about austerity, starting with forced drawdowns of vacation pay and eventually moving to the painful prospect of pay cuts and mass layoffs. This didn't feel like the HP Way at all.

As times got tougher, Fiorina talked more and listened less. She became Antigone again, speaking her mind, standing apart from the crowd—and letting her opponents know that she was afraid of nothing. At Lucent, she had won people's hearts by spending hours with them. "If there was snow and it looked as if the airport might close," one consultant recalled, "Carly would say, 'Don't worry, Margaret, you can stay at my place.'" As HP's boss, Fiorina couldn't free up hours of time for everyone who might want to chat with her. A handful of people in her inner circle got to see her

Bill Hewlett mingling with production workers in the 1940s. He invented HP's first product, led the company's push abroad, and was an early champion of women's rise into management ranks. HEWLETT-PACKARD ARCHIVE

Dave Packard handing out bonus checks in 1954. He was the iron-willed patriarch, building one of the world's most successful companies—and tearing apart flawed products with his bare hands. HEWLETT-PACKARD ARCHIVE

Dick Hackborn (*right*) sharing some business pointers with protégé Rick Belluzzo in 1991. Hackborn led HP's entry into the printer business; admirers credited him with "building the family fortune."
DENNIS AHERN,
HEWLETT-PACKARD

Carly Fiorina and Lew Platt fielding media questions on the day in July 1999 when it was announced she would be the company's new chief executive.
STEVE CASTILLO, HEWLETT-PACKARD

Carly Fiorina standing before a mock-up of the original HP garage. Even before she joined Hewlett-Packard, she knew she wanted to draw on the company's legendary heritage to redefine its mission going forward.
ANDY GOODWIN

Walter Hewlett, Carly Fiorina, and Dick Hackborn. The three directors smiled together for the 1999 annual report— a friendly pose that wouldn't be possible two years later.
ANDY GOODWIN

David Woodley Pack-
ard. The only son of
Dave Packard, he
taught ancient Greek
and opened his own
revival movie theater.
After the HP-Compaq
merger was announced,
he accused Fiorina of
distorting his father's
words to justify the
deal. THOR SWIFT

Susan Packard Orr. The third of Dave Packard's four children, she was the one
her father entrusted with the chairmanship of the family foundation. At its
peak, the Packard Foundation had $18 billion in assets. SCOTT LEWIS, SILICON
VALLEY BUSINESS INK

HP director Jay Keyworth.

HP director Bob Knowling.

Walter Hewlett running in the 1964 Boston Marathon as a Harvard sophomore. His time of 2:32 was the fastest ever by a nineteen-year-old.

The counting room. In the upper photo (*left to right*), Larry Sonsini, Carly Fiorina, and Bob Wayman wait tensely for Alan Miller (*far right, foreground*) to call a winner in the grueling HP-Compaq proxy contest. The bottom photo was snapped seconds after Miller declared: "You're good to go."

DOUGLAS L. PECK, HEWLETT-PACKARD

Delaware Chancery Court, where Walter Hewlett filed a last-ditch suit seeking to stop the HP-Compaq merger. Hewlett attorney Stephen Neal's opening statement sent stock traders racing out the door thinking that the suit might prevail. But as Fiorina and then Hewlett testified about the long merger battle, Judge William Chandler decided that Hewlett-Packard had won cleanly. DRAWINGS BY SUSAN SCHARY

Carly Fiorina attracting a hero's welcome at Compaq headquarters in Texas, just after the merger with Hewlett-Packard was completed. Michael Capellas, Compaq's CEO, is two steps behind her. DAVID NANCE, HEWLETT-PACKARD

Carly Fiorina ringing a bell to celebrate completion of the merger. Hewlett-Packard traded in its old stock symbol, HWP, in favor of a new one, HPQ, that reflected both companies' heritage. ANNE KNUDSEN, HEWLETT-PACKARD

warmer side; most others regarded her as brisk, efficient, and remote. The emotional connection was gone.

One of the clearest breakdowns of trust came on Hewlett-Packard's electronic message boards. Traditionally, employees had posted anonymously, creating an online version of the old-timers' suggestion box next to the foreman's office. By spring 2001, some of the message-board postings read like angry scrawls on a bathroom wall, with Carly Fiorina as target No. 1. "It had devolved into a public gripe session that was dominated by a very, very small group of people," said Yvonne Hunt, HP's head of internal communications. Disgusted by this turn of events, Hunt announced that anonymity was over. Only signed postings would be allowed. The new rules cleaned up the message boards, but they didn't get rid of the underlying problem.

As business kept slumping, HP's top executives realized they needed to slash payroll costs in drastic, unprecedented ways. They now faced what Dick Hackborn later called "the worst downturn I've seen in forty years in the computer business." The head of human resources, Susan Bowick, earlier had drafted a list of fifteen ways to reduce employee costs. All the gentle steps at the top of her list had been tried but weren't sufficient. It was time to look at steps 14 and 15: across-the-board pay cuts and mass layoffs. Based on her twenty-four years of experience at the company, Bowick recommended a mandatory 10 percent pay cut, accompanied by a warning that if conditions worsened, layoffs might follow. But Fiorina wanted employees to administer some of the painful remedies themselves. Instead of shrinking paychecks by fiat, Fiorina proposed asking employees to surrender money voluntarily.

"I was among the group that felt: 'Man, this is a big gamble,'" Bowick later said. "We got so much from the workforce already. I thought this was really pushing the organization and the goodwill."

Fiorina disagreed. "Don't underestimate the workforce we have here—and what they will do," she told Bowick. In early June, Hewlett-Packard sounded a call for voluntary sacrifice. People weren't obligated to do anything, but if they cared about the company, they could help by forfeiting paid vacation time or 10 percent of their pay. Back in 1970, Bill Hewlett had created a similar program to help the company squeak through a mild recession without layoffs. Fiorina's plan elicited concessions from an astonishing 86 percent of employees, saving Hewlett-Packard $130 million. The chief executive did her part as well, passing up a $625,000 bonus that had already been approved. "It says a lot about trusting employees," a company spokeswoman said. "It really goes back to the company spending an awful lot of time, right back to the founders, valuing the individual's contribution."

Then came the layoffs. On July 26, Hewlett-Packard announced it would fire 6,000 employees in a bid to cut costs $500 million a year. The high-tech slump by now was so severe that HP's action didn't even merit its own article in many newspapers. The Associated Press now provided a daily "layoff roundup," which on that particular day happened to include 25,000 other sackings at Alcatel, Avaya, Infineon, International Rectifier, JDS Uniphase, and Quantum. But for HP employees—particularly those who hadn't read the voluntary-sacrifice memo carefully—the job cuts felt like treachery. The selfless concessions of June hadn't really accomplished anything; the latest dismissals just proved that management wielded all the power and would use it ruthlessly.

At genteel Hewlett-Packard, every aspect of the layoffs shocked employees. Managers were given emotionless scripts to be read to affected workers. Outplacement consultants from Lee Hecht Harrison were brought on-site to warn fired workers that it might take thirty interviews before they could find another job. At most locations, workers got a few days to clear out their desks and say their good-byes at farewell lunches. Even so, stories spread of workers being turned into "unpersons" that day, told to go home and never return. Downsizing had become an accepted fact of life at many big companies, but at Hewlett-Packard it was all new and horrible. In nervous watercooler chatter, employees couldn't discern a clear basis for who got fired. Decisions weren't being made by people's immediate bosses; it seemed to some bitter employees as if a random-number generator had decided who would go and who would stay. Many people with poor performance ratings on the company's one-to-five scale were sacked, but Susan Bowick, the head of human relations, later acknowledged that at least sixty stars—people with "fives"—were sent packing as well.

For Carly Fiorina, this was no time for tears. "I was very focused on the need to get it done quickly," she later said, "because I knew it would be a huge trauma to the organization. They had never done something like this before. I was also concerned, frankly, about the ability of management lower down to handle it. It was a new thing." Later, Fiorina would concede that the layoffs could have been handled better, particularly by giving lower-level managers a bigger say in how the cuts were made. But at the time, she was stubborn, strong, and unrepentant. Even some ousted employees remained in awe of her. "After I lost my job," one HP employee later recalled, "my financial adviser said: 'Sell your stock in the company. You've been kicked in the teeth. Just put it behind you.' And I said, 'You don't know Carly. She's so strong-willed. She'll get things done.' So I kept all my shares."

Some of the harshest reactions came from HP's powerful alumni in Silicon Valley, who took lifelong pride in their connections to the company's glory years of the 1950s to 1980s. Many of them regarded Fiorina as a human wrecking ball, destroying the team spirit they cherished—and the value of the Hewlett-Packard stock they still owned. They barely knew her and they didn't have up-to-date information about the company's operating problems, but they believed she was utterly clueless about the HP Way they had helped create. At a Silicon Valley charity ball in spring 2001, several members of the old guard buttonholed *Forbes ASAP* editor Michael S. Malone, a onetime HP employee himself. "All of them were in tuxedos," Malone recalled. "And all of them were leaning on me: 'Mike, we've got to do something about what's happening at HP. Mike, you've got to write something. You've got to stop this.' " Malone took his time, but he eventually weighed in with devastating critiques of Fiorina's impact on a company he loved.

Even journalists with only passing interest in Hewlett-Packard began viewing Fiorina in a tough new light. They could see the stock was down. They heard rumblings of discontent, and they knew the notion of "Carly in trouble" was a headline-grabber. Fiorina had enjoyed wonderful beginner's luck with the press, delighting *Fortune* magazine in 1998 with candid stories of her life journey. But reporters in 2001 didn't want to be charmed. They were writing about the collapse of the New Economy, and Fiorina was newsworthy only when she stumbled. Uneasy with this "gotcha" journalism, Fiorina became testy with reporters—and that, too, became part of the story. The glamorous new CEO of Hewlett-Packard was being recast as the Ice Queen.

To the horror of Hewlett-Packard's press department, a few analysts and writers began to suggest that Fiorina's job might be in jeopardy. Rob Enderle, an analyst at Giga Information Group, led the charge, telling print journalists in July that HP and Lucent were on the same bumpy path. He then appeared on CNBC on August 10, telling journalist Maria Bartiromo that Fiorina was "the CEO most at risk and the one most likely not to be around at the end of the year." Left undisputed, such chatter could spread to top-tier magazines, newspapers, and Wall Street research departments. Then it would be impossible to dismiss.

Communications chiefs Allison Johnson and Suzette Stephens decided to move fast. They contacted Louise Kehoe, Silicon Valley bureau chief for the *Financial Times*, and urged her to write a story stating that the HP board remained 100 percent supportive of Fiorina. "I'm not interested in doing the story unless you can get me interviews with every single director," Kehoe shot back. Within forty-eight hours, her wish was largely granted. Director Sam Ginn praised Fiorina for reviving HP's culture and inventiveness, saying the company's overall health is "much better than it was two years ago." Fellow director Jay Keyworth averred that the recent layoffs were "a restoration of the true HP Way" because they were making the company stronger. Dick Hackborn, Phil Condit, Pattie Dunn, and Bob Knowling all phoned or e-mailed Kehoe with reminders that the company's problems were deep-seated and Fiorina deserved a lot of time to fix them. Only Walter Hewlett couldn't be produced; he was driving across America in a recreational vehicle with his family.

In the *Financial Times's* August 19 issue, Kehoe wrote the story that HP's press office had requested but followed up the next day with an extremely perceptive piece about Fiorina's knife-edge existence. In that article, Kehoe observed that Fiorina's first two years at Hewlett-Packard could hardly be called a success. The stock had fallen, the new chief executive's reinvention plan had faltered, and doubts persisted about promised gains in financial performance. Yet Fiorina still had the board's total confidence. In the article, Fiorina was quoted only briefly, but she offered a melodramatic thought that Kehoe used to conclude the article. "I keep asking myself what Dave would say if he looked down and saw what was happening," Fiorina said. "He'd look at it and say: 'This is the company I wanted to lead. Sure it's in turmoil, but it's going in the right direction.'"

There was a lot more Fiorina could have said. But she wanted to keep the board's next project absolutely hidden from outsiders for just a little bit longer.

A half mile from Carly Fiorina's Palo Alto office is a low-slung building now occupied by HP Labs, but best known as the place where Dave Packard and Bill Hewlett worked in their prime. Both of the founders' offices are preserved with museum-quality care. The linoleum floors, laminated desks, and simple ranch artwork on the walls are barely altered from the 1970s. A wooden door at the edge of Packard's office leads to the old boardroom, which has been treated with the same time-capsule deference. In the boardroom, beige wall-to-wall carpeting rests under a long wooden table and sixteen pale gray leather chairs that don't really match anything else.

For most of the John Young and Lew Platt eras, the old boardroom sat vacant. Directors opted for more elegant quarters in what is known as Building Twenty, in the midst of the executive office wing. Then, a few months after joining Hewlett-Packard, Fiorina steered directors' meetings back to the old boardroom in Building Three. She liked the connection to HP's history. She didn't mind the homey look. And she relished the room's best feature: immense sliding-glass doors that opened onto a quiet patio. During the daytime directors could enjoy plenty of natural light in the boardroom. In the evening they could dine informally on the patio, a setting that combined candor, power, and friendship.

On the afternoon of July 19, 2001, Fiorina began the most important board meeting of her career. From midspring onward, she had been mentioning to directors that archrival Compaq Computer might be interested in combining forces with HP. Everything had been hazy and preliminary at first. But exploratory efforts were moving fast enough that it was time for the board to learn everything it could about the potential deal—and then act.

Looking around the room, Fiorina saw only three directors clearly intrigued by the merger prospect. Dick Hackborn liked it. So did Jay Keyworth and Bob Wayman. Four others were neutral or wary. Across from Fiorina was an empty chair where Walter Hewlett normally sat. He was skipping the meeting in favor of a personal commitment known only to a few directors. Colleagues counted him in the skeptics' camp; during the spring, he had voiced concern that any giant acquisition would limit HP's mobility. But Hewlett lately had dropped out of the board dialogue, missing an important conference call July 10 because of a communications mix-up.*

"I will not talk you into this," Fiorina told directors at the start of the meeting. She clicked through eight PowerPoint slides about HP's strategy,

---

* Hewlett had told HP board aide Rosemarie Thomas that he would visit his Lake Tahoe cabin during the Fourth of July weekend. Believing that Hewlett would return to Silicon Valley immediately after the holiday, she left scheduling messages only at his Palo Alto home. As a result, Hewlett never got word of the conference call.

all presented in reassuring blue and green colors. She reminded directors about the growing importance of computer services. Then, in her last five slides, she presented a blunt portrait of a company at risk. "To execute this strategy, we must fill some holes," she told directors. Now she summoned an alarming slide printed on a stark red background. Hewlett-Packard needed to get stronger in software, outsourcing, storage, and high-end printing, she declared, and it needed to cut costs.

Fiorina's final three slides were outright dire. "Our current PC position is unsustainable," she told directors. Hewlett-Packard was falling behind in the Dell-style art of selling personal computers directly to consumers. PCs couldn't be viewed as a stand-alone business that could be lopped off without harm to the rest of Hewlett-Packard; both the printer and server businesses were tightly linked to personal computers. Even worse, Fiorina declared, "Our server business is losing momentum." Servers were meant to be a profit engine and a crucial part of HP's Internet strategy, but Hewlett-Packard was making the wrong kinds of machines and might not be able to afford the costs of staying competitive in next generation R&D. "How do we regain momentum in the server business?" she asked.

With that, three McKinsey consultants stepped forward. After spending two months learning about the Houston company's operations, they had found a startlingly good mesh between the two organizations. Hewlett-Packard was strong in Unix-based servers, weak in the Windows NT market, weak in storage, strong in consumer PCs, and feeble in Dell-style direct selling. Compaq was just the opposite. Put the two companies together, and the combined lineup looked a lot stronger than what either company could do alone. Furthermore, the McKinsey consultants identified at least $2.5 billion a year in costs that could be pruned out by fiscal 2004—largely by eliminating duplicative spending in key business areas. The two companies fit together like a zipper.

Sam Ginn voiced his doubts about moving deeper into personal computers. "We've never made much money at it," he said. "Our returns are lousy and so are theirs." The McKinsey experts retorted that HP and Compaq had much less at stake than most people realized. Together, the two companies rang up $20 billion a year in revenue selling personal computers. But they didn't make the hardware or software; they didn't even assemble the machines. Intel, Microsoft, and contract manufacturers such as Flextronics handled such chores. The PC business consisted mostly of brand-name sizzle and some legal agreements in a file cabinet. If the two companies could coax out a few marketing efficiencies and post even a slim profit, that would translate into a decent return on invested capital.

As the afternoon played out, Dick Hackborn became one of the most vocal proponents of the deal. He had been arguing for years that industry standards almost always won out over proprietary architectures in the computer business. As a result, he believed, Hewlett-Packard ought to seize command of the standardized—and increasingly popular—Windows NT server market and rely less on its customized Unix machines. An HP-Compaq combination would finally get the company pointed in the right direction. The two companies certainly would lose some business as they took time to mesh together. Hackborn wanted McKinsey to quantify that risk, but if it wasn't too big and if it appeared likely that most of the lost business would be concentrated in the companies' least profitable areas, he was ready to champion the deal.

Pattie Dunn had been doubtful at the start. "There's scant history of these things working," she said. "What will make our odds better?" When the McKinsey consultants started talking about $2.5 billion a year of cost savings, her face lit up. That was a huge number. If one fresh fact could put her mind at ease, that was it. Consolidation mergers often worked out well in the long run, she knew. Her own industry, banking, had seen plenty of them. Merged companies were most vulnerable in the first year or two. If there were big cost savings to be reaped right away, she was starting to feel a lot better about the deal.

At dinnertime, directors moved out to the patio for swordfish, rice, and green beans. Skepticism was starting to soften. The combination of McKinsey, Dick Hackborn, Jay Keyworth, and Pattie Dunn made the deal sound more intriguing. When directors returned to the boardroom after dinner, Fiorina handed each of them a sheet of paper with three questions. First: Do you think the IT industry needs to consolidate and if so, is it better to be a consolidator or a consolidatee? Second: How important is it to our strategic goals to be number one or number two in each of our chief product categories? Finally: Can we achieve our strategic goals without a complete scene changer?

The questions were both innocent and ingenious. Carly Fiorina wasn't pushing directors to do anything. "I'm not trying to talk you into this," she reminded them. She just wanted them to mull these issues overnight in their hotel rooms so that they could provide their insights when the board meeting resumed the next morning. In conjunction, however, the three questions framed the debate in a fascinating new way. Anyone who cared about Hewlett-Packard's standing in the world was bound to see the company as a natural consolidator, destined to be a market leader, that needed to do something decisive to get back on track. Embrace those answers, and directors would be a big step closer to authorizing the Compaq deal.

The next morning at 8 A.M. the directors reconvened, and two more skeptics came on board. Sam Ginn went first. "I've thought about it carefully," he said. The PC business still concerned him, but he had decided that wasn't the prime issue. Competing with IBM was his ultimate goal, and merging with Compaq could help. Phil Condit was similarly encouraging. "I've been through a lot of mergers," he said. "This feels very analogous to what I've been doing. It is difficult. History is not particularly kind to a lot of mergers. So don't approach it casually. But if you are really focused, it can be successful. If you believe you're up for it, then I think it's worth doing." Bob Knowling remained hesitant. "I agree we've got to do something," he said. "I'm just not sure this is it."

Next up to speak was Walter Hewlett, who had quietly slipped into the boardroom a few minutes earlier. His personal commitment the day before had been fulfilled; he was ready to help govern HP again. Hewlett asked for a moment to collect his thoughts, so Jay Keyworth, the last person due to speak in the clockwise chain, offered a ringing endorsement of the deal. "The overarching thing is, we've got to do something," Keyworth declared. "We're not going to succeed without a scene changer."

Now Walter Hewlett weighed in with a message that was both low-key and incredibly jarring to his peers. "We really need to think this through," he said. "I don't think this is the right choice." The Compaq deal flunked all the tests that mattered to him. It meant a much bigger bet in PCs, an industry that he thought was highly problematic. It meant combining genteel HP with the much scrappier culture of Compaq, which he felt would be disastrous for employees and ultimately bad for shareholders. To his consternation, all the other directors appeared to be racing ahead on the HP-Compaq merger without him. Walter Hewlett wanted to slow things down.

"I wish you'd been here yesterday," one of the other directors shot back, "because we spent about ten hours covering all that." The HP boardroom was a polite place, but all around the table other directors were visibly exasperated at Hewlett's stance. Most of them were intensely busy people who had cleared out extra time to help Carly Fiorina sort through her strategic choices. Phil Condit had flown in from Chicago, putting all his regular Boeing business on hold for two days. Pattie Dunn was in the midst of trying to negotiate a management buyout of her investment-management business, but she had turned off her cell phone and was concentrating on nothing but HP's needs. It galled them that Walter Hewlett wanted to drag the entire debate backward—after missing the previous day's crucial talks—just so that he could reenter the discussion at a more fundamental level.

When directors found out why Hewlett had missed the Thursday board session, they were even more flabbergasted. He had been playing the cello at an outdoor concert staged at the Bohemian Grove, the summer home of the men's club that his father and Dave Packard had enjoyed for decades. Faced with a schedule conflict between his cello and the HP boardroom, the cello won.

To Walter Hewlett, his absence ought to be seen in a different light. He had given his word eleven months earlier that he would play in the Grove's biggest concert of the year. His presence was needed, and he didn't break his promises. He had genuinely thought that Hewlett-Packard's Thursday-afternoon board session would involve only routine committee work, something that he could skip with minor regrets. Somehow, he hadn't fully absorbed Dick Hackborn's decision a year earlier to start using the Thursday-afternoon sessions as high-level strategic reviews. "If I had known what an important board meeting this was, of course I would have been there," Walter Hewlett said more than a year later. "They never told me." He would wonder from that time onward whether his fellow directors had deliberately kept him in the dark about the importance of their Thursday meeting.

During a break Friday morning, Dick Hackborn tried to reengage with Walter Hewlett. The two men had been friends for years; Hackborn also was Carly Fiorina's mentor and the most prominent booster of the HP-Compaq deal. If anyone could smooth the waters, Hackborn was the one. He asked Hewlett to talk a bit more about what was bothering him. "We're acting like we're in a crisis and we're not," Hewlett said, adding: "It sounds like a bad idea. There's no way I could go to the Hewlett Foundation and recommend it." When Walter Hewlett made that comment, he believed he was simply expressing the depth of his concern to a friend. But after Hewlett's awkward investment in Indigo stock earlier that year, fears abounded that proprietary information might be leaked or misused. Hackborn mentioned his conversation to Fiorina. Moments later, she tracked down Hewlett and read him the riot act.

"Walter, don't you dare go tell anybody about this!" Fiorina said.

"This is private information! This is confidential. You're not supposed to tell anybody. You can't go to the Hewlett Foundation and tell them we're talking about this." She wanted to scorch him with anger, not because she didn't like him but because she couldn't bear the thought of an ill-timed leak undermining the entire deal. Hewlett absorbed his scolding without getting angry at Fiorina. She was just doing her job. But he seethed with indignation at Hackborn. "For him to turn around and report to Carly," Walter Hewlett later said, "I felt this was betrayal."

Regardless of Walter Hewlett's frame of mind, other directors were ready to move forward. When the boardroom discussion resumed, Dick Hackborn turned to two HP computer executives who had been sitting quietly along a side wall of the boardroom and asked them what they thought of the deal. Ann Livermore voiced strong support. So did Duane Zitzner. That reassured everyone else in the boardroom. At the end of the meeting, directors agreed to hire Goldman Sachs & Company, one of Wall Street's top firms, as the board's financial adviser. It was time to assemble the classic deal-doing entourage: consultants, lawyers, and investment bankers. From this point onward, these advisers would form an almost unstoppable juggernaut committed to getting the transaction negotiated, announced, and completed.

"We had already worked for quite awhile on the incrementalist strategy," director Pattie Dunn later remarked. "There weren't a lot of viable alternatives. The key question to me was: 'Is management going to turn itself inside out to make this deal work?' And I thought both the HP and Compaq managements had a huge stake in making the merger work. If you believed that something transformational was required, then it all fell into place."

At Compaq's headquarters in Houston, a similar epiphany was taking place. The company was much younger and brasher than Hewlett-Packard, but it, too, had lost its way after a glorious beginning. Founded in 1982 by three Texas Instruments employees meeting in a Houston pie shop, Compaq was a creation of the PC era. Rod Canion, William Murto, and James Harris could see the incredible potential of IBM's freshly launched personal computer. They also believed that a scrappy little company could match IBM's basic design at lower cost and win a lot of customers by selling what would become known as "PC clones." Over the next dozen years, Compaq roared to prominence in the clone business, elbowing aside dozens of rivals. Insiders thought of Compaq as the Wal-Mart of technology: not trying to impress the elite, but unbelievably adept at serving ordinary folks' needs. Then, in 1997 and 1998, Compaq CEO Eckhard Pfeiffer announced acquisitions of two sophisticated computer companies, Tandem and Digital Equipment, in the belief that Compaq now could expand its way into the corporate-data-center market. When merger integration went badly, Pfeiffer lost his job in early 1999. Compaq's chief information officer, Michael Capellas, took over.

In an industry full of rock-star CEOs, Capellas came across as the diligent road-show manager who did all the little things right but wouldn't ever evoke the crowd's roar just for walking onstage. Blind in one eye from a childhood accident, Capellas regularly told interviewers about an incident of teenage persistence that defined the rest of his life. When his high-school football coach told him he wasn't tough enough to be a linebacker, Capellas went on a weight-lifting binge, bulked up, and got to play the position he wanted. He became co-captain of the team and ultimately led Warren G. Harding High School to the Ohio state championship in 1971. Capellas did the same thing in his career. Starting with a business degree from Kent State in 1976, he joined Republic Steel as an accountant and inched his way forward with twenty-two different jobs at six different companies. "I always wanted the toughest job," Capellas told *BusinessWeek* after taking command at Compaq.

As Compaq's new chief executive, Capellas did his best work in fixing business basics at what was now a 65,000-employee company that had grown too fast for its own good. He repaired relationships with key suppliers such as Microsoft and Seagate, which had eroded under previous leadership. "I don't think anybody could have made a better start," Microsoft CEO Steve Ballmer declared in mid-2000, a year into Capellas's tenure. Capellas also owned up to Compaq's troubles competing with Dell; in late 1999 he paid $370 million to buy the PC-distribution arm of Inacom, which specialized in selling computers directly to consumers.

Because of Capellas's hard-grinding background, however, he got tagged right away as "not a visionary." No matter how much Capellas tried to convince Wall Street and the media that he did have big ideas, the less-glamorous image persisted. He talked briefly about refocusing Compaq around computer services. Then he championed Internet appliances as the company's driving force. A year into his tenure, investors couldn't tell where he wanted to take Compaq.

Inside the Compaq boardroom, directors fretted. "As you start to slide downhill, a number of things become pretty obvious to you," Compaq director Larry Babbio later remarked. "Number one, it becomes more and more obvious that your course profile isn't good. It becomes very obvious that there are too many players in the industry and that consolidation is absolutely critical if the industry is going to survive." What's more, some directors believed that HP's name had enormous cachet in the market, even though some of the California company's operations were stumbling. By contrast, the name *Compaq* didn't make anyone's heart beat faster, even though the Houston company owned some excellent technology. Put the two operations together, call the combined company Hewlett-Packard—and a lot of problems would be fixed at once. Such a transaction would mean that Compaq's acquiring days were over. It would take refuge inside a bigger company and vanish as an independent entity. But that was tolerable. The next step was to fathom Hewlett-Packard's frame of mind.

In early June 2001, things got serious. In the midst of the Unix technology-licensing conversations, Capellas told Fiorina that sharing licenses and competing for the same customers didn't really make sense. Maybe it was time for the two companies to work much more closely together. "Is your board prepared for such a broad-based conversation?" Capellas asked. "Well, Mike," Fiorina replied, "I'm not sure I'm ready to have this kind of conversation." She wanted him to signal a bit more about Compaq's intentions. "If you are, call me back," Capellas said.

A few days later, she did.

It didn't take long for top executives at both companies to decide they liked the business logic of a merger. On the HP side, the decisive nod came from finance chief Bob Wayman, who in late June held several secret meetings with Michael Capellas and Compaq CFO Jeff Clarke at the law offices of Wilson Sonsini. Before the talks started, Wayman had expected pathetic posturing from the Compaq executives—the equivalent of "putting lipstick on a pig." Instead, Wayman came away impressed with how well the two companies' operations fit together and how much cost-cutting a merger would allow. He also was startled to see how quickly Compaq had built up a Dell-like ability to sell PCs directly to consumers, something that continued to be maddeningly elusive for Hewlett-Packard. After two rounds of talks, a freshly converted Wayman went to Fiorina and declared, "There's a lot to work with."

Deciding what to do about Michael Capellas was much harder. He hoped to be co-CEO of the combined company. People on the HP team thought that was preposterous. They offered him what amounted to a ticket out of the company: running merger integration for a year, with no clear prospects of anything to follow. Capellas balked—and so did his directors. Not only did they want Hewlett-Packard to treat their CEO decently, they also wanted to ensure that other senior executives at Compaq thought they had a future in the combined company. If HP hogged all the good jobs for itself, the merger wouldn't produce a stronger company. As talks bogged down, Capellas decided to call Fiorina on August 5 and tell her that the whole deal was off.

Right from the start, Fiorina assumed that Capellas was negotiating. If he wanted to slow down the talks and send a signal to the HP board, she could respond appropriately. "I'm disappointed," she said. "But if you want to break off discussions, so be it." She finished the phone call within seconds and then wondered, with a sly sense of amusement, how long it would take for Capellas to pick up the dialogue afresh.

Fiorina didn't have to wait long. On Wednesday evening, August 8, the San Jose Technology Museum hosted an immense dinner party to celebrate the twentieth anniversary of the personal computer. Organizers put Compaq founder Rod Canion, Microsoft founder Bill Gates, and Intel chairman Andy Grove onstage for a freewheeling discussion of the early days. At the dining area's head table, top executives of leading PC companies—including Carly Fiorina and Michael Capellas—were asked to sit side by side and enjoy the show. Capellas began the rapprochement, greeting Fiorina with a hug the moment they saw each other. A top Compaq executive, Shane Robison, slipped next to Fiorina a little later and whispered, "We've got to keep talking." She told him, "Don't worry. It's all going to be OK." During dinner, Fiorina and Capellas scrupulously avoided talking about the merger directly, but they enjoyed friendly chat about the economy, their spouses, and the performers onstage. At the end of the dinner, Fiorina turned to Capellas and said, "Let's stay in touch."

"I would really like that," Capellas replied.

By late August, the leadership issues had been resolved in a thoughtful compromise. Capellas would become president of the combined company, reporting to Fiorina and overseeing the main operating units. Five of his key lieutenants—Peter Blackmore, Jeff Clarke, Bob Napier, Shane Robeson, and Mike Winkler—would join nine HP executives to form the new company's executive team. When lawyers needed code names for their paperwork, Fiorina decided that HP should be called "Heloise" and Compaq

"Abelard." The cultural allusion baffled most of her advisers, who were told that the love letters of Heloise and Abelard were an important part of French medieval literature.★

Plans were made to announce a merger agreement immediately after Labor Day, on September 4. Lawyers and investment bankers still had some haggling left about the exact purchase price and the companies' strategy to win antitrust approval of the deal, but all the essentials were in place. Assuming that antitrust authorities blessed the deal (which was considered likely but a potential nail-biter) and that shareholders of both companies approved the merger (which was considered a formality), the two companies could expect to be fully united some time in the first half of 2002.

As friction points got smoothed away, Hewlett-Packard's top outside attorney, Larry Sonsini, noticed something odd. While eight of HP's directors enthusiastically supported the deal, Walter Hewlett did not. "It was becoming clear that Walter was troubled by the deal," Sonsini later said. "He was unable to articulate why, other than that it was a very big merger and he was afraid that big mergers didn't work." At first, Sonsini recommended that Hewlett be given a bit of breathing room, in the belief that he was a straggler who eventually would catch up of his own accord. "We thought: This is a change for HP," Sonsini later recalled. "Walter's tied to the HP Way. He will get through this. Don't pressure him. Let him work it through."

At an August 31 board meeting, Sonsini informed all the Hewlett-Packard directors that they would soon be asked to sign the formal merger agreement and that both companies were expecting unanimous approval from the two boards. "This is very, very usual," Sonsini said. It's a way of showing board cohesiveness, he explained, adding that it would help the "optics" of the deal—a quaint way of saying that unanimous endorsement by directors would look good to Wall Street. At that meeting, Walter Hewlett said: "I'm obviously troubled by the merger. What are you guys doing? Look at the terrible position you're putting me in."

When the board meeting broke up, Sonsini walked out with Hewlett and told him, "Walter, I know you're working this through. You're a member of the board. I represent you on this. I want you to know that you can separate, from a legal viewpoint, a decision as a director acting in the inter-

---

★ One extra-curious adviser wandered onto the Internet to learn more about the medieval couple, only to discover that Abelard ultimately was castrated when Héloïse's family grew angry at him. That fact was kept hidden from Michael Capellas until September 2002. When he learned of Abelard's fate, Capellas said, "I'm glad I didn't know."

est of all shareholders and your decision managing your own stock position." In oblique terms, Sonsini was telling Hewlett: Vote quietly against the deal, if you want, with your personal HP shares (which amounted to a modest 401,000 shares, or 0.02 percent of the company). Just announce that you're supporting the deal as a director. That's what management cares about.

"Thank you," Walter Hewlett replied. "That's very helpful."

Three days later, on the eve of the merger announcement, Hewlett-Packard's directors staged a conference call to ratify the fully drafted deal. Once again, Sonsini went through the need for a unanimous vote. Once again, Walter Hewlett anguished about what to do. Finally, Hewlett decided to embrace the Sonsini compromise.

"I am voting for this as a director." He was still trying to sort out his own beliefs, and as much as he felt inclined to vote his own shares against it, he wanted to see what the wider world would make of the merger. Perhaps he was overly fearful. No one asked him to elaborate; there was something uncomfortable about hearing Hewlett make a contorted attempt to soothe both his fellow directors and his conscience. For a company eager to launch the Compaq merger plan with the best possible face to the public, the Sonsini compromise was perfect enough.

In New York, Carly Fiorina, Michael Capellas, and dozens of aides got ready to announce the merger to the world on Tuesday, September 4, as planned. Fiorina and Capellas both believed the combined companies could achieve great things. But Goldman Sachs had confirmed Fiorina's concern that investors weren't likely to share that enthusiasm. Acquiring companies' stocks often dropped 5 or 6 percent on the day a major takeover bid was announced, the investment bankers observed. In this case, Wall Street was likely to fixate on the view that two struggling makers of personal computers were pairing up—and creating a bigger, sicker PC business in the process. Even if Fiorina and Capellas believed that view was absurd, it was likely to dominate investors' thinking for at least the first few days. In that case, the advisers said, HP's stock might fall 10 percent or more. A drop of 15 percent was conceivable.

Over the holiday weekend, Carly Fiorina alerted her team to some of the investor apprehensions that were likely to arise. "This will not be a deal that is well understood or well liked," she warned. "It is only a matter of how bad it gets before people start to see what the deal is all about."

Chapter 8

WALTER HEWLETT'S REBELLION

Walter Hewlett had been coming to the San Felipe Ranch almost all his life. Even as a teenager, he understood the rhythm of the place better than any of the other Hewlett and Packard children did. He was a capable rifleman, a good listener when the campfire stories began, and an engaging free spirit. During the deer-hunting weekends of the 1960s and 1970s, he woke everyone before dawn with unbearably loud music, played on whatever instrument he favored that year—usually an accordion—so the hunt could begin on time. When Dave Packard died and Bill Hewlett became wheelchair-bound, people wondered if the great traditions of the San Felipe Ranch would perish. They didn't. From the mid-1990s onward, the old ways stayed alive because of the dedication of Bill Hewlett's oldest son.

So the evening of Friday, September 7, 2001, began as so many had in the past. A barbecue was sizzling; sunset was approaching. Walter Hewlett and a dozen guests clustered near an enormous black hearth, where they could enjoy the ranch's best views. In front of them stretched an endless panorama of rolling hills, dark green shrubs, and parched yellow grasses. This was a perfect place to eat outdoors—and to talk. This was where Dave Packard and Bill Hewlett had done some of their best strategizing over the years.

Standing beside two of his father's longtime friends, Walter Hewlett confided his deep uneasiness about the Compaq deal. He worried that the giant merger would trap Hewlett-Packard deep in the profitless mess of the personal-computer business. He viewed the deal as an alarming departure from the way that HP usually did things, and a risky gamble that two big technology companies could be fused together. Any way that he looked at it, HP-Compaq felt like bad business. To his embarrassment and shame, Walter Hewlett hadn't been able to convince anyone in the boardroom that this $20 billion leap into the unknown was wrong. He had spoken against it repeatedly, but no one had taken his objections all that seriously. He had been outmaneuvered so crushingly that in the end, he didn't even have the courage to vote against the deal. His point of view had been dismissed; his dissent bottled up.

Now that the merger plan had been disclosed to the world, everyone else seemed to regard it as a disaster, too. Hewlett-Packard and Compaq had announced the deal on Tuesday, September 4, with all the ebullience they could muster. (Carly Fiorina told investors it would "create tomorrow's leader today." Michael Capellas added: "I'm absolutely psyched.") None of that bravado impressed the stock market. When trading opened that day, HP's stock tumbled 19 percent, to $18.87 a share. Investors from coast to coast began spitting HP out of their portfolios as if it were a moldy piece of fruit. Each bit of public criticism only intensified Walter Hewlett's dilemma. He had missed his chance to stop the deal before it was announced. From the official public record, investors and HP's 87,000 employees would think that he actually *liked* the deal. That was a grotesque misrepresentation of his true feelings. So now, should he keep quiet about his qualms? Was he tangled up in worries that ultimately didn't matter? Or was it time to take a stand?

"You're absolutely right to be concerned," one of the other hunters replied. It was Jim Gaither, managing director of Sutter Hill Ventures and a longtime trustee of the Hewlett Foundation. A quick-witted, silver-haired lawyer by training, Gaither in recent years had begun a second career as a venture capitalist. He watched the ebbs and flows of Silicon Valley every day, and what he saw gave him plenty of reason to be jaundiced. "Technology mergers of this type generally don't work," Gaither said. "Look at Compaq itself." In Gaither's eyes, Compaq's 1998 purchase of Digital Equipment had produced nothing but chaos and eroding shareholder value. What's more, Gaither argued, HP's pursuit of Compaq wasn't just a minor dalliance. It was such a big bet that if it went wrong, it could jeopardize the future of HP itself.

Then Arjay Miller, a former dean of the Stanford Business School, weighed in. He was a big-company man, with a résumé that included a half-dozen blue chip directorships and a stint as president of Ford Motor Company in the 1960s. "It's awfully tough," he said. "The hardest thing to do on a board is to go against your peer group. But I don't agree with a lot of these big mergers. There needs to be a dominant company to make things succeed." Miller ticked through a handful of examples he knew well from his own directorships or auto-industry experience. Wells Fargo and Crocker Bank worked out tolerably. Daimler-Benz and Chrysler was a mess. Then he zeroed in on the most fundamental issue of all.

"What would your dad do?" Miller asked. After the tiniest pause, the retired dean answered his own question: "There's no doubt in my mind. Your dad wouldn't have voted for this deal."

The road to rebellion started slowly. A few days after the deer-hunting weekend, Walter Hewlett talked again with Jim Gaither, this time about all the complications of being a director, a shareholder, an executor of his father's estate, and chairman of the family foundation. "With all the hats you're wearing," Gaither told him, "you ought to get a lawyer." He recommended Stephen Neal, the top partner at Gaither's old law firm of Cooley Godward, in Palo Alto. Neal was a savvy corporate attorney who had handled complex cases for the likes of General Motors and USG. But he also was feisty enough to defend convicted S&L swindler Charles Keating in the mid-1990s when no one else wanted to touch the matter—and to win acquittals or mistrials in the most crucial cases. As Gaither figured it, Stephen Neal was exactly the kind of fierce, protective advocate that Walter Hewlett needed.

A week passed. Then on Sunday morning, September 23, Walter Hewlett visited Cooley Godward and finally found lawyers who listened. They talked in a small conference room for five and a half hours. Out came a waterfall of unhappiness and frustration that touched on everything: Compaq . . . the vote . . . Larry Sonsini's advice . . . Dick Hackborn . . . Phil Condit . . . and most of all, a feeling of having been railroaded into a directors' vote that didn't express his true beliefs. "Walter clearly needed to unload," recalled Keith Flaum, a younger Cooley partner present at the meeting. "For the first few hours, we just listened." In some capacity, it was clear, Walter Hewlett wanted to speak out against the deal, if only to clear his conscience. But how could he do that and still handle all his obligations to the trust and the foundation?

Stephen Neal began to craft a plan. Walter Hewlett could be a much more powerful factor than the other directors realized, as long as everything got done in the right order. Don't criticize the Compaq deal in public just yet, Neal advised. Don't breathe a word of your concerns to Carly Fiorina. Cut back on contact even with friends such as David Woodley Packard. Keep everything on hold until the Hewlett Foundation and Bill Hewlett's estate (the Hewlett Trust) conducted their own reviews, aided by independent experts. "We got things in the right sequence," Neal later said. It was a disarmingly modest comment. Just three weeks earlier, Larry Sonsini had stymied Walter Hewlett's concerns in a boardroom where eight other HP directors wanted to do the deal—and only one had qualms. Now, everything was being reassessed with the opposite perspective in mind: *What if Walter Hewlett turned out to be right and all the other directors were wrong?*

If Walter Hewlett needed any more reason to be apprehensive about HP's expansion plans, he could find it every time he picked up a newspaper. In late September, HP stock skidded to $12.50 a share, partly because of investor jitters about the deal and partly because of a wider sense of despair sweeping through the United States. Terrorists had demolished the World Trade Center in New York a week after Fiorina and Capellas announced the merger agreement. Anthrax scares broke out soon afterward, further darkening the national mood. At a time when even the most routine activities, such as opening the mail, seemed scary, hardly anyone was inclined to endorse a giant and risky business combination. As the influential "Lex" column in the *Financial Times* put it on October 2: "Both companies have a good excuse for walking away from this merger."

Walter Hewlett's older sister, Eleanor Gimon, called from Connecticut, bitterly unhappy about what the Compaq announcement was doing to HP's share price. "I was horrified," she later recalled. "What a bad deal! I asked Walter, 'Aren't you going to do something?' Clearly something had to be done. I asked him, 'How could you have voted for this?' He said he was pressured into it."

By early November, all the pieces necessary for a Hewlett counterattack were in place. Both the Hewlett Foundation and the Hewlett Trust were firmly in the No camp, bolstered by sturdy reports from outside experts. Their charts and financial data vehemently argued that buying Compaq would hurt the Hewlett entities' big investments in HP. Now Walter Hewlett could start putting pressure on other people. With the help of Stephen Neal and a new media adviser—savvy New York publicist Joele Frank—Walter Hewlett drafted the first press release of his new life. He, his sisters, the Hewlett Foundation, and the Hewlett Trust all would be opposing the Compaq acquisition. His reasons were expressed as flatly and unemotionally as possible: "I believe that Hewlett-Packard can create greater value for stockholders as a stand-alone company than as a company combined with Compaq." There was a sly code to these sorts of announcements: The most stunning messages always were couched in the blandest language. Public reaction would make headlines soon enough. Plans were made to distribute the release at 10:30 A.M. Pacific time on Tuesday, November 6. Half an hour beforehand, from a small conference room next to Stephen Neal's office, Walter Hewlett phoned Carly Fiorina to let her know what was coming.

In a few stark sentences, he told her that the Hewlett interests would be voting no, and that an announcement was imminent. His tone was unyielding and terse; this was a courtesy call in name only. "I don't understand why you're doing this," Fiorina said, in a stunned voice. She asked if he could hold off the announcement for a little while. The answer was no. Joele Frank wanted Walter Hewlett's perspective to dominate the first day's press coverage, before HP figured out its full response. "This isn't going to help the stock," Fiorina declared. Hewlett didn't respond. "The decision is what it is," he said. With that, it was time to say good-bye.

Half an hour later, the financial community was sizzling with the news. CNBC, Bloomberg, and Dow Jones poured reporters onto what suddenly was the hottest business story of the day. HP's stock skyrocketed 17 percent, finishing the day at $19.81. Maybe the summer's push to combine Hewlett-Packard and Compaq could be stopped cold simply because a powerful director didn't like the merger. Keith Flaum, the junior Cooley Godward lawyer in the room, was beside himself. He leaped out of his chair and turned toward Walter Hewlett. It was time for high-fives.

The uprising had begun in earnest. This time Walter Hewlett couldn't be dismissed as a melancholy heir, unable to find his way in a high-powered boardroom. He was recasting himself as a man of principle, speaking out in an effort to prevent HP from making a horrible mistake. "This is a bad transaction," he told Bloomberg Business News. "The sooner it ends, the better." He hammered home that point in a half-dozen other interviews the afternoon of November 6. If people wanted to know his strategic thinking, he explained that buying Compaq would increase HP's exposure to the dismal personal-computer sector and dilute the lucrative printing business. If people searched for personal grudges that might be fueling his opposition, he swatted away their questions. "This isn't about Carly," he told *USA Today*. "This is about the transaction." Commentators in almost every newspaper found him persuasive and powerful.

What had changed? In the two months since the deer-hunting weekend, Walter Hewlett had pulled together a small army of people who could help him fight the legions at Carly Fiorina's disposal. He had hired a lawyer who could joust with Larry Sonsini. He had enlisted a small San

Francisco investment bank, Friedman, Fleischer & Lowe, that intended to talk back to Goldman Sachs. He had signed up a brilliant media adviser who could sharpen his rhetoric so that he might be as persuasive as HP's charismatic CEO. With their help, he was a new man: bolder, brasher, and more combative than ever before.

All this help wouldn't come cheap. Over the next eight months Walter Hewlett would dip into the Hewlett trust for more than $30 million to finance his opposition to the Compaq deal. It was his readiest source of cash—and it was perfectly legal. His new investment bankers, Salomon Brothers alumnus Tully Friedman and Morgan Stanley alumnus Spencer Fleischer, calculated that the value of HP's stock could be boosted $5 a share or more if the Compaq deal were stopped. That would make a $500 million difference to the eventual value of the Hewlett Foundation. On the face of it, there was something odd about using millions of dollars from a dead parent's estate to fight a takeover battle, rather than just letting the money go straight to the foundation. But if Walter Hewlett's financial advisers were accurate about the potential payoff to the foundation, he was doing the right thing.

In private moments, Walter Hewlett was searingly honest about his own limitations. "You've got to look at my personality," he said, after the HP-Compaq battle was over. "Look at my strengths and weaknesses. I'm fond of saying that all the power in the world belongs to people that like to talk. I don't like to talk. I'm not highly verbal, and my father wasn't either. It can take me an hour of preparation just to come up with one minute of spoken remarks. I told the board members what I thought, but I wasn't a Daniel Webster making my case." All summer, he had been outmaneuvered by people more persuasive than he was. On his own, he could never prevail. "I'm not afraid of making decisions," he continued. "But what I'm not good at is writing letters. On the verbal side, I needed help. So Steve Neal, and Joele Frank, and Spencer Fleischer, and Tully Friedman—they added the outward coating of radicalism. But I made the decisions. On the rabble-rousing, the saber-rattling, I had a lot of help with that. Not in a thousand years—I couldn't have done that without the help I had."

In a way, Walter Hewlett became an organist. He knew the composition that he wanted to play. He believed it should blast forth as powerfully as possible. When he hired his advisers, he found the business world's equivalent of sixteen-foot Bourdon pipes that would bellow forth his message. All he needed was to touch the right keys, and the thundering would begin.

Within hours after his phone call to Carly Fiorina, Walter Hewlett realized that he hadn't broken his opponents' resolve after all. Fiorina put out a statement saying she was "disappointed but not surprised" by his opposition, and that she remained strongly in favor of the deal. The other HP directors were even more forceful. In a joint press release, they reaffirmed their "enthusiastic support" for the merger and endorsed Fiorina's leadership. The first testimonial in the statement came from Dick Hackborn, who called the merger "the very best way to deliver the value our shareowners expect." Privately, he told Fiorina he was outraged that the Hewlett Foundation had decided to oppose the deal without hearing his perspective as a foundation director. Positions had hardened. Both sides were inching toward a protracted fight, with the fate of the merger ultimately to be decided by a shareholder vote in early 2002.

How hard did Carly Fiorina and the other directors want to battle to complete the deal? Walter Hewlett didn't know. "I'm not sure whether I'm dealing with John Paul Jones or General Custer," he told one journalist at about this time. He had started with high hopes that the mere news of his opposition might cause the deal to collapse. If that wasn't going to happen, he might well need to take his case to HP's other major shareholders over the next few months. That would require a savvy campaign manager, who could court key voters with phone calls, visits, and endless mailings, while keeping the momentum going with endless tactical thrusts at the opposing side. Walter Hewlett had no idea how to find such people; he had spent much of his life without even knowing that they existed. But the New York law firm of Wachtell, Lipton, Rosen & Katz, which was working for his new investment bankers, Friedman, Fleischer & Lowe, was full of experts in this arena. Its advice: Sprint to hire Dan Burch, before the other side gets him.

If Hollywood central casting had gone looking for a campaign operative, it couldn't have done better than Dan Burch. He was a stocky man in his midfifties, with untucked shirttails, a penchant for gossip, and a hushed, conspiratorial voice that suggested he knew where all the bodies were buried. He had been orchestrating takeover campaigns since he was a college student in the 1960s. In the 1980s he worked for corporate raider T. Boone Pickens on some deals—and against him on others. As long as the action was hot and the pay was good, Burch and his small firm of MacKenzie Partners were willing to harness their skills to the highest bidder. MacKenzie's New York offices were slightly shabby and disheveled, but takeover veterans knew that was a good sign. So many partisans were clamoring to hire Burch that there just wasn't time to clean up the last battle before starting the next.

There was something about Walter Hewlett that fascinated Burch. As a boy, Burch had helped his father train horses for the Mellons and Vanderbilts. He had always admired America's aristocrats. Now, at last, he was getting a chance to help Old Money fix the family company in the midst of a crisis. He couldn't have asked for a better assignment.

A few days after Hewlett announced his opposition, Burch flew to California to brief the dissident director and his other advisers about what might be involved in an all-out battle for shareholders' votes. Such tussles were called proxy contests, and they were the business community's version of pro wrestling matches in a cage. No matter how civil everyone might be before a proxy contest started, things almost always turned ugly, fast. Both sides would start running full-page ads in the newspapers, denouncing their opponents. Private detectives might be hired to dig up dirt. Daily press releases and fax campaigns would appeal to voters' avarice one day and evoke their basest fears the next.

Burch said he didn't want to step beyond his client's requests. But he knew how the game was played, and if Walter Hewlett really wanted to win an all-out battle, Burch had some powerful tactics at his disposal. The Hewlett camp could nominate its own full or partial slate of directors, asking shareholders to kick out Dick Hackborn and other incumbents in favor of people Walter Hewlett would rather see in the boardroom. In addition, Walter Hewlett could demand private meetings with members of HP's leadership team, quizzing Carly Fiorina's lieutenants to see if any of them wanted to join him in fighting the Compaq deal. Finally, he could plunge the Hewlett Trust into debt by borrowing as much as $1 billion so that the trust could buy another fifty million HP shares. That might imperil the trust's finances, but it certainly would increase his voting clout, giving him another 3 percent of the shares outstanding.

The possibilities were endless. For a while, Walter Hewlett sat still and listened. "This was all foreign to him," Burch recalled. "He was being a sponge." Then, at a certain point, Walter Hewlett decided to draw the line. Several people later recalled him saying, "Let's stick to the high road." As Walter Hewlett later explained, the most aggressive tactics just didn't feel right. "I felt like I was speaking for a certain set of values," he said. "What good does it do me to descend below those values if that's what I'm trying to protect?" Even so, on Friday, November 16, Walter Hewlett filed paperwork with the Securities and Exchange Commission, saying that he might lobby other shareholders. A proxy contest was imminent.

That Friday happened to be the date of a Hewlett-Packard board meeting. Other directors had been mulling over Walter Hewlett's uprising for ten days now. Their feelings ranged from exasperation and bewilderment to some glimmers of hope that face-to-face talks might make everything all right again. Early in the board meeting, fellow directors asked Walter Hewlett to explain why he opposed the Compaq deal so much. Their questions may have been too sharp-edged; his answers may have been too oblique. In any case, both sides came away disappointed.

"Walter never looked up at us," fellow director Bob Knowling recalled. "His eyes were looking down the whole time. You could tell he was very uncomfortable. He kept referring to 'my advisers.' He didn't have an alternative to the Compaq acquisition. When we pressed him for details of his opposition, he mentioned the number of layoffs involved with the merger. And he said, 'This isn't what my father would have wanted done with the company.' He had never really talked about his family or his father in the boardroom before. This was the first time I'd heard it."

After the meeting, Dick Hackborn and Jay Keyworth thought they saw an opportunity. They asked Walter Hewlett to join them for a chat in his father's old office, just down the hall. It had been faithfully preserved as Bill Hewlett left it, with yellow linoleum tiles on the floors, five sharpened pencils arranged side by side in the middle of a tidy desk, and a tiny paperweight model of HP's first product—the audio oscillator of 1939—in clear view. This wasn't just an office anymore; it had become a full-fledged shrine. As the three men stepped inside, Hackborn asked the question no board member had dared raise earlier in the day: "Walter, have you thought about what might happen if you win?"

Rather than let Walter Hewlett answer, Dick Hackborn sketched out a series of dire possibilities. Various directors might quit. Top management might walk away. The struggle to beat back the Compaq deal might destroy HP's leadership just as the company most needed firm guidance. It was a scary prospect, and it took Walter Hewlett by surprise. He had always assumed that if the Compaq merger were voted down, directors could roll the clock back to June 2001. They could think afresh, as one unified team, about what to do next. "I worried for a moment that the top management would quit and I'd be sitting there with shareholders on my head," the founder's son later said. "Everybody would be pointing at me, saying, 'Look what you did to this company!'" Uncertain what to say, Walter Hewlett stalled for time. He said he was going to keep an open mind. He said he hoped that Hackborn and Keyworth would too. "It's really important that we keep the door open," he said, and he asked for a few days to collect his thoughts.

During the next few days, as Walter Hewlett and his top advisers played over that conversation, they decided that Hackborn and Keyworth were bluffing. Hewlett-Packard's longtime managers were dedicated professionals whose loyalty was to the well-being of the company, not to any particular takeover strategy. Everyone except Carly Fiorina almost certainly would stay. The other directors had a fiduciary duty to work in shareholders' interests. Storming off in a pout about a failed merger wasn't going to serve that obligation. Yes, directors were highly emotional about what they regarded as an assault on Carly Fiorina's leadership. For now, however, there was no reason to assume that turning down the Compaq deal would cause mass upheaval inside HP. When Keyworth left a message a week later saying he wanted to talk further, Hewlett didn't return the call.

Meanwhile, the Packard Foundation was trying to decide how to vote its huge block of HP stock: 10.4 percent of all shares outstanding. If the foundation lined up with management, Walter Hewlett's protests would probably prove futile; the deal would prevail. One of his advisers, in fact, worried that "Walter will look as if he's tilting at windmills." But if the Packard Foundation decided to vote no, then the full weight of the founding families would be opposed to the merger. In that case, Wall Street analysts predicted, the deal almost certainly would collapse.

What did the Packards want to do? The oldest of the Packard siblings, David Woodley Packard, had already announced that he hated the deal. But he didn't control much stock; his Packard Humanities Institute owned just 1.3 percent of HP shares. When he spoke out, his reasons made him sound like the champion of a high-minded but doomed cause. "I sort of care about some of the old-fashioned cultural values more than I really should," he told the San Jose *Mercury News* in early November. He lashed out at the layoffs expected in an HP-Compaq merger, saying that his father "never developed a premeditated strategy that treated HP employees as expendable." It was a sincere argument, but it wasn't likely to influence the institutional investors that owned most of HP's stock. It wasn't even likely to persuade his three sisters.

Nobody outside 300 Second Street in Los Altos could get a clear read on the Packard Foundation's intent. Walter Hewlett's advisers made a detailed presentation in mid-November and came away stumped. "They asked very few questions," investment banker Tully Friedman recalled. "The questions they asked were studiously neutral. We couldn't read them at all—and we worried they might not be voting our way." Carly Fiorina and her team made two presentations, in September and December. "We thought we made some headway," recalled HP investor-relations chief Steve Pavlovich. "But we couldn't really tell anything."

Inside their headquarters, though, Packard Foundation executives and trustees were in agony. They had scrambled throughout 1999 and 2000 to organize one of the biggest foundations in America so that they could deal with all the money that Dave Packard had left them. They had hired program officers by the dozens. They had sketched out beautiful, ambitious responses to overpopulation on three continents. Now, with HP stock in its worst slump ever, their goals were being decimated. After the merger announcement sent the stock reeling even further, Packard Foundation CEO Dick Schlosberg was forced to slash the overall budget for 2002 a third time. Projects were dying. Program officers were coming into his office, saying, in effect: *My group's budget is in tatters. There's no money for me to do what you hired me for. I can't cut any more without ruining what we're doing.*

Every time that HP stock dropped another dollar, the assets of the Packard Foundation shriveled by $218 million. If HP stock kept skidding, Dave Packard's philanthropic legacy would be destroyed. The morning of September 4, right after the HP-Compaq deal was announced, Schlosberg got his first sickening glimpse of that danger. He was eating breakfast at home, with the kitchen television set tuned to CNBC. Before he had finished his coffee, broadcasters told him that HP stock had skidded $5 a share. Doing the math in his head, Schlosberg realized: *I've just lost $1 billion!* Later that day, the foundation's chair, Susan Packard Orr, called him. "What are we going to do?" they both wondered. Vote the stock wisely, they decided, and recognize that on a deal this controversial, their stance might determine the merger's fate.

In the early autumn, Schlosberg, a football fan and onetime air force pilot, told his colleagues: "We may need to go into a hurry-up offense." He asked McKinsey or Bain to help analyze the deal, but he discovered to his chagrin that both consulting firms already were on HP's payroll. In mid-October, he lined up Booz Allen Hamilton instead, drawing on the expertise of Bruce Pasternack, a top consultant at the firm who knew HP well. For the next six weeks, Booz-Allen consultants talked confidentially to top executives at Microsoft, Intel, and other key players in the high-tech world, trying to gauge whether the deal made sense. Each interview yielded its own story, but the assessments included serious doubts about the combined company's maneuverability. Meanwhile, David Woodley Packard dropped off two hundred letters from HP employees and retirees voicing dismay about the merger. The pieces were coming together. At a board meeting on December 7, Schlosberg decided, the Packard Foundation would make up its mind and announce its position to the world.

Hours before that board meeting, Walter Hewlett got a final chance to influence the Packard Foundation's vote, and he almost let it slip away. On the afternoon of December 6, Hewlett was in San Francisco, visiting friends at the Bohemian Club. When he got back to Palo Alto at about 5 P.M., he found a frenzied stack of messages asking him to come to Packard Foundation headquarters at once. There, sixty-nine-year-old Dean Morton, a top HP executive in the John Young era, was leading a meeting in his capacity as chair of the investment committee. Joining him were four other trustees—Susan Packard Orr, Lew Platt, Cole Wilbur, and Dick Schlosberg—along with a twenty-three-year-old grandson of David Packard who would be a silent observer. For twenty minutes, Walter Hewlett ticked through his reasons for voting no. Then Morton posed a shrewd question: "What if everything works out the way that management hopes? What would your opinion of the deal be in that case?"

"I think it's highly unlikely that it will work out that way," Walter Hewlett replied. "But in fairness, let me try to answer the question. I think that HP is fundamentally a technology company. It's always been able to move wherever the technology is on the cutting edge, whether that's instruments, or computers, or printers. I think that if this merger goes ahead, it will trap HP in this particular part of the computer business forever. We'll become a captive company, attached to one particular industry. Before, we could run. Now, we'd be frozen." It was the argument he had tried to articulate—to no avail—in the HP boardroom all summer. Walter Hewlett was groping for his words then, and even if he had found them, it probably wouldn't have mattered. Most of HP's directors had a big-business focus. Their mission was to build a dominant, enduring company in a few core industries; they really weren't interested in trying to preserve the agility of HP's youth. But in Los Altos, at last, Walter Hewlett found a powerful audience that shared his starting point. Dean Morton and Lew Platt had come of age when HP was small and nimble. Cole Wilbur knew that era too; his father had been HP's personnel director in the 1950s. They bought into Walter Hewlett's argument, and a majority No vote began taking shape.

As discussions continued, Susan Packard Orr was in the hardest position of all. Over the past two years, she had become friendly with Carly Fiorina, cheering her on. In September, after the merger was announced, Susan Orr had phoned Fiorina to tell her she was choosing the right course and should stand firm. Now, David Packard's daughter was being tugged hard in two opposite directions. Vote yes? Vote no? Ultimately, she decided, she needed to put personalities aside and do everything possible to protect the foundation: the living extension of her parents' great civic spirit.

The next morning the Packard Foundation's finance committee officially voted to oppose the Compaq merger. It was unanimous. An hour or two later, the entire board of trustees concurred. A three-paragraph news release was drafted, to be released after the close of stock-market trading. Only the final sentence hinted at the foundation's panic over HP's falling share price: "Grants awarded totaled approximately $614 million in 2000, and the foundation expects to make grants of approximately $460 million in 2001." The money was running out.

All that remained was for Susan Orr to make a courtesy call to HP headquarters. She excused herself from the board meeting and headed into a small adjoining office, where she closed the door and phoned Fiorina. "This is a very difficult call to make," Orr began. There was no script this time—just a heart-to-heart talk that left both women moved. Groping for the right words, Orr explained that the foundation's vote wasn't meant as personal criticism of Fiorina or her leadership. "I believe in what you're trying to do," Orr said. "I wish I had a tenth of your courage."

When the call was over and Orr stepped back into the boardroom, she couldn't hide her feelings. "One look at Susan, and you knew it had been a difficult call," the foundation's chief financial officer, George Vera, later remarked. Dick Schlosberg was more explicit. "Susan was tearful," he said.

Hewlett-Packard rushed out its own press release that afternoon, saying it was disappointed with the Packard Foundation's decision and would continue communicating the merits of the deal to the company's "broad shareholder base." Even so, many onlookers decided they had just witnessed a knockout blow to the merger—and to the female CEO who championed it.

"I'd say it has about a five percent chance of happening now," declared Gartner Group analyst Todd Kort. Even blunter views came from Ashok Kumar, an analyst at U.S. Bancorp Piper Jaffray. "It's dead," he told one reporter the evening of December 7. "It's safe to say that Carly is on her way out," he remarked in another interview. For them to continue this charade would be like having two clowns without a circus." Even the normally cautious editors at *BusinessWeek* decided they had seen enough. They weighed in a few days later with a grim cover photo of Fiorina headlined CARLY'S LAST STAND.

In Silicon Valley itself, the most jubilant reaction came from David Woodley Packard. On the night of December 7, several hundred moviegoers came to the Stanford Theatre to see two British films from the 1940s— *A Canterbury Tale* and *The House of Fear*. Just before the evening screening started, Packard stepped onstage to offer his commentary on the HP-Compaq deal. "I feel as if I've been living in *The Wizard of Oz*," he said. He gave attendees a moment or two to remember the film's villain: the Wicked Witch of the West. A moment later, he said something that attendee Dick Rosenbaum took as a direct allusion to the uprising against Carly Fiorina: "I think we've slain the witch."

In a far more serious vein, Walter Hewlett wondered if the Packard Foundation's No vote finally could compel HP and Compaq to abandon the deal. "The handwriting is on the wall and it is clear," he declared in an open letter dated December 12 to both companies' directors. "If the merger is brought forward for a vote, there is a very high probability it will be defeated." The rest of the letter was part strident, part pleading. It wasn't Walter Hewlett's cadence at all, and in fact he later acknowledged that the bulk of the letter was Stephen Neal's handiwork. But it was a powerful message. Pressing on with the proposed merger, he argued, would cause both companies to waste money, degrade employee morale, and confuse customers. He finished by calling for a "speedy, mutual unwinding of this transaction."

Ironically, the letter only made HP's directors and top executives even feistier. In a rapid response, the company blamed its troubles on "the actions of Mr. Hewlett." Walter Hewlett glanced at the statement and wondered what each director really thought. He liked his letter. He believed that his arguments were strong enough that even if he couldn't budge the entire board, it might be possible to pry away one or two other directors. All the way into January, he kept hoping that Bob Knowling, Pattie Dunn, or some other director would rally to his cause, but no boardroom ally ever emerged.

If directors wouldn't listen, perhaps major shareholders would. From late November onward, Walter Hewlett and his advisers took to the road, visiting portfolio managers with anywhere from 4 million to 50 million shares of HP, urging them to vote no, too. The shy software developer was striding into bank buildings in Boston, New York, Philadelphia, and Chicago pitching his story. Dan Burch took command of logistics, booking five-star hotels, renting limousines, and chartering a small Beechcraft plane for short hops up and down the East Coast. (For long-haul travel from California to the East Coast, everyone flew first class on United Airlines.) It was a weird new world for Walter Hewlett, whose usual travel habits involved wrangling cheap fares in coach and taking his children on driving vacations that involved stops at roadside Dairy Queens. But this was the way investment bankers did things. If he wanted to look sharp and be on time for these city-to-city sprints, he needed to live large. So he did, reluctantly at first, then with a certain bemusement about it all. "I feel as if I've stepped into an alternate universe," he told friends.

The first few meetings went wonderfully. "You're preaching to the choir," investors told him, even before he opened his mouth. "Thank you, Walter, for doing what you're doing," they said, as he wrapped up. In the endlessly cheery world of financial analysis, Walter Hewlett offered a stunningly pessimistic contrast. HP couldn't compete effectively in the PC market even if it did buy Compaq, according to binders prepared by his advisers at Friedman, Fleischer. The deal wouldn't make HP into a powerhouse in computer services or enterprise computing either. Instead, it would dilute earnings from the printer business and bring little in return. If there was ever a season for such wary views, this was it. Technology stocks had been slumping for more than a year, with no relief in sight. Big investors were tired of hearing from CEOs who kept asking for patience and promising that things would get better. What's more, in October 2001 Ford had kicked out its chief executive, Jacques Nasser, when he lost the loyalty of the founding Ford family. In the depressed markets of early 2002, this seemed like a good time to bet against expansion-minded CEOs and side instead with more conservative founding families.

If anything, investors were annoyed that Walter Hewlett hadn't spoken out aggressively much earlier. "Shareholders were impatient for HP to fix its problems," Tully Friedman recalled. "They were quite critical of the board—including Walter—for not getting HP's act together. This was a four- to five-year frustration. The board had had a long time to sort it out." On the road, Walter Hewlett acknowledged those concerns with an earnestness that was refreshing and occasionally eerie. When analysts at one investment firm asked why he hadn't fought the deal much harder before it was approved, Walter Hewlett didn't skate around the issue with a smooth but empty response. Instead, he told the analyst: "You know, you're right. I'll have to think about that."

A terrifying moment occurred on February 11, just after the Hewlett team's Beechcraft plane had taken off from Atlanta, heading for Pittsburgh. Investment banker Spencer Fleischer peered out a passenger window and saw thin streams of clear fluid running along the wing. A part-time pilot himself, Fleischer knew there was only one possible explanation: a fuel leak. As calmly as he could, he walked up to the cockpit and told the pilot of the danger. "We're going to be turning around," the pilot announced. For the next three minutes, everyone on the plane sat dead still, hoping that a sudden fire or complete rupture of the fuel tank wouldn't end their lives. When they landed, Hewlett and Fleischer rented a different plane and got airborne an hour later. They were shaken, but they weren't about to quit.

Overall, Hewlett found the road warrior's life exhilarating. "It energized Walter," his father's friend Arjay Miller observed. "It was a life-changing event." Early in 2002 Walter Hewlett bought a Blackberry e-mail pager and became addicted to it. He acquired the rights to www.walterhewlett.com and www.votenohpcompaq.com and filled both Web sites with regular updates on his proxy campaign. During limousine rides, he bantered with Spencer Fleischer about everything and nothing. At one point, they matched wits to see who could figure out how far light travels in a nanosecond.

Media interviews became a regular part of his week, and Walter Hewlett gradually came to enjoy the half hour of repartee with each curious new reporter. His public-relations adviser, Joele Frank, helped him rehearse for interviews. "You are my sword and my shield," he told her. But some of his best preparation took place at home in the evening, when his wife, Esther, pretended to be a journalist quizzing him—until they both felt he was in command. When *Wall Street Journal* reporter Pui-Wing Tam asked him at one point if he thought HP and Compaq's cultures were compatible, he quipped, "About like Athens and Sparta." The classical allusion delighted the *Journal's* graphics department, which produced a sketch depicting him as an armored warrior in ancient Greece. Hewlett liked the image enough to tape it to a kitchen cabinet in his Palo Alto home.

In the process, Walter Hewlett began to toughen his views of Carly Fiorina. At first, "we wanted to tread lightly on the Carly issue so that this didn't become a 'lynch Carly' vote," proxy solicitor Dan Burch recalled. As the Hewlett team traveled around the United States, however, some of the big shareholders most inclined to vote no on the Compaq merger also wanted Fiorina ousted. Their views might have been persuasive in their own right, or the Hewlett camp may have decided to start echoing its best constituents' rhetoric. Such things happen in political campaigns. Either way, Walter Hewlett's newspaper ads began to include more jabs at Fiorina. And in his Wall Street presentations, he began showing a politician's ability to attack an opponent while appearing merely to be taking note of public concerns. "Investors are regarding this as a referendum on Carly, in light of her intransigence and her unwillingness to look at the facts," he began saying. "It's a very bad deal. It's hard for me to see how she will survive if the deal is voted down."

Unhappy HP employees began reaching out to Walter Hewlett, too, in gestures that further hardened his resolve. Throughout January and February, a steady trickle of employees phoned or wrote to his proxy solicitors and media advisers to complain about poor morale within Hewlett-Packard. ("I think we're all going to get jazzed," one employee said, spoofing Fiorina's upbeat vocabulary. *Jazzed* wasn't a happy word anymore; it had turned into a mordant new term for being fired.) On another occasion, an anonymous HP employee went much farther, e-mailing some of HP's confidential financial modeling to Walter Hewlett's media advisers in New York. That report depicted a piece of the merger integration that didn't appear to be going well at all. While there's no evidence that the Hewlett camp ever shared that gloomy document with the media, proxy solicitor Dan Burch later recalled members of the Hewlett team alluding to it in at least one meeting with key institutional investors.

HP returned the favor with ever-harsher ads and shareholder letters attacking its dissident director. One two-page ad in *The Wall Street Journal* was headlined FLIP. FLOP, and it listed a half-dozen seemingly contradictory positions that Walter Hewlett had taken on various issues in the past six months. The Hewlett Foundation's investment chief, Laurie Hoagland, was breakfasting with Walter Hewlett at the Palace Hotel in New York the day the ad appeared, and Hoagland was fuming. The ad seemed so mean—and unfair. Hoagland was about to offer some sputtering sympathy and indignation to his boss, when he noticed that Walter Hewlett was smiling. Hoagland's boss didn't really care what HP's ad agency or Carly Fiorina's loyalists were saying about him. They had passed into the realm of people who didn't matter. "Well, well," Walter Hewlett said, with a brief wave at the ad. "Why talk about that? Let's talk about what we're going to do today."

Only one part of the feud really gnawed at Walter Hewlett: his relations with Dick Hackborn. What had once been a fine friendship was in tatters by now. The two men couldn't sit together anymore as Hewlett Foundation trustees; Hackborn had quit in mid-December. Publicly, Hackborn said he couldn't be part of Walter's "ill-advised proxy campaign." Privately, he told friends he felt shabbily treated by the foundation's decision to oppose the merger behind his back, without giving him a chance to defend the deal's merits to the trustees. "Maybe Hackborn wasn't in the inner loop," Walter Hewlett later said. "But based on the way he behaved, did he deserve to be?"

Their relations turned even icier in early February, when *Business Week* profiled Walter Hewlett. The article's eighteenth paragraph consisted of a stunningly precise account of the November 16 visit to Bill Hewlett's office. An unidentified source said that Walter Hewlett "turned ashen" when confronted with the prospect of a leadership meltdown at HP. The article's sourcing was clearly second- or thirdhand; Dick Hackborn himself hadn't talked to the magazine. But somehow, Hackborn had let the secret out, and Walter Hewlett was furious. A man he once considered one of his best friends at HP was violating the principles of conflict resolution by unilaterally making parts of their private talks public. Months later, Walter Hewlett still would seethe about that breach. "These people aren't interested in having some door open," he said. "Forget it. They can't be trusted."

On the road, Walter Hewlett kept such personal concerns as hidden as possible, talking strictly about the merger's apparent failings in his meetings with investors. When shareholders asked about his father—and whether family pride was spurring him to step forward—he answered carefully. "Walter would tell them that he had learned a lot about values from his dad," recalled Larry Dennedy, a top aide to proxy solicitor Dan Burch. "In the Hewlett family, loyalty and responsibility were very important. He would explain that he had a responsibility to the foundation. He didn't think this deal was in the best interests of the foundation, which has a significant stake in the company. By speaking out about the deal, he was trying to protect the value of the foundation's investment." It was a carefully constructed answer that genuinely did explain Walter Hewlett's chief reason for waging the proxy fight. But that answer also pulled the curtain shut on matters that weren't meant to be discussed with strangers.

With the most trusted members of his team, though, Walter Hewlett opened up far more about his legacy, and when he did, the images were unforgettable. On a plane trip with Tully Friedman, Walter Hewlett was leaning back in his seat, eyes closed, with headphones piping in music from a compact-disk player. He peeled off the headphones and passed them over to Friedman. "What do you think of this?" Hewlett asked. Friedman listened for a few seconds to a dazzling cascade of organ music. "It's beautiful," the investment banker said. "What is it?"

"It's César Franck's Chorale No. 3 in A minor," Walter Hewlett replied. "It's one of my favorite pieces. We played it at my father's memorial service. I'm playing the organ in this recording. It's from twenty-five years ago."

At last, Walter Hewlett was a man with a mission. He was rallying together everything in his life—his passion for Hewlett-Packard, his music, his devotion to his family, and his stamina as an athlete—to fight for a cause. He was doing his best, at age fifty-seven, to stand firm against what he regarded as a business blunder. As he went into battle, he was becoming a revered figure in the eyes of many HP retirees, employees, and front-line managers. One day in the winter of 2002, he drove into downtown Palo Alto to get a haircut and parked his red electric car on a side street. When he came back, there was a handwritten note slipped under his windshield wiper. It read: "Thank you, Walter, for doing what you're doing. Your father would be proud of you."

Chapter 9

THE CRUSADE OF HER LIFE

For Carly Fiorina, the autumn of 2001 was a period of nonstop peril. She had spent more than two years crafting a fresh strategy for Hewlett-Packard, looking for ways to execute it, then settling on the Compaq transaction as the best hope of shoring up the company. Everything had seemed crisp and logical in the summer's secret talks, but once the acquisition plan became public, things got ugly. She had to convince shareholders, employees, and customers to embrace the deal, too, but from the moment that the merger plans became public, pessimism and distrust abounded in every group that Fiorina hoped to court.

Traveling as briskly as ever immediately after the deal's announcement, Fiorina tried to persuade people to see things her way. By mid-October, she had touched down in Los Angeles, Minneapolis, New York, Monaco, Japan, and South Korea. No matter how rapidly she traveled, she couldn't arrive early enough to frame the conversation her way. "Volumes have been written about the combination . . . but most of those stories, frankly, miss the point," she told European customers at a Monaco technology conference in mid-September. At employee events, she was blunter still, carping about unfair and inaccurate press coverage. There weren't many chances to be warm and funny. All too often, she sounded brittle and exasperated. In her speeches, she tried hard to rebut each piece of criticism, and sometimes she did so with great skill. All the same, the more time she dissipated in explaining what wasn't wrong with the deal, the more she was trapped in a loser's game.

In a mid-October visit to South Korea, she opened her remarks to several hundred employees by thanking them for cutting the workforce earlier in the year and trimming other costs in tough times. She tried to explain how much the Compaq merger could help Hewlett-Packard strengthen its global position. When she opened up the meeting for questions, however, anxious employees quizzed her about one danger after another. Would the merger crimp research spending? How would it affect the HP Way? Should employees think about bolting to another job to avoid the next wave of layoffs? After several attempts to reassure workers, Fiorina asked for more questions and got only silence. "Did the audience get shy?" she asked. "I guarantee you, you'll be more uncomfortable with the silence than I will." A moment later, she got a safe wrap-up question, answered it, and then headed off for a customer visit.

What Fiorina really wanted to do was change the conversation, infusing each audience with her conviction that Hewlett-Packard could be a stronger, bolder, *nobler* company by acquiring Compaq. She needed to win people's loyalty around the world with a soaring vision of better times ahead. In her talks, she could pop in brief allusions to operating synergies, Linux, critical mass in enterprise computing, or whatever details might resonate best with each audience. But her core message had to transcend financial models and computer jargon so she could convey the enormous potential of the HP-Compaq combination.

Her early attempts misfired badly. Soon after the terrorist attacks of September 11, she likened strong-minded CEOs like herself to New York City firemen, dashing into the burning World Trade Center in hopes of saving lives. Fiorina was so wrapped up in the drama of her own story that her analogies defied belief. Once Walter Hewlett's opposition to the deal became public, though, Fiorina began framing her arguments much more effectively. "This is all about building the future," Fiorina explained in a stump speech several months into the proxy contest. "We cannot sustain our company by standing still, but by moving forward with courage and determination. In an industry that is changing as rapidly and fundamentally as ours is, there is no future in the status quo. . . . To the skeptics who say it won't work, it won't sell, it won't succeed, it's not the HP Way, I say: 'You don't know the people of the new HP.' "

Fiorina wasn't being strident or defensive anymore. She was recasting herself as a brave woman, alone on a podium, crusading for the dreams and aspirations of her entire company. If people thought she was vulnerable, all right—she was. Before her opponents fully realized what had transpired, she had turned that appearance of vulnerability into her greatest asset. In a widely quoted speech to software developers in January 2002, she portrayed the HP-Compaq deal as a breakthrough too audacious to win the establishment's support. "Everyone who has made an impact in this industry remembers what it was like at one time to be an outsider with a big dream, facing long odds," she said. "Success is anything but inevitable." She was campaigning as the outsider and the underdog, bolstered only by a messianic conviction that she was right—and that eventually most of her shareholders, employees, and customers would agree. In an interview a month after announcing the deal, she declared: "The company's success will be my legacy. The company's failure will be my failure, with all the predictable consequences."

In her most audacious move, Fiorina began invoking the early careers of Dave Packard and Bill Hewlett as justification for the HP-Compaq merger. With the founding families strongly opposed to the merger, it seemed mind-boggling that she could ignore their grievances and lay claim to the fathers' intentions instead. But she did it anyway. She latched onto a legendary Dave Packard quote—"To remain static is to lose ground"—and made it the centerpiece of two-page newspaper ads. She created plausible but unwitnessed conversations from long ago, in which the founders spoke her language. As she told the software developers, "To every single person who said, 'It's never been done before,' Bill and Dave replied, 'Yes, but there's never been a company like HP before.'"

Could she pull it off? She faced a daunting set of tasks, knowing that if she stumbled anywhere, she failed at everything. She needed a majority of shareholders to vote with her, and she needed to keep the top members of her executive team loyal. She needed to connect with customers, to defend Hewlett-Packard's core businesses, and to regain her employees' trust as best she could. As much as she publicly insisted she was speaking for all employees, it was clear she wasn't. HP's own surveys showed that at least 30 percent of employees didn't like the deal, and outside assessments funded by David Woodley Packard suggested that opposition in some key HP locations ran as high as 63 percent. If Fiorina hoped to survive, she couldn't just dash from meeting to meeting, improvising strategy as she went along. For a contest this long and grueling, she needed a formidable power base that her opponents couldn't touch. Walter Hewlett had originated his VOTE NO campaign from the safety of the San Felipe Ranch and the stronghold of his father's stock holdings. Fiorina needed her own stockpile of credibility and strength to tap for months to come.

Fortunately for her, Fiorina had secured the best stronghold of all: the Hewlett-Packard boardroom. Directors had hailed her as the finest CEO candidate in America in the summer of 1999, even before she started the job. They had rallied round her in the notorious executive-session meeting of September 1999, in which Lew Platt questioned her competence before she had unpacked all her boxes. As she settled into the job, directors had come to regard her as the embodiment of all their hopes and goals for Hewlett-Packard. She was their instrument, charging into work every day trying to make HP a more modern, more competitive business. When things went badly for her—as they did with the front-end/back-end reorganization or with the sudden economic slump of 2001—it just meant that the problems she faced were even tougher than directors had realized. In months of closed-door deliberations all summer, she hadn't arm-twisted board members to approve the Compaq merger. If anything, Dick Hackborn and a few other directors had taken the lead, hoping that the giant combination would help solve Fiorina's problems. All the independent directors except Walter Hewlett cherished Carly Fiorina. They had bet the company on her. For reasons of pride, ideological conviction, and maybe even old-fashioned gallantry, they weren't about to back down.

When the Packard Foundation opposed the merger on that first Friday in December 2001, Fiorina didn't waste a moment in turning to her boardroom allies. By 7 P.M., she had connected with each director except Walter Hewlett in a brief phone conversation. All the independent directors were disappointed and baffled by the deepening opposition to the deal, Fiorina later recalled. Each director agreed to caucus over the weekend by telephone. On Sunday morning, Fiorina sat in a small first-floor study in her home and began a crucial conference call. Within moments, Dick Hackborn, Sam Ginn, Phil Condit, Pattie Dunn, Jay Keyworth, and Bob Knowling were on the line. After the briefest of hellos, Fiorina asked each board member to give her a yes or no answer to three questions: Should we stop? Should we go on as is? Or should we go on in a modified way, perhaps spinning off the personal-computer businesses before completing the merger?

Decisive answers came back, almost in unison. "We're going on!" the directors told Fiorina. No one was more adamant than Dick Hackborn. "Let's get back to the question Why are we proposing this in the first place?" he said. His answer: "It's the best solution for fixing the whole computer business." By the end of the call, directors were so confident about their decision that they could afford to worry about Fiorina's well-being. They asked if she felt comfortable proceeding in what would surely be a long struggle. When she said yes, the decision was sealed.

Shortly afterward, Hackborn took his point of view public in a *New York Times* interview with veteran technology reporter Steve Lohr. Carly Fiorina had learned the industry with "lightning speed," he said. The merger would put the new Hewlett-Packard "on a comparable footing with Intel and Microsoft." If shareholders didn't approve the merger, he warned, "They will have to get a board and a management to fix the PC business and these other problems." Mindful of Hackborn's reputation in the computer industry, Lohr observed that the former chairman's endorsement might be HP's biggest asset in courting people who otherwise didn't care much for either the merger or Fiorina.

Other directors aimed heartfelt testimonials at HP employees who mightn't fully appreciate Carly Fiorina's courage and commitment. In a public letter to HP employees, Bob Knowling wrote: "I've known your CEO for years. It pains me to see the negative publicity, but this comes with the territory of being the CEO. Through it all, I've not once seen her whine about how she is being treated. She's never shown me anything but grit and determination to win. . . . I believe in her. I trust her and I am confident she will lead this company to the next level of greatness."

Such endorsements couldn't single-handedly bring Fiorina closer to victory, but they had enormous psychological importance for Fiorina's top aides and advisers. At a moment when the pro-merger camp might have been on the brink of panic—when people could have been so consumed by thoughts of defeat that they couldn't do their jobs—the directors helped establish a calmer tone. One of the company's outside attorneys, Marty Korman of Wilson Sonsini, instantly noticed the newfound resolve among HP's leaders when he came to headquarters during the week of December 10 to review five strategic options with regard to the HP-Compaq merger. Options one through four kept the deal alive; option five involved abandoning the deal. Advisers had barely handed out their briefing sheet when Fiorina interjected, "Option five is off the table. We aren't going to do that. So let's move on."

Only Compaq hadn't got the message. Immediately after the Packard Foundation's decision to vote no, Compaq's directors were told by their investment bankers that the merger had only a 15 percent prospect of going through. By the following Monday, the chances had been upgraded to 40 percent. That was still too dicey for Michael Capellas's tastes. In an e-mail he told employees that Compaq had a solid future whether the merger happened or not. It was prudent advice for employees, but a dangerous message in the hands of journalists and the financial markets. This was the first time that anyone at the top of either company had spoken about the merger's prospects with less than absolute certainty. If doubts were creeping in, they might spread. Then there would be a stampede to be the first journalist—or the first stock trader—to let everyone know that the merger was doomed.

Compaq director Tom Perkins tried to patch over the doubts as fast as possible. In a Reuters interview five days after the Packard decision, he said that neither company had any plans to walk away from the deal. But inter-company harmony was much too crucial to be sorted out by e-mails and wire-service interviews. A few days later, Capellas and Perkins headed to Dick Hackborn's home in Boise, where they were joined by Fiorina and one more director from each company. The six men and women met for three hours in Hackborn's den, sipping coffee and talking through fine points of merger tactics until they felt they understood one another perfectly. "It was very focused, very friendly, and very straightforward," Capellas later recalled. "We said, 'We're in a proxy fight. What do we need to do to win?'"

Ultimately, the deal's fate was in the hands of Hewlett-Packard's shareholders. They wouldn't vote until March 19, 2002, but with a few nimble calculations, it was possible to tell, almost minute by minute, what investors were thinking. If investors felt confident that the merger would go through, then HP and Compaq shares would trade in close harmony, reflecting the two companies' eventual promise to cash out Compaq holders and give them a preset number of HP shares instead. It would be as if HP were a locomotive climbing a hill, and Compaq a freight car coupled tightly to it. Every bump in HP's share price should be matched by a similar move in Compaq's, but if traders believed that the merger agreement was doubtful or hopeless, the freight car would be cut loose. Without support from HP, Compaq's shares would tumble.

Anyone checking stock prices in December saw the financial equivalent of a runaway freight car crashing into a canyon. HP stock meandered safely in the low $20s during the entire period, but Compaq, which reached nearly $12 early in the month, skidded as low as $9.02 after the Packard Foundation decided to vote no. On Wall Street this interplay was known as "the spread"—a measure of how deeply Compaq was trading at a discount to the stated value of the merger terms. In perfectly secure situations, the spread might be as little as 2 percent or 3 percent. In mergers with dicey prospects or long delays, the spread could reach 10 percent or more. On December 14 the spread on the HP-Compaq merger was 28.6 percent.

Just at that nadir, a visitor arrived at Hewlett-Packard headquarters with a surprisingly upbeat message. He was Alan Miller, the company's recently hired proxy solicitor. With his scruffy white beard and his fondness for tropical-print shirts, Miller looked much too counterculture to be taking command of the campaign for shareholders' votes. But he and his New York firm of Innisfree M&A had been fighting—and winning—big shareholder battles for nearly a decade. He had studied HP's shareholder register. He had examined the spread. And there was something he wanted Carly Fiorina and the HP finance department to know.

"I believe this is very winnable," Miller declared. Step by step, he took them through his analysis of HP's shareholder base. As HP executives knew, more than half the company's shares were owned by mutual funds, trust departments, and other institutions. Such investors were analytical and open-minded. Most of them were based thousands of miles from Silicon Valley. They might be mildly intrigued by the founding-family drama, but it would not decide their votes. They just wanted their stock to go up. In the flurry of trading since the Compaq merger was announced, the institutions that truly loathed the deal probably weren't shareholders anymore. Most of the ones that remained had a history of siding with management, as long as management could make a strong case.

What's more, Miller observed, a huge block of votes was up for grabs, in a process that could work out very well for HP. Many big shareholders relied on a little-known advisory firm for voting guidance on complex issues. Win an endorsement from this firm—Institutional Shareholder Services of Rockville, Maryland—and as much as 23 percent of all shares could pour into the Yes column. ISS was founded and run by lawyers who didn't know an enormous amount about the high-tech sector, but they were diligent people who were very attuned to the fine points of corporate governance. Visit them early, Miller advised. Visit them often. "If you've got them," he said, "you've got a very good chance of getting over the top."

More glimmers of hope emerged from Steve Pavlovich, Hewlett-Packard's head of investor relations, as he started talking with HP's major shareholders. Perhaps one-quarter of them owned so much Compaq that they were inclined to vote for the deal in spite of its risks, hoping it could rescue their slumping investments in the Houston computer company. Furthermore, he found, just about every big shareholder was willing to meet with Carly Fiorina. "Their rule was 'You never turn down a meeting with a CEO,'" Pavlovich later observed. Investors might just gawk at America's most powerful female boss or pester Fiorina for insights about other companies in their portfolio, but as long as they were eager to schedule meetings, Fiorina had a chance to tell her story one-on-one to the voters whose support she needed most.

In early January, Fiorina started visiting some of HP's biggest shareholders in New York. Some were dubious about the deal; others noncommittal. But Lewis Sanders, vice chairman of Alliance Capital Management, welcomed her. "I've already made up my mind about the deal," he told her.

"I'm voting for it. Don't bother making your presentation. Let's talk about the industry." He had pegged the personal-computer industry as ripe for consolidation, and he figured that a combined HP–Compaq ought to fare better against industry leader Dell Computer. Similar "roll-up" plays had worked well for him in the auto–parts and drug-distribution businesses. It hardly amounted to a ringing endorsement of Fiorina's strategy, but she wasn't picky. Alliance owned about 50 million shares of HP, 3 percent of the total company. Any rationale that brought a big investor into the Yes camp was wonderful.

As the proxy contest intensified, Fiorina and her media advisers made a crucial modification to their message. In November, when the Packard Foundation hadn't decided how to vote, Fiorina insisted that the merger wasn't meant to be a triumph of new over old. She tried to define it more narrowly as a chance to build a world-class computer company that could rival IBM. But now the vision-versus-nostalgia demarcation looked alluring, especially to Allison Johnson, the company's head of brand strategy and communications. "When it was clear that the families were going to align against the deal, I knew we could take it beyond a financial story," Johnson later said. "This would be about the future instead of the past."

As the ultimate custodian of the Hewlett-Packard archives, Fiorina could bolster her case by invoking the most treasured images of HP's early days. These photos and epigrams, which had become almost religious relics to some, now were part of *her* heritage and legitimacy. Knowing that, her first major newspaper ad displayed Bill Hewlett's original audio oscillator from 1939, next to the headline WHAT IF WE HAD STOPPED HERE? Another ad showed the founders working in the lab right after World War II. Everything about the ads projected a simple confidence: the big photos, the abundant use of white space, and especially the short, simple messages. "Bill Hewlett and Dave Packard understood that in the face of change, HP could choose to lead or to follow," one ad declared. "Always they chose to lead. . . . The merger of HP and Compaq is a renewal of HP's traditional aims, adapted to new technological times."

The ad campaign infuriated Dave Packard's son, David Woodley Packard. In a retaliatory advertisement in *The Wall Street Journal*, the sixty-one-year-old son accused Fiorina of "misappropriating my father's words." The famous quote—"To remain static is to lose ground"—bore no relevance to the proxy contest, he asserted. Fiorina was betraying her background as a marketing executive, he contended, by trying to cloak her argument in the words of an admired person.

Fiorina didn't back down one bit. She didn't even give David Woodley Packard the satisfaction of a response. She and her ad agency advisers at Goodby Silverstein & Partners in San Francisco had framed their message perfectly, and if her opponents didn't like it, that was all the more reason to stick with it. Fiorina began mentioning Bill and Dave in her speeches as if they were her own uncles or grandparents. She kept running ads about tradition and transformation in the major newspapers. In all her references the founders were brave, smart, and forward-looking—and they were quoted with comments that somehow amounted to endorsements of the Compaq deal. She was overpowering opponents by making stunningly sweeping assertions, again and again, in a tone that brooked no dissent. David Woodley Packard kept carping about her in a half-dozen more ads over the next two months but Fiorina owned the airwaves, at least on this issue. She believed the merger was perfectly in keeping with the HP Way. And she believed that current executives—not the heirs—were the right people to make that judgment call.

At HP headquarters, a handful of key aides thrilled to the fight. Allison Johnson, Steve Pavlovich, attorney Charles Charnas, and a half-dozen colleagues set up a war-room caucus every day at 6 A.M. "We told each other what issues were likely to come up," Johnson later recalled. "We corrected any factual errors in press coverage. We advanced certain story lines and deflected others." There was a new scrappiness to Hewlett-Packard that hadn't been part of the culture in the Lew Platt years. The company wasn't taking its cue from mild-mannered engineers anymore; its aggressive new public posture was being set by lawyers and public-relations specialists who enjoyed the fray. On the days she was in Palo Alto, Fiorina stopped by the war room at least once or twice with a kind word, a goad, or just a request for an update. Late at night, she talked strategy with HP's top outside attorney, Larry Sonsini. He was the somber one, with grim updates about each potential deal opponent. Fiorina was the mischievous one, interrupting his commentary to ask, "Larry, can't you be a little more *creative* in your descriptions of these people?"

Most of the time, Fiorina was on the road, courting the same big investors that were seeing Walter Hewlett. As the incumbent, representing one of the world's largest companies, she traveled in style. One of the Gulfstream IV jets that she had encouraged Hewlett-Packard to buy in 1999 whisked her to each appointment; she needn't hew to United Airlines' schedule for long-haul travel or worry about the dangers of a hastily rented little Beechcraft. At each stop, the limos were waiting; the hotel rooms were ready as promised. There wasn't any of the ragged improvisation that marked the Hewlett campaign. HP's on-the-road logistics were immaculate; all the details were in the capable hands of Goldman Sachs, the company's investment bankers, who knew how to tend to traveling executives.

In her investor meetings, Fiorina brought out many of the same arguments that had circulated since the McKinsey presentation of the previous July. The merger would vault the combined company to the No. 1 position in several key markets. She predicted it would produce at least $2.5 billion of cost savings by fiscal 2002, while jeopardizing at most 4.9 percent of the combined companies' revenue. It might improve earnings per share as early as fiscal 2003, although that couldn't be predicted with certainty. Overall, she had a plausible but not mesmerizing business case for the deal. If everything worked out as she hoped, Hewlett-Packard would be bigger and stronger. And everyone was working very hard on merger integration. She could sell investors on the numbers to some extent, but what she really wanted to convey was her own commitment and passion. Fiorina believed in the deal—and that should be highly persuasive in its own right.

By mid-January, HP stock had inched up to $22.42 a share. The spread had narrowed to 21 percent. The merger's prospects remained dodgy, but thanks to Fiorina's hard work and savvy positioning, things didn't look nearly so bleak. Meanwhile, moral support was pouring in from welcome places. Her former boss at Lucent, Henry Schacht, phoned with his best wishes. More calls and e-mails came from Carlos Gutierrez at Kellogg, Steve Case at AOL Time Warner, and Sandy Weill at Citigroup. Carly Fiorina had entered Hewlett-Packard as a standard-bearer for ambitious women around the world. Now, weirdly, she was a role model for middle-aged male CEOs. They couldn't help but wonder whether her all-out battle to stay in command might be more than an isolated event in the executive suite; it might be a harbinger of what any high-profile leader could face when the cheering stopped. At one point, Jeff Bezos, the CEO of Amazon.com, called in a giggly mood to say, "I just thought you needed a hug. Consider this a telephonic hug!"

With the constant demands of the proxy contest, Fiorina fell badly behind in a less visible but equally crucial part of her job: keeping the loyalty of rank-and-file employees. Many of them remained bitter about the previous summer's big layoffs. No matter how much executives tried to position the merger as good for the company overall, there was no denying that HP and Compaq together had announced plans to cut another 15,000 jobs, equal to 10 percent of their combined workforce. "Morale is as low as

I've ever seen it," a veteran HP manager told *The Wall Street Journal* in November 2001. "People don't want this acquisition to go through."

Despite periodic attempts to hear workers' concerns and offer them candid updates, HP executives retreated at times into a Dilbert-like world of starchy e-mail blasts to all employees. "The rumor mill is alive and well," one management missive declared. "You should not consider any merger-related communication official unless it comes from Carly Fiorina, the Management Committee, or the Integration Office." With many corporate memos reading more like regulatory filings than heart-to-heart communications, most employees turned to their local newspaper or to Internet chat boards to find out what was really going on.

Quick visits to Hewlett-Packard facilities helped Fiorina win some friends but also deepened her opponents' distrust. In December 2001, Fiorina popped into Vancouver, Washington, for a classic HP "Coffee Talk." Company organizers cabled together chairs in the cafeteria where she spoke, as a fire-safety measure; they also put out plastic knives and forks in lieu of the usual metal cutlery, thinking it would make it easier for employees to take half-finished meals back to their desks. Dissidents regarded both steps as evidence of management paranoia. "So much for trust!" one HP veteran declared in an Internet posting afterward. At the session, employees asked Fiorina why she was so critical of Walter Hewlett and why the company had laid off people with sterling performance ratings. Fiorina answered as best she could. In surveys after the meeting, some employees said the visit left them feeling better about the merger. But on the flight home, Fiorina and HP's head of employee communications, Yvonne Hunt, agreed it had been a brutal trip.

Fiorina fared poorly, too, with Hewlett-Packard's retirees, many of whom still hadn't made peace with the Agilent spin-off or many other changes of recent years. She tried to brief two retiree groups about the merits of the merger, showing them video clips of directors endorsing her action, including a testimonial from Dick Hackborn. Most retirees were civil to her face but afterward muttered that she didn't understand the real HP. In the Agilent employee population, which served as a reliable barometer for the sentiments of HP traditionalists, the merger ultimately was opposed by an eight-to-one margin.

All the same, Fiorina's poor standing with employees and retirees didn't immobilize her one bit. There was still time. She needed investors' loyalty first or else there wouldn't be a merger. But once she got the deal approved, she believed she could go back and rebuild morale. It might take awhile, but employees would come to see the merger's benefits and would rise to new heights of productivity. The ones who didn't, she reasoned, just weren't suited to make the journey. Besides, her biggest career accomplishments at Lucent and AT&T often had occurred just when opponents thought she was doomed. "People have always underestimated me," she told one of her HP's outside consultants, Keith Yamashita, in the midst of the proxy contest. "I've learned that this can be a great advantage."

Hewlett-Packard's directors weren't blind; they could tell partway through the proxy contest that Fiorina wasn't a hero in everyone's eyes. But fellow board members remained as loyal as ever, and in mid-January, they endorsed their handpicked CEO in language so strong they could never back down. The occasion was Fiorina's annual performance review, conducted by the eight other directors—including Walter Hewlett—without Fiorina in the room. The heads of the governance and compensation committees, Sam Ginn and Phil Condit, ran the meeting, and fellow directors showered them with kind words and support for an embattled friend. "She's doing most of what the board hired her to do," Pattie Dunn remarked. "She's come in to change the company. If a few eggs are being broken, that's not a surprise." Bob Knowling was just as loyal, praising Fiorina for her toughness and her focus on transforming HP. Dick Hackborn gave her high marks for strategy, vision, and communicating her message inside and outside the company. Even Walter Hewlett acknowledged her strengths as a communicator.

The cheering could have gone on forever. But directors still had to confront the aspects of her job that weren't going well. Sam Ginn identified the key issue right away: some in Hewlett-Packard regarded Fiorina as an "imperial CEO," aloof and out of touch. He recommended more brown-bag lunches with employees so that she could connect with everyday workplace concerns. In a similar spirit, Bob Knowling suggested that employees needed to see the warm, touchable side of Fiorina. "The emperor is human," he said, explaining that Fiorina needed to visit the HP labs and field offices and be a down-to-earth person there, too. Directors wanted so much to help Fiorina become a beloved CEO within her own company that they kept pushing the same remedy: a bit more shop-floor bonhomie. If she could just share her warmth with employees, everything would be all right.

Dick Hackborn was the one director ready to tackle tougher issues. At his home in Idaho, he had been receiving dozens of letters, calls, and e-mails about the previous summer's layoffs. Some HP employees weren't just annoyed about Fiorina's demeanor; they felt deeply frightened about the way she was managing the company in a downturn. These issues couldn't be papered over with twenty minutes of cafeteria banter. As lay-offs continued, he contended, Fiorina would need to lessen the pain in var-ious ways so that lopped-off workers and the survivors believed the system was fair. Hackborn wanted Fiorina to be the company's most effective CEO since Dave Packard and Bill Hewlett ran the show. In many ways, he believed, she was closer to that goal than ever. But there was a hole in her handling of employee issues, and it needed to be fixed, fast. The merger would work, he warned, only if it had the loyalty of HP's entire workforce.

Walter Hewlett listened quietly to most of the discussion, contributing little. Near the end, he offered what struck other directors as surprisingly mild comments. Calling the merger a very big step for HP, he said, "If we had to do it, I wish we were doing it later, when she had more experience." With that, the closed-door session was over. The directors had sized up Fiorina as candidly as anyone, giving full credit for her greatest virtues and blunt guidance on dealing with her biggest flaw. "It was very objective and even-keeled," Knowling later remarked. "She didn't get eight people singing the chorus that she's the greatest thing to walk through the valley since Christ himself."

Even so, HP's directors had learned that in the midst of a proxy con-test, rock-solid certainty meant everything. With Walter Hewlett abstain-ing, the directors decided to tell the outside world that Fiorina had won their highest endorsement. They awarded her an A-plus for leadership.

The day after the directors applauded Fiorina, they decided to assail Walter Hewlett with their harshest language yet. Back in the summer, other directors had deemed Walter Hewlett to be a harmless straggler who was having trouble understanding the benefits of the Compaq deal but who surely would catch on eventually. Even in the autumn, Fiorina and Hackborn believed his dissent was tied to a simpleminded view of HP's past that ultimately wouldn't thwart the deal. Other directors, such as Pat-tie Dunn, saw Walter Hewlett as a bit of an oddball, forever defined by his decision to forgo the McKinsey board meeting the previous July in favor of playing the cello at a Bohemian Grove concert. But the directors had badly misjudged the situation. The mildest man in the boardroom some-how had turned into a Ninja warrior hell-bent on stopping the Compaq merger. The way things were going, he might prevail.

Suspicions and theories about Walter Hewlett's newfound forcefulness abounded. Jay Keyworth cooked up scenarios in which David Woodley Packard was putting incendiary thoughts into Walter Hewlett's head. Other people close to the HP board devised conspiracy theories involving every-one from former CEO Lew Platt to investment banker Tully Friedman. "I believe Walter is a man who can be influenced," said Larry Sonsini, the powerful Palo Alto lawyer advising the board. The directors and their ad-visers had pegged Walter Hewlett as a weak man fighting a strong deal, and they were so certain of their position that it seemed inexplicable for him to be mounting such an effective attack without some secret string-puller in the background. Fiorina at one point shrugged her shoulders and said, "I can neither justify nor explain it."

Yet for most of Silicon Valley and a meaningful part of Hewlett-Packard's own workforce, the dissident director had become Saint Walter. People saw him as a reluctant hero, stepping out of his simple private rou-tines to stop his father's company from making the worst imaginable mis-take. This was a story of American courage, akin to the film *Mr. Smith Goes to Washington* or the sight of Judge John Sirica in the 1970s calling the Wa-tergate burglars to task. In fact, some confused shareholders thought that Walter Hewlett *was* his father. HP's investor-relations department was fielding calls from angry shareholders wanting to know why the company was at war with Bill Hewlett. "It's Walter Hewlett, not Bill," the investor-relations specialists explained. They were spooked by the notion that some shareholders might vote against the deal without even knowing who was leading the opposition.

It was time to set the record straight. Proxy solicitor Alan Miller was the hard-liner, telling one HP executive, "It's politics. It's negative cam-paigning. You have to go there." Investors ought to know that Walter Hewlett, at age fifty-seven, hadn't ever worked full-time for a major com-pany, Miller said. Once this fact was unforgettably in the public domain, he predicted, HP's job would get much easier. "I thought we needed to cut the legs out from under this guy before he got going," Miller later re-marked. So Miller and a few other New York advisers proposed sending a directors' letter to shareholders, deriding Walter Hewlett as nothing more than an heir, an academic, and a musician.* Some directors blanched at first. For a company as genteel as Hewlett-Packard, this was nasty language, especially in regard to a co-founder's son. The phrase "academic and musi-cian" was taken out, put back in, taken out—and finally reinstated for

---

* The first draft actually referred to Walter Hewlett as "a musician and a paleontologist." In Miller's rush to get the counterattack started, he had mistakenly turned his opponent into a fossil collector as well as a cellist. "I was just throwing out ideas," Miller later said. "I felt: 'Whatever he is, that's what we should call him.'"

good. When directors approved release of the letter on Friday, January 18, they blasted Walter Hewlett for ignoring the wiser counsel of eight other directors with three hundred years of business experience among them.

Journalists salivated. This was far more than a dispute about business strategies in the computer industry; it had turned into personal taunting in a takeover battle with billions of dollars at stake. Meanwhile, Walter Hewlett's loyalists seethed. In their eyes, Carly Fiorina and her board friends were insulting a brave and decent man. That meant she was debasing Hewlett-Packard and the HP Way even more than the traditionalists had thought. For the next three months the phrase "academic and musician" became the bloody shirt waved by leaders of the rebellion.

For all the uproar, the letter to shareholders hit its mark. It forced investors—especially top-tier portfolio managers—to pay attention to a new question: Did Walter Hewlett really have the authority and expertise to override the rest of the board? If the answer was "Not really," then HP's brief flirtation with negative campaigning had paid off. Alan Miller agitated for more efforts to undermine Hewlett's credibility, and the Goodby Silverstein advertising agency worked up a prototype of a wickedly snippy ad about boardroom attendance, headlined WHERE'S WALTER? But Fiorina and Johnson told their wordsmiths to stop. Blunt attacks weren't needed anymore. The "experience" issue was in plain view now, and it could be delicately exploited from this point onward.

For most of the winter, Carly Fiorina matched Walter Hewlett's dash across the United States, as each of them hunted for big investors' votes. On February 7, Fiorina started the day in New York, joining General Electric's legendary former CEO Jack Welch for a televised chat about the deal. (Welch complimented her on winning European antitrust approval for the merger, something that had eluded him on his attempt to buy Honeywell. "You're smarter than I am," he declared.) Moments after the show was done, Fiorina hopped on the HP jet and flew back to Palo Alto for a midday meeting with retirees. Using the time change to her advantage, she flew on to Hawaii later that day for a dinner meeting with local managers and customers. Other people could marvel at executives who worked twenty-four-hour days—thanks to clever maneuvering across time zones, she had put in a thirty-hour day.

Was either side gaining an edge? The clearest clues came from the stock market, and anyone looking at the spread saw a tense, sawtooth pattern that looked like Gallup Poll results in the closest of political campaigns. In early February, Fiorina narrowed the spread for three days in a row, pushing it as low as 9.5 percent. Later in the month, Walter Hewlett punched it as wide as 20.3 percent. For all the intense struggles, the two sides had practically neutralized one another. Each side was scrambling for a breakthrough; neither had achieved one.

The next decisive moment was coming March 5, when the ISS advisory firm would announce its recommendation on the deal. ISS's head of corporate programs, Patrick McGurn, had sneered at the HP-Compaq merger at first, telling reporters in November that "the timer has popped on this turkey." But ISS officials redefined themselves as studiously neutral once they started dialogues with the Fiorina and Hewlett camps. Handicappers on both sides agreed that if ISS sided with Hewlett, the merger would be crushed in a landslide of No votes. Even if ISS endorsed the merger, Hewlett might prevail. But Fiorina would have her best chance yet.

Unsure what factors would be most persuasive, each side sent a procession of representatives to Rockville. Carly Fiorina made the opening presentation in January, and she was followed in the coming weeks by HP's investment bankers, merger integration specialists, and two independent directors—Phil Condit and Sam Ginn—to explain all the hard work and care that the board had invested in the merger. Dick Hackborn phoned in at one point to offer his thoughts about both the merger and Walter Hewlett's frame of mind. Meanwhile, the vote-no camp countered with Walter Hewlett himself, followed by his investment bankers, top officials of the Hewlett Foundation—and two surprise visitors: Packard Foundation trustees Lew Platt and Dean Morton.

Throughout the proxy contest, the Packard Foundation had been almost invisible, at the request of Susan Packard Orr. Her foundation would vote no, but she didn't want to stir the waters any further. All the same, Platt and Morton had spent their entire careers at Hewlett-Packard. They cared deeply about the company's fate, and they believed that the merger on balance was a grave mistake, even if HP was trying hard to make it work. Morton was the more aggressive critic; Platt told business associates at the time that he would choose his words very carefully. "I don't want to do anything to hurt Carly Fiorina," he remarked. That was the old-school HP way of doing things. Platt had recommended her for the job and he knew that his current boss, Susan Orr, liked Fiorina. As much as possible, Platt vowed to be the voice of dignified dissent. Orr wasn't thrilled to see two of her trustees lobbying in any form, but she respected their right to make a few low-key appearances against the deal.

As experts marched through Rockville, both sides realized that ISS wasn't deeply immersed in strategic issues affecting the computer industry. The ISS analytical team was headed by Ram Kumar, a one-time student at the University of Southern California law school,* who was all of thirty-two years old. Most of the small firm's staffers were well schooled in corporate-governance issues but much less attuned to servers, printers, personal computers, and the troubled history of high-tech mergers. That lack of technical expertise dismayed the Hewlett camp, but caused far fewer problems for Fiorina's allies. The centerpiece of the vote-no campaign was a belief that high-tech mergers seldom worked, and that the business rationale for the HP-Compaq deal was especially feeble. If ISS's experts weren't ideally equipped to assess that perspective, the Hewlett camp would be forced to fight without its best weapons. HP's experts thought they could win on any battleground, including the contested turf of the deal's business rationale. But Fiorina and her advisers felt especially confident about their chances if ISS focused on other issues, such as the board's diligence in considering the merger or the integration team's hard work in figuring out how to put the two companies together.

In its final report, ISS declared after fifteen pages of analysis that both sides' business cases were plausible and that it would take a leap of faith to pick one over the other. From that point on, Kumar and his colleagues offered Hewlett some minor compliments, saying he had "served an immensely productive role in stoking up a debate about the merger's merits." But on what ISS now regarded as the decisive issues—merger-integration planning and boardroom processes—Hewlett-Packard got an enthusiastic thumbs-up. Even two snippets of the Packard Foundation testimony were cited in support of HP's merger-integration efforts. As ISS heard things, Dean Morton and Lew Platt had traveled all the way from California to tell the advisory firm that the merger planning was "good" and "better than anything" they had seen before.

At HP headquarters on the afternoon of March 5, two dozen aides crowded into Carly Fiorina's office to watch CNBC coverage of the ISS press conference and to listen to a speaker-phone conversation with proxy solicitor Alan Miller. (He somehow had obtained an advance text of the ISS remarks a few seconds before the press conference began.) To most

---

* In September 2002, *Smart Money* magazine reported that Kumar had dropped out of USC law school without graduating. ISS officials read that article and immediately asked Kumar to resign or be fired. He chose to quit. A few days later, ISS executive Patrick McGurn defended his firm's HP–Compaq analysis as untainted by the scandal, adding, "It is an organizational position that we still stand behind."

Americans, the live telecast was a truly obscure bit of corporate maneuvering. But to the executives in the room, this was as exciting and nerve-wracking as game seven of the World Series. As soon as people heard that ISS executive Patrick McGurn was recommending shareholder approval of the HP-Compaq deal, an enormous cheer swept through Fiorina's office. The merger agreement wasn't on the brink of collapse anymore. There were fourteen days left before the big shareholder vote, and Fiorina's comeback appeared nearly complete.

"Now we're ready," Fiorina told her friends. "Let's go out and win this thing."

Chapter 10

INTO THE COUNTING ROOM

In 1976, Jimmy Carter and Gerald Ford spent $34 million apiece in their race for the presidency. Nearly three decades later, that still ranks as one of the most expensive political campaigns of all time, displaced only by more recent presidential contests and a few ultracostly Senate races. With $68 million to disburse between them, the Carter and Ford campaigns bought countless television and radio ads, hired dozens of speechwriters and consultants, and flew the candidates and their entourages to cities all over America. Something as simple as bumper-sticker distribution became an obsession, with millions of motorists getting decals that proclaimed they were Carter or Ford supporters.

Even allowing for twenty-six years of inflation, it was hard to imagine that a single company's business dispute could touch off a bigger spending spree. By early March 2002, however, it was clear that the HP-Compaq contest was headed for the record books. Eventually, Walter Hewlett would spend $36 million on the vote-no campaign. Hewlett-Packard would shell out $75 million on behalf of its proxy contest and related merger expenses. As the combined spending surged toward $100 million, both sides became swept up in something that truly did resemble a full-fledged presidential campaign.

Each side had its strategists creating powerful, overarching stories that were meant to transcend the immediate dispute and connect with voters' hearts and pocketbooks. By these accounts, Walter Hewlett wasn't just campaigning against the merger, he was championing sound judgment, tradition, and the honor of the founding families. He was Jimmy Carter in 1976 or John McCain in 2000: a principled man in reckless times. Meanwhile, Carly Fiorina wasn't just arguing for the Compaq transaction; she was urging people to step into an exciting, uncharted future with her. She was John F. Kennedy in 1960, or maybe Bill Clinton in 1992: the charismatic young leader who vowed to get things moving again.

As the campaign dragged into the exhaustion zone, each side looked for quick tactical thrusts that could exploit the opponent's most vulnerable spots. Each side insisted that it wasn't entering the nasty swamp of negative campaigning and character assassination. It was just trying to set the record straight on areas that had become unfairly muddied by an opponent's action. Yet as bickering intensified, what had begun as a courteous boardroom debate was turning into what *The Wall Street Journal* referred to as "smash-mouth politics."

Shortly before the ISS decision was due to be announced, Walter Hewlett in an SEC filing accused Hewlett-Packard of attempting to "hide the ball" with regard to the pay packages of Carly Fiorina and Michael Capellas after the merger. The company at one point had considered awarding packages valued at a combined total of more than $115 million for the two of them if the merger was carried out. Hewlett faulted the company for not disclosing the proposal months earlier, when Fiorina had said she would pass up $8 million in retention pay under her existing contract. Her sacrifice might not seem so magnanimous if shareholders knew how much the deal might enrich her. "We wanted to disclose that," Hewlett attorney Stephen Neal later said.

Hewlett's disclosure infuriated the Fiorina camp, but it didn't do much to sway ISS. In its write-up of the deal, the advisory firm noted that HP's directors hadn't ever approved the controversial options package. In fact, in January 2002 the board's three-person compensation committee unanimously voted not to proceed with the options package, with Hewlett, Ginn, and Condit casting the votes. The company's decision not to disclose the aborted pay package "falls far short of the good governance ideal," ISS wrote, but if directors had decided that Fiorina wasn't going to get the money, the issue was moot. Hewlett hadn't achieved his big objective of budging ISS from its support of the deal; all he had gained was a minor pat on the back from ISS, which suggested in its report that he stay on the board as a shareholder advocate.

Meanwhile, Fiorina's aides showed that they could play hardball too. On March 12, minutes before Walter Hewlett was due to address nine hundred investors in a giant conference call in New York, Hewlett-Packard released a list of questions that investors ought to ask the dissident director. The queries were strident as could be, accusing Hewlett of mishandling his board duties and not having a coherent plan for Hewlett-Packard if the merger were voted down. Many investors disregarded them, but a few of the questions did make it into the conference call in some form. And for Walter Hewlett, who never liked public speaking at any stage of his life, the notion of addressing a vast, unknown audience that had been primed to hate him was visibly unnerving. "There was this feeling that he was going to be shown to the multitudes," one adviser remarked. "Walter isn't a well-spoken Wall Street type," another adviser added. "It was hard for him to steer the conference call back to what it needed to be."

Could either side find a decisive edge in the final two weeks? In the final weeks of any neck-and-neck political race, campaign veterans watch three things. First, which side is better at old-fashioned machine politics, especially when it comes to rounding up voters struggling the hardest to make a choice? Next, which candidate's will to win is strongest when exhaustion sets in and the rawest emotional issues come into play? And finally, what unexpected events could send shock waves through the electorate, giving one side a last-moment edge?

All three factors were at play in the final days of the HP-Compaq campaign. Two of them benefited Carly Fiorina. One of them decisively aided Walter Hewlett. The result was an election so close that both sides went to bed the night before the election unsure who was going to win.

For Walter Hewlett's campaign manager, Dan Burch, the ISS decision was very bad news, but not devastating. Like everyone else, he watched the spread abruptly narrow to 11.4 percent on March 7, the day after ISS's recommendation. Hewlett-Packard stock was at $20 a share now; Compaq was tagging along at $12.65. The newly narrowed spread was one of Fiorina's best ratings in the marketplace since Walter Hewlett's challenge began. Burch was determined to make that her high-water mark and to chip away at her support, hour by hour, until shareholders went to the polls.

On Friday, March 8, Burch sent Walter Hewlett to Boston to meet with Putnam Investments, one of HP's biggest shareholders and an early supporter of the merger. By midafternoon Hewlett was on a plane again, this time to visit another big shareholder, State Farm Insurance, in Bloomington, Illinois. Hewlett got home after 10 P.M. that Friday evening and had barely a day at home to catch his breath. Then at 6 A.M. Sunday a limousine was waiting at his door to whisk him away to the San Francisco airport for another week of East Coast lobbying. The final days of the campaign would be consumed by a blur of big-investor lobbying, with visits to Zurich Scudder . . . Mellon . . . GE Asset Management . . . Fidelity . . . Boston Partners . . . Glenmede Trust . . . Union Bank of Switzerland . . . Och Ziff . . . and phone calls to countless others.

Partway through this whirlwind, fatigue began to set in. At one juncture, Dan Burch handed Hewlett a list of seven or eight institutional investors that were willing to take a phone call from the candidate. Hewlett looked at the list and grimaced. "I hate doing this," he said. "I'm not very good at it." Then he rallied, declaring, "It needs to be done. I'll do it." Near the end of the campaign, after a marathon lobbying day in Boston, members of the Hewlett party stood in the lobby of the Four Seasons Hotel, waiting for a limousine. One of Dan Burch's aides, proxy solicitor Larry Dennedy, turned to the candidate and said, "Walter, how are you holding up?" Hewlett replied, "I want this over. One way or another, I just want this over."

Burch had no choice but to push Walter Hewlett in front of the company's biggest shareholders as much as possible, no matter how exhausted the candidate was. But for smaller investors, Burch built a vote-getting machine that wooed them assiduously without requiring any effort by Hewlett himself. A half-dozen times in the campaign, Burch's firm of MacKenzie Partners sent vote-no mailings to all 900,000 HP shareholders—from the biggest institutions to the tiniest individual investors. Each package included a form letter from Walter Hewlett, a financial analysis of the merger's purported flaws, and a green voting card that could be mailed back to the proxy firms.

All winter, Burch hired dozens of college students, out-of-work dot-com employees, and other New Yorkers to come to his slightly disheveled offices at 105 Madison Avenue and a satellite facility in California. Their job: to phone investors. Each of these phone solicitors was given a script to help in this get-out-the-vote exercise. "Did you get our latest mailing?" the phone solicitors asked. "Have you voted yet?" "Do you have any questions?" By early March, Burch had people working the phones from 7 A.M. to 11 P.M., calling investors in all fifty states. In a routine proxy contest, MacKenzie's battalions might be asked to contact only holders of 1,000 shares or more. This election required something extra, so Burch told his part-time workers to call everyone owning 300 or more shares. All told, MacKenzie put 180 part-time workers on the job, ordering them to place nearly 500,000 phone calls to HP shareholders. It was inconceivable to Burch that HP's campaign could do anything more.

A mile uptown, HP's proxy solicitor, Alan Miller, threw an even bigger army into battle. His firm of Innisfree M&A hired four hundred people to get out the Yes vote by penetrating even farther into HP's shareholder ranks. In conjunction with another proxy-solicitation firm, Georgeson & Company, Miller wanted his people to court voters with fewer than one hundred shares—the "odd-lot" investors who ordinarily didn't matter to anyone. This was the political equivalent of going door-to-door in North

Dakota farm country, rounding up even the tiniest bundles of votes, on the belief that even the slightest edge might be decisive. A flabbergasted commentator, *Reason* magazine correspondent Mike Lynch, figured that the two sides were spending more than $100 per voter—easily forty times what both presidential candidates had spent per voter in 2000. "We probably changed people's minds in only a small percentage of the calls," Miller later said. "But we knew this was going to be an amazingly close election. I thought we couldn't afford to overlook anyone."

Neither side could be certain how everyone was voting, but both could make sharp guesses based on fragmentary information. Institutional investors sent their votes directly to a neutral tallying firm, Automated Data Processing. Those were the easiest to track; ADP told Miller and Burch once a day exactly how the ballots were running. Individual shareholders generally mailed back voting cards to the proxy solicitors; these votes eventually would be tallied by neutral parties as well. As a practical matter, most small investors in favor of the merger submitted white HP ballots to Miller's firm, while opponents sent green Hewlett ballots to Burch's firm, even though it was possible to vote yes or no on either ballot. Shareholders typically voted once and let that decision stand, but some kept casting new ballots, either reiterating their views or switching sides. Only the most up-to-date votes counted, forcing Miller and Burch to keep revising their tallies of ballots already cast. Each side knew a lot; neither side knew everything.

Meanwhile, Miller was rushing to put his candidate in front of as many voters as he could. To his delight, Carly Fiorina and HP's chief financial officer, Bob Wayman, were proving to be a spectacular one-two combination. Fiorina delivered the big-picture vision of the combined company and stayed above the fray. Wayman fleshed out the numbers with the authority of a man who had been CFO for eighteen years. If investors seemed to be taking Hewlett's glum financial analysis seriously, the silver-haired Wayman could stare at them and say, "Those numbers aren't reliable. Let me show you why." Each evening, Miller sent Fiorina a list of eight to ten big shareholders to phone the next day. He expected her to flinch. She didn't. "Is this list long enough?" she asked one evening. "Do you have anyone else you'd like me to call?"

As the long campaign drained both sides' energies, something unthinkable was happening. Carly Fiorina—the newcomer, the person with less than three years' experience at Hewlett-Packard—wanted to win more than Walter Hewlett did. Both of them were locked in the fight of their

lives. She was traveling to the point of exhaustion, pressing her case repeatedly to anyone who might listen. He was, too. Going into the battle, it
seemed as if nothing could trump Walter Hewlett's commitment to his
cause. He had grown up with the very best of the old HP Way all around
him. His family name was on the front door of the company. He was the
last guardian of the founding families' role in the boardroom, and no one
dreaded the possible collapse of Hewlett-Packard more than he did. When
he told people that he regarded the Compaq deal as "bad business," he was
speaking with every ounce of conviction in his body.

Carly Fiorina was driven by something even fiercer. She had come
into Hewlett-Packard insisting that there wasn't a glass ceiling anymore for
female executives. She had maintained again and again that gender didn't
matter, as if she could sweep away centuries of prejudice just by declaring
victory. That blithe stand was just for public consumption, however. All
through the proxy contest, she knew, anonymous posters on Internet message boards were denouncing her as "the bitch from New Jersey"—and
worse. Ever since she arrived at the company, HP's security team had intercepted threats from an alarming number of "crazies." Fiorina was more
visible and more vulnerable than ever. On the brink of her greatest career
triumph, the faceless enemies were terrifyingly close to pulling her down.
She had to outrun them.

Director Bob Knowling, the only African-American on the HP board,
was one of the very few people to peer this deeply into Fiorina's psyche. "I
know what it's like to trek in new spaces, where you're different," Knowling later said. "It's lonely at the top. It's even lonelier for some of us, as the
minority. She's carrying a banner for a lot of people." Partway through the
winter of 2002, Knowling called Fiorina and talked a bit about the frustrations she faced. Then he said, "I know it ain't in you, but you could always
walk away from this."

Her response: "I can't ever do that, Bob. If I do, they've won."

Inside HP headquarters, employees didn't know all the reasons why
Fiorina was fighting so hard, but they knew she was hammering for better
results with an intensity that was both awesome and terrifying. In early
March, Duane Zitzner, head of the company's computer-systems group,
sent Fiorina a series of morose updates by e-mail. He called his group's
February's financial performance "really terrible," adding, "I feel we have a
meltdown in the front end." If he expected sympathy—or a similar sense
of panic—from Fiorina, he was badly mistaken. She dismissed his com-

plaints as "histrionic," adding in a later court deposition that "Duane always sends complaints of where the business stands. He is a Chicken Little kind of guy."

Day by day, Carly Fiorina was fighting her way through problems that would have destroyed most other chief executives. Dick Hackborn understood this better than anyone. Years before the proxy contest, Hackborn had been inside the Microsoft boardroom when company founder Bill Gates burst into tears, overcome with frustration about government antitrust investigations that were hobbling his company and vilifying Gates himself. "The whole thing is crashing in on me," Gates said at the time. "It's all crashing in." Eventually, Gates stepped aside as CEO and opted to be chairman only, a less stressful role. Carly Fiorina faced an even more ferocious assault on her legitimacy. She withstood everything her opponents could throw at her. "I've seen very few CEOs capable of doing that," Hackborn said. "She's one of them."

Carly Fiorina's willpower helped her even more in a crucial bit of brinksmanship with Walter Hewlett himself. Late in the campaign, it became clear that some big shareholders who were queasy about the Compaq deal itself couldn't bring themselves to vote no until they felt confident about the company's fate if the merger plan failed. Would Fiorina stay or go? What would other directors do? And top executives? In essence, was there a safe alternative to the deal? Or, as one commentator put it, were shareholders faced with "this—or the abyss"?

Fiorina could have made the investors' lives easier (and helped her rival) by publicly spelling out what she thought might happen if the deal got voted down. She never did. In part, she wanted to project constant certainty that the HP-Compaq merger was the right choice for the company and that she was confident most shareholders would agree in due time. Any sign of wavering or contingency plans would hurt her cause. But she also realized that the specter of turbulence aided her cause greatly. Each investor on the verge of voting no would have to think through a half-dozen or more scenarios, with no clear idea of what would happen and every opportunity to get spooked by some aspect of the unknown. In the final weeks of the proxy contest, nervous portfolio managers at State Farm in Illinois, Wellington Management in Boston, and State Street Bank in Boston all traveled partway down the path toward no—and then ran back to the safety of endorsing the deal.

Forced to develop their own strategic roadmap, Walter Hewlett and his investment-banker advisers put forth a plan in late February 2002 called "Focus and Execute." They urged Hewlett-Packard to invest heavily in imaging and printing, while cutting back its commitment to personal computers, especially for business users. They suggested making some minor acquisitions in software and services and thinking about spinning off the printing business as a separate company in a year or two. Each of the specific steps was eminently defensible, but the overall plan lacked excitement and vision. It consisted of a series of alternatives; it didn't amount to *the* alternative. Even as Hewlett and his aides talked up their plan, they felt they were being dragged into more precarious territory. As investment banker Spencer Fleischer later put it: "Our original position was: 'We don't have to present an alternative plan. That's management's job.' We didn't think it was appropriate for Walter to deliver a strategic plan. He was at pains not to run the company. Only when the company effectively built this campaign of 'It's this or the abyss' did we realize that Walter would have to say what the stand-alone view was."

Now Hewlett was presenting a bigger target for attack, and the vote-yes team wasted no time in firing back. If Hewlett thought spinning off the printer business was such a good idea, HP strategists asked, why hadn't he proposed that in board meetings over the past few years? If the company were to wind down part of the PC business, how many layoffs would be involved? Without detailed access to internal company data and management expertise, Hewlett's answers were bound to seem murky.

Tully Friedman, one of Walter Hewlett's investment bankers, tried to help in the final week of the proxy contest by sounding out Lew Platt on whether he would be willing to run Hewlett-Packard again, this time on an interim basis if a No vote on the merger suddenly left the company leaderless. Platt wasn't eager for the job. He had moved to Sonoma County, north of San Francisco, and he was deeply involved in his longtime hobby of wine-making. Moreover, people in the Fiorina camp still saw Platt as a lingering menace, and that bothered him. Shortly after his visit to ISS to argue against the HP-Compaq merger, Platt got phone calls from Bob Wayman and Larry Sonsini suggesting that he should back off. Platt regarded their calls as vaguely threatening, even though, ironically, he had probably done more to help than hurt Fiorina with his ISS visit. Platt believed it was his right to speak out discreetly about the merger, and the company's attempt to muzzle him left him feeling ill-treated. In this new frame of mind, Platt told Friedman that if absolutely necessary, he would try to be "helpful." News of that conversation made its way into the *Finan-*

cial Times, and suddenly the Fiorina camp had a new campaign issue. Did voters really think that HP's interests would be advanced by bringing Lew Platt back? If that was Walter Hewlett's best idea for new leadership at HP, could investors really feel secure with the dissident director calling the shots?

In the final days of the campaign, board members made two extraordinary personal appeals on behalf of Fiorina and the merger. On March 11, Sam Ginn and Phil Condit staged a conference call for investors, in which the two directors expressed their worries about the company's future if the merger didn't pass. "I won't walk away and pout," Ginn said. He vowed to look hard for a proper replacement if he left. But Ginn cautioned that if the deal were voted down, "you [would] create an inherent conflict for the existing directors." Meanwhile, Dick Hackborn weighed in with an open letter to shareholders and employees, telling them about his struggle to get HP to embrace the laser printer in the early 1980s and suggesting that the merger was "in the best spirit of the imagination, daring, and determination that made this company such a treasure in the first place." It was an openly sentimental appeal, crafted in part by the HP press office, with images of Bill and Dave listening patiently, smiling, and nodding before telling Hackborn to proceed. It was meant to connect with the group of voters Fiorina couldn't reach by herself: longtime HP employees who might otherwise be tempted to side with Walter Hewlett.

Fiorina was winning on multiple fronts, yet in the campaign's final ten days, the spread unexpectedly widened in Walter Hewlett's favor. The reason had nothing to do with the HP-Compaq battle itself and everything to do with investors' growing dismay about business scandals making headlines across the United States. Government investigators and whistle-blowers were flushing out the most astonishing tales of financial mischief at Enron, Global Crossing, Arthur Andersen and other once well-regarded enterprises. In each case, time-honored systems of corporate governance weren't working. Shareholders at scandal-plagued companies had no idea what was going on. Boards of directors weren't spotting problems. Top executives' upbeat public statements were laughably at odds with the darker activities transpiring inside such companies. The more that major investors read about these scandals, the more angry and embarrassed they felt. Were they just patsies in someone else's enrichment scheme?

Walter Hewlett and his vote-no campaign had shown up at just the right time. No one was suggesting that Hewlett-Packard should be lumped in with the Enrons and Andersens of the world. All the same, some big shareholders wanted to prove that they could act tough if necessary. So one after another, big state pension funds, which had long seen themselves as activist investors, lined up on Hewlett's side. All of them said that their decision to vote against the HP-Compaq merger was based purely on the merits, but unlike most institutional investors, which wanted to keep their decisions private, the state funds were quite willing to make a splash, with public announcements and TV interviews. For their own reasons, it was time to make a statement. First came an endorsement on March 8 from the giant Calpers fund in California. In the next few days other hefty state retirement plans in California, Ohio, Colorado, New York, and Texas announced that they didn't like the merger either. None of these plans was a giant HP shareholder, but their stakes of 0.7 percent, 0.3 percent, or even 0.1 percent were welcome allies to the Hewlett camp, one by one. Taken as a group, the state funds' support gave Hewlett a lot of urgently needed momentum.

In any extremely close campaign, the district that teeters longest between the two choices becomes famous for years afterward as the place where the whole contest was decided. In the 1960 presidential campaign, people became fascinated by Illinois, which ultimately went for Kennedy over Nixon by a margin of less than 0.2 percent. Forty years later, Florida became the nation's hot spot, as Al Gore and George W. Bush battled for more than a month over recounts that would decide who got the White House. In the Hewlett-Packard proxy contest, the final swing vote turned out to be Deutsche Bank, a giant German bank that owned twenty-five million shares, or 1.3 percent of the company's stock. Both sides thought they had its support; both sides thought they lost it. It would take an extra month—and millions of dollars—to find out who was right.

The tussle for the German bank's loyalty began in earnest on Friday, March 15, just four days before the election, with Hewlett investment banker Spencer Fleischer sitting in a rented private jet on a New Jersey airstrip. Fleischer had been trying for weeks to get an indication of how Deutsche planned to vote its shares. Now he finally had the bank's investment chief, Dean Barr, on the phone. When Fleischer hung up, he had good news for his colleagues. Deutsche Bank planned to vote against the deal, Fleischer declared. But he warned them that the bank's investment managers were jittery that pro-merger forces might put pressure on them once their voting stance was known.

Fleischer asked the Deutsche Bank executive to make a public statement in opposition to the deal. That tactic had been working beautifully for Fleischer with public pension funds. But commercial banks were different. They weren't trying to send anyone a message about corporate ethics. They didn't like publicity about their investment decisions. And while portfolio managers like Barr officially operated completely independently from the rest of the bank, there was no denying that many of Deutsche Bank's commercial lenders had deep business relationships with HP's current leadership and wanted to see the merger approved. Even so, Fleischer believed that a public statement would be coming in half an hour. By the end of the day, it was clear that Deutsche Bank wouldn't be saying anything in public. News of Barr's preliminary decision to vote no had spread inside Deutsche Bank, with damaging repercussions to the Hewlett camp. Word trickled out to HP's proxy solicitor, Alan Miller, that Deutsche Bank was planning to vote against the deal.

Miller was chagrined beyond belief. For the past ten days he had marked Deutsche Bank down as a certain Yes, knowing that the bank subscribed to ISS, which had just endorsed the deal. Scrambling to recoup, Miller passed along word to Hewlett-Packard over the weekend that the Deutsche vote at best was up for grabs—and at worst was hopelessly lost. On Sunday evening, Fiorina phoned her chief financial officer, Bob Wayman, to figure out what to do next. She got only his answering machine and left a stubborn, forceful message, saying that HP needed to do something extraordinary to schedule a last-moment conversation with Deutsche Bank, in hopes of getting the big investor "back where we want them to be."

The next day, Monday, March 18, top executives at Hewlett-Packard prepared feverishly for two meetings that would take place within twenty-four hours. One was the long-awaited shareholder vote, which would bring the 160-day proxy contest to a close. HP would be hosting that 8 A.M. meeting at the Flint Center in Cupertino, a good-sized Silicon Valley auditorium with 2,400 seats. Most major shareholders already would have voted electronically and wouldn't attend in person. But thousands of individual shareholders would come, and most were likely to be Walter Hewlett supporters. Hewlett would be there, too, and he wanted a few minutes to address the crowd. Meanwhile, Fiorina would preside for the entire session, fielding an hour or more of questions while allowing voters to make one last pass at the ballot box before she declared the polls closed. No matter what happened, it would be a tense public finish to an extraordinarily hard-fought campaign. As if that wasn't enough to worry about, Alan Miller was booking a 7 A.M. conference call for Fiorina and Wayman to address Deutsche Bank portfolio managers in New York and Germany. This would be a private caucus backstage at the Flint Center, and it would be sure to have its own drama as well, just minutes before the start of the public meeting.

The evening before the vote, both sides huddled with their advisers, trying to handicap the election. At HP's offices, Fiorina, Wayman, and investor-relations chief Steve Pavlovich looked at tallies that showed their side ahead by a razor-thin margin. But they were working with guesses; the best tallies were in the head of Alan Miller, and he was en route from New York in a private HP jet. He wouldn't touch down at San Jose International airport until 11:45 P.M.

Within the Hewlett camp, meeting at Stephen Neal's law offices, the mystery was even deeper. Spencer Fleischer thought his side had enough votes to win. Some of Dan Burch's colleagues thought they trailed by a whisker but could still win if Walter Hewlett could rally one more big investor in phone calls he would make just before the shareholder meeting started. The only clear pessimist was Dean Morton, head of the Packard Foundation's investment committee. *Things aren't falling into place the way we'd like,* he told himself.

As voting day arrived, crowds began forming outside the Flint Center before 6 A.M. The first rays of sunrise hadn't yet broken through the nighttime sky, and already this corner of Silicon Valley was full of noisy, heartfelt support for Walter Hewlett—and utter scorn for Carly Fiorina. One former Hewlett-Packard worker marched back and forth, banging a giant drum in mourning for the end of the HP Way. Just outside the auditorium doors, French unionists unfurled a banner that read CARLY'S DREAM IS A NIGHTMARE FOR WORKERS. Farther back in line, HP retirees talked about a company in danger of losing its soul. Many men wore green blazers or green neckties; women sported green scarves or shoes. Like hard-core football fans, they had taken the color of Hewlett's proxy cards and adopted it as their tribal marker.

"I'm voting no," Warren Hargrave told one writer. "I don't want to see more people lose their jobs." He was a twenty-seven-year HP veteran who had retired in the 1990s and now owned 10,000 shares of the company's stock. To him, the company's heyday would always be the period when the founders walked the halls and made personal connections with lab technicians like him. "If Dave and Bill hadn't passed away," he said, "none of this would have happened." Carly Fiorina's boosters were scarcer but determined to hold their ground. "A lot of old-time HP people say this company used to be run like a big family," said Andreas Hotea, an HP engineering manager. "That might have been fine twenty years ago, but the time when someone can have a job guaranteed for life is over. People have to realize this isn't a social club. We're talking about running a business."

When the Flint Center doors finally opened, security guards watched all entrances. A stern sign barred cameras, bottles, backpacks, computers, and weapons from the premises; metal detectors made sure no one tried anything sneaky. For the past few days, both HP and the Hewlett camp had worried that the meeting might degenerate into an Old West shootout. At one point, Walter Hewlett's attorneys asked permission to bring four armed bodyguards. The guards could come, HP decided; the firearms couldn't.

Fiorina had barely slept the night before. Just before 7 A.M., while the crowds poured into the Flint Center, she and Wayman settled into a small backstage office to begin their conference call with Deutsche Bank. It was a chaotic exchange. People were walking in and out of conference rooms at each location. Introductions were haphazard. No one at Hewlett-Packard really knew who the bank's key decision-makers were. In any case, Wayman and Fiorina offered their stump speeches with as much vigor and clarity as they could muster. The merger was the best alternative for HP. It could improve earnings, making the company No. 1 in some key markets and perhaps shoring up the PC business. Near the end, Wayman tried his version of "this or the abyss," declaring: "We are going to have a real tough six to twelve months if this deal gets voted down."

Two miles away, Walter Hewlett was working the phones, too, aided by investment banker Spencer Fleischer. They were operating out of the Hilton Garden Inn, a traveling salesman's hangout with cold Budweiser bottles stacked up in the lobby and brew-your-own-coffee machines in each room. It was a crazy place for campaign headquarters, but it was the best they could find. HP's law firm, Wilson Sonsini, had snapped up almost everything usable on the De Anza College campus that surrounded the Flint Center. Still, the Garden Inn's rooms had long-distance phone service, and that sufficed. Every few minutes, it was time to dial East again, to see if one more institutional investor could be brought around. Hewlett persuaded Jennison Associates, a major New York investor that managed money for the Hewlett Foundation, to switch about 15 million shares to No. He tried—and failed—to budge State Street Bank in Boston, which owned about 50 million shares and was voting Yes. And he did his best with Deutsche Bank, telling its fund managers in a hurried fifteen-minute presentation that a No vote might help Hewlett-Packard extricate itself from some of the worst parts of the PC business. Add it all up, and his last-minute phoning spree had clearly helped the cause. No one on his team knew whether it would be enough.

At about 7:40 A.M., Walter Hewlett arrived at the Flint Center, where admirers and the media mobbed him. As he stepped out of his limousine, television crews thrust toward him, asking anything to get a sound bite. "How are you feeling, Walter?" "Do you think you're going to win?" He smiled, waved, and didn't say a word. As he got inside, he relaxed a little. Two rows of seats had been set aside for him and his friends, relatives, and advisers. Now he was surrounded by almost all the people who had helped him come this far: Stephen Neal, Tully Friedman, Dan Burch, and other key advisers—but also his wife, Esther, his younger brother Jim, and other longtime friends. Only David Woodley Packard wasn't there; he told Walter Hewlett that he found such meetings too stressful. As the forty members of the Hewlett party settled into their seats, shareholders approached the dissi-dent director, clutching HP stock certificates and asking for his autograph. He obliged, making a personal connection whenever he could. "I think of all the time you put in over all these years," he told one retiree. "This is the least I can do."

The meeting was due to start at 8 A.M., but HP announced a brief delay so that latecomers could make their way out of the parking lots and be seated. Then, at 8:26 A.M., Carly Fiorina stepped on stage and called the meeting to order. She was standing alone, at a pale wooden lectern, isolated from everyone else. She looked weary: Her face was gaunt, her eyelids puffy, her eyes darting back and forth erratically. She had dressed elegantly, wearing a purple suit with a high-neck white blouse and a small pendant on a gold chain. But everything about her body language and appearance said: *I've been doing this for many months. It's been a long, grueling campaign and I am beyond exhaustion. What you're seeing is the ultimate expression of willpower, and the hope that a few people in the next hour will hear something that will make them vote yes.*

In the press tent just outside the Flint Center, journalists were told to unplug their video recorders from the master control board. Reporters could watch a live video feed of the meeting, but they couldn't walk away with their own frame-by-frame versions of what was about to unfold. Print accounts and secondhand summaries on the evening news would be barely tolerable. Journalists were being kept out of the meeting hall itself. By im-plication, powerful people within Hewlett-Packard had decided that the next ninety minutes shouldn't be too vividly known to the wider world.

If Carly Fiorina had had any hope of a friendly audience, that prospect was dashed within the first five minutes. After announcing that 1,949,477,350 shares were eligible to vote, she began introducing HP executives in the audience. "Please hold your riotous applause while I introduce them all," she said. It was a rueful comment; HP's leaders attracted a few tepid claps but nothing more. Then she officially opened the polls and invited Walter Hewlett to speak about his proposal. Just as Fiorina finished introducing her rival, a roar burst forth throughout the auditorium. All eyes turned to Walter Hewlett. Rows of people jumped to their feet; green shirts and green jackets seemed to be everywhere. A jubilant woman swung a green necklace above her head. In the press tent, someone blurted out, "Oh, my God!" Someone else muttered, "That's riotous applause." Everyone could hear high-pitched, jubilant welcomes for Bill Hewlett's oldest son. But a lower-pitched growl rumbled through the hall, too: the sound of an angry mob eager to take down Fiorina.

Walter Hewlett savored the cheers for a few moments; he couldn't stop them even if he wanted to. He smiled and waved. He had been awake since 4 A.M., but he looked calm and in command. With a fresh haircut, a blue-gray suit, and a conservative tie, he carried himself like a man who should be running a giant corporation. The only clue betraying his true position was a small green button on his lapel, with the inscription DISSIDENT. As the crowd finally quieted, he began reading from a small stack of index cards that he had prepared in close cooperation with Joele Frank's speech-writing team. His delivery was a little ragged. His pitch was flat, without any of the crescendos and diminuendos of a trained orator. But he nonetheless was delivering the speech of his life, and he knew it. This wasn't a strident campaign speech, hustling for last-minute votes. It was a salute to the Hewlett-Packard that he loved, coupled with an affirmation of the reasons why he had stepped out of anonymity to take a stand. Win or lose, this was the way he wanted to be remembered.

Partway through, Walter Hewlett called HP "a symbol of the best that an American company can be." As the crowd burst into applause, even Carly Fiorina joined in. He framed the proxy contest in the broadest terms possible, as a debate about the soul of Hewlett-Packard and what it meant for America. Then he deftly put himself on the side of the angels. "I want you to know that the HP Way is not a relic for another time," he said. "It's not a piece of trivia, relevant only to the Hewlett and Packard families. It is alive in our employees, in our stockholders, and in our customers." The whole speech lasted less than five minutes. By the time the last cheers faded away and Walter Hewlett sat down, it was clear his listeners had found their hero.

Now it was Carly Fiorina's turn to stand alone and endure everything a hostile crowd could offer. Several dozen shareholders queued up beside large microphones mounted in the aisles so that they could challenge the HP chief executive. The opening question was tough: "If the merger isn't approved, what are your plans?" And the ones that followed were even harsher. Why is HP overpaying for Compaq? Why will so many jobs be lost? What does this down-and-dirty proxy contest say about the HP Way? Why are you paid so much? Why are so many people in the HP retirement plans voting against the merger?

Each time, Fiorina held her ground. She was civil when she could be; chilly when she couldn't. She said she agreed wholeheartedly with Hewlett on the importance of legacy and traditions, adding that she regarded layoffs as a last resort. She insisted that the majority of HP employees supported the deal, even if retirees didn't. When the audience booed, she shot back: "Ladies and gentlemen, that is a fact!" At every opportunity, Fiorina defended both the Compaq merger and her own legitimacy. "The board of directors has considered a whole host of alternatives," she said. "If this one is voted down, we'd look again at all the others. We think this is the single best opportunity."

Then came the hardest exchange of all. A broad-shouldered man in his early forties stepped to the microphone. He introduced himself as Dan Dove, a twenty-two-year veteran of the company, working in Roseville, California, as a network-infrastructure specialist. Coming to Hewlett-Packard in 1979 had pulled his life together, he said. He was unemployed at the time with a pregnant wife; now he was a respected engineer with eight patents to his credit and a university degree he had earned with HP's sponsorship. "I've had many, many opportunities to go to start-ups," Dove said. "Some of my friends are multimillionaires, [but] I said no, because I saw the opportunity here to work for a great company." But in the past year, he had seen colleagues fired almost at random. This wasn't the HP he cherished. "I oppose this merger," he declared. "I don't trust the organization that's pushing it. And if it goes through, I will not be an employee of Hewlett-Packard for very much longer. I regret that because I do love this company very much."

As the applause died down, Fiorina blinked. She looked downward. Some onlookers thought she was going to cry. Then she pulled herself together with a no-nonsense answer that included just the faintest wisp of an apology for the previous summer's firing spree. "I'm certainly sorry that you feel that way," she said. The layoffs weren't pleasant for anyone, and in some cases HP made mistakes about individuals, she acknowledged. "In many of those cases we ended up correcting those mistakes. Our goal . . . was to move with speed." She lingered over her answer a minute or two longer, but the message didn't change. No matter what her opponents threw at her, Carly Fiorina wouldn't break. They could insult her, boo her, or even appeal to her tender side. It wouldn't work. She would emerge from this meeting an iron-willed survivor.

If people thought her hard-hearted at that particular moment, so be it.

Two more shareholder questions followed. But now the final drama of the meeting was taking place in whispered cell-phone conversations among top members of the HP team. Backstage, proxy solicitor Alan Miller was watching an immense bank of twenty fax machines and keeping track of last-minute vote changes. He didn't have total visibility into the No camp, but he could see most of the votes that were switching to Yes. Overall, Miller's best judgment was that the Yes cause was picking up about seven million votes as the meeting unfolded. Most of Deutsche Bank's shares were switching his way, and that would more than offset Walter Hewlett's gains at Jennison. Shortly after 10 A.M., Miller phoned HP's top legal adviser, Larry Sonsini, who was stationed on the floor of the auditorium. As Sonsini later remembered it, Miller told him, "I think the blocks that we wanted have come in. What you ought to do is consider wrapping up."

Those were magic words. Sonsini quickly passed the message to HP lawyers onstage, who slipped a handwritten note to Fiorina. Moments later, Fiorina declared the polls closed and the meeting over. The official vote results wouldn't be announced for weeks. But both the dissidents and HP management headed into closed-door huddles, where they pieced together their best estimates to see if anyone felt confident enough to declare victory.

Fiorina headed backstage to the Flint Center counting room: a high-walled chamber designed for theater-set storage. There, an eerie sight greeted her. Alan Miller was sitting at a large table, with at least a dozen people clustered around him. He had flown in from New York on an HP jet the evening before; he hadn't slept all night. Clutching a yellow No. 2 pencil, he was talking on the speakerphone to Art Crozier, one of his proxy-solicitor colleagues at Innisfree's New York offices. In front of Miller was a half-eaten bagel, a nearly empty glass of orange juice—and a single scratch sheet, with working totals penciled in for HP's white voting cards, Walter Hewlett's green voting cards, and three other smaller sources of votes. The numbers weren't adding up.

"What the fuck is going on?" one of the Innisfree executives screamed over the speakerphone, before Miller hurriedly picked up a handset and muted his partner's voice. Everyone else looked on in silent dismay, as if they were in a hospital operating room watching a heart-surgery case that was starting to go very badly. "No, no, no, that can't be right!" Miller snapped at one point. For all their tight scrutiny, Crozier and Miller had fallen out of sync as they each tried to track 13 million shares that might be voted against the merger. Had they counted them once? Twice? Not at all? They picked through the numbers again and again, trying not to panic. Finally Miller's numbers worked. So did Crozier's. They checked the tallies again. Everything still worked. Miller swallowed hard and turned to Fiorina.

"You're good to go," he said. "It looks like at least a twenty-five-million-vote margin, and more likely forty-five million or fifty million."

After months of being told that their cause was hopeless, Carly Fiorina and her loyalists had pulled off one of the most stunning comebacks ever seen in a merger contest. They had shrugged off the opposition of HP's founding families and found many thousands of other shareholders who believed in them—and in their vision for a combined HP-Compaq. The celebration might have lasted longer, but Walter Hewlett's team had just issued a press release saying it felt "optimistic" about the outcome. It was a tepid statement indicating that the Hewlett camp couldn't make its tallies add up to victory. But it was creating enough confusion that it was time to tell reporters the real outcome. Fiorina's communications chief, Allison Johnson, had drafted three possible statements ahead of time, designed to cover every conceivable outcome. The MERGER DEFEATED release could be torn up; it would never be needed. The TOO CLOSE TO CALL release wasn't necessary either. But what exactly should a victory release say? Should HP management claim victory by nearly two percentage points? At least one percentage point? Some twenty-five million votes?

"Whatever way you look at, it's a slim margin," someone blurted out.

"Slim but sufficient," Sonsini replied.

Moments later, Carly Fiorina headed back onstage to tell the world that the HP-Compaq merger had prevailed by a "slim but sufficient" margin. This time her voice sounded warmer. Her eyes weren't veering about any more. As reporters quizzed her, she was calm and even a little playful. When asked if an ultraclose final tally might generate a recount, just as the

2000 presidential election had in Florida, she laughed off the prospect. "We don't have dimpled chads or hanging chads or pregnant chads," she said. "This is pretty simple." All the same, she had serious things to say. She thanked shareholders for embracing change, and her employees for standing strong. She told her opponents, "When the ground has cooled, I hope we can put the rancor of this campaign behind us." And she offered a peace gesture to the Hewlett and Packard families. "This company will always be proud to bear your names," she said. "We want to be faithful stewards of your legacy." For Fiorina, it was a perfect finish: victory on her terms and a message of reconciliation for the founding families. When asked what she had learned from the five-month proxy contest, Fiorina replied, "I've learned how much I love this company, and how much I'm willing to fight for what I think is right for this company."

Now the spotlight turned to Walter Hewlett. In a midday press conference at the Hilton Garden Inn, he said it was "simply impossible to determine the outcome." He sounded so calm and reasonable that reporters' pens barely stirred when he added that he planned to keep his options open regarding a challenge to the vote. Most journalists focused instead on his wry assertion that at some point "I will resume my life as an academic and a musician." It was a charming quip; it just didn't speak to what was really going on inside the Hewlett camp.

Chapter 11

SEARCHING FOR VINDICATION

Anyone following the proxy contest knew that Walter Hewlett had been a gifted runner as a young man. His performance as a Harvard sophomore in 1964—when he completed the Boston Marathon in two hours thirty-two minutes—was immortalized in a Harvard documentary, known simply as *Marathon*. The film showed Hewlett gaining speed in the late stretches, running confidently and beautifully on a miserable rainy day. Hewlett's eighteenth-place finish, which won him a medal, became a constant item in his biography, upheld as proof of his character and stamina.

Very few people knew what happened a year later, in the 1965 Boston Marathon. Once again, Walter Hewlett outpaced almost everyone. A hundred yards from the finish line, he was in twenty-first place, with another runner a dozen steps ahead. Summoning one last kick, Hewlett tried to outrace the man ahead of him. As Hewlett neared the finish line, race officials looked suspiciously at this sprinting young man in a Harvard shirt. So many college students had been sneaking onto the course just a mile from the finish that judges regarded Hewlett as another cheater. They disqualified him, handing his medal to someone else. Hewlett wanted to protest. He had trained for months; he had picked up an official entry number at the starting line; he had run the full 26 miles 385 yards in the same impressive 2:32 time that he had posted the year before. But as other runners kept crossing the finish line and getting the last few medals, Hewlett realized it would be an enormous disruption to insist on the prize he deserved and force the reassignment of fifteen other medals. He gave up and walked away. It didn't seem to matter much at the time.

Decades later, digging through a box of memorabilia, Hewlett found his 1964 Boston Marathon medal and wondered what had happened to the 1965 medal. Then he remembered: It didn't exist. "The way I left things," he later said, "there was no record of me ever having run that race."

Now, a much bigger race was over, and Walter Hewlett had to decide whether it had been settled fairly. Once again, he had competed with everything he could muster. He had spent more than $30 million trying to convince other investors that the HP-Compaq merger ought not to take place. He had contacted nearly one hundred major shareholders in person, continuing to fly from city to city even after a near-death experience on a private jet. He had argued the vote-no case on the phone incessantly, even when he was worn out and just wanted to go home. In the final minutes of the campaign, he had gone toe to toe with Carly Fiorina in seeking one more voter, and he had seemingly battled her to a draw. Was it good enough? On the afternoon of March 19, Hewlett's proxy solicitor, Dan Burch, staunchly told reporters that Hewlett-Packard's claims of victory were premature. Privately, though, Burch conceded that Hewlett was behind, perhaps by a percentage point. If those numbers held up, the vote-no campaign had narrowly failed, unless there was something so terribly wrong about the company's conduct that the vote totals ought to be overturned.

Hewlett's advisers already had their suspicions. Hours after the shareholder vote wrapped up, a dozen members of the team, led by Stephen Neal, Dan Burch, Spencer Fleischer, and Joele Frank, gathered at Neal's law offices in Palo Alto. The last-minute voting switch by Deutsche Bank rankled all of them. They ignored Hewlett's offsetting capture of the Jennison vote and decided instead that Deutsche Bank's decision had tipped the election to Fiorina. As soon as he knew the vote had switched, Fleischer frantically called the bank's investment chief, Dean Barr, for an explanation. But his calls weren't put through. From the Hewlett team's perspective, it was impossible to believe that Deutsche Bank's decision was based on the merits of both sides' presentations. Instead, some Hewlett advisers wondered if powerful magnets under the table were yanking voters' allegiances around.

For Stephen Neal, one of the best courtroom lawyers in Silicon Valley, the remedy was obvious: Sue Hewlett-Packard on allegations of vote tampering. In his mind, a winning lawsuit could undo the merger vote and force the company to start over or admit defeat. No one in the Hewlett camp knew everything about Deutsche Bank's decision process, but a belief took hold that there were grounds for a suit. Besides, now that the election results were clear, the Hewlett advisers had run out of options. If Walter Hewlett agreed, the best hope of keeping the crusade alive would be in the courthouse.

Ironically, just a few doors away at Cooley Godward, HP director Sam Ginn thought he was hammering out a peace accord with Hewlett himself.

The gentle tone of Hewlett's midday press conference had impressed Ginn, to the point that he had asked Fiorina whether it might be worth renominating the dissident director in April for another one-year term. Just a week earlier, when it looked as if the merger might be voted down, Fiorina and the other directors had been adamant about their desire to banish Hewlett from the boardroom. But in victory, it was easier to be magnanimous. Bill Hewlett's son certainly had enormous credibility among longtime employees. Enlisting him as a backer of the merged company might help a lot of the company's worst morale issues fade away.

"Go see Walter," Fiorina had told Ginn. "If he can be a productive member, and if it can heal some of the wounds, it may not be a terrible idea."

So Ginn made his way to Cooley's offices around 2 P.M., where he offered Hewlett a deal. Ginn wanted Hewlett to accept that HP had won, to support the company's merger strategy going forward, and to give Carly Fiorina a chance to implement that strategy. If those conditions were acceptable, other directors would be proud to have Bill Hewlett's son stay on the board.

"I think I can be helpful," Hewlett replied. "I'm willing to give Carly a chance to succeed." Hewlett said he did want to reserve his right to challenge the shareholder vote. In his mind, the outcome wasn't totally settled yet, and he thought he was spelling out a vital qualifier to his generally friendly thoughts. But if Hewlett was passing along a coded message, Ginn missed it. "He did have the option under the rules to ask for a recount," Ginn later recalled. "That's what I assumed. Never once did I assume that he was talking about legal action." The only sharp words came when Ginn accused Hewlett of leaking confidential board documents and asked him to forswear such conduct. Hewlett said a higher duty to board integrity had forced him to disclose private pay discussions. After a few minutes of sparring, they agreed to put the past behind them and agree simply that there wouldn't be any leaks going forward.

At the end of their meeting, Ginn and Hewlett shook hands and parted ways. But their memories of their ambiguous conversation brought them into two utterly different camps. Within HP's leadership, it was assumed that the old board harmony could be put together again, with Carly Fiorina firmly in charge and Walter Hewlett quietly rejoining the team. But within the Hewlett camp, the drumbeats for a lawsuit kept growing louder. "They wanted Walter to keep quiet and just be a good boy in the corner," remarked Jim Gaither, the former Cooley Godward partner and a longtime director of the Hewlett Foundation. "That was unacceptable."

It took Walter Hewlett several days to decide what to do. He wasn't eager to sue at first. But in talking with his advisers, "there was a sense that the company had pulled a fast one," he later recalled. "No one had a clear idea what exactly it was. It was a picture that would take awhile to put together." As Hewlett ruminated, he began focusing less on Wall Street's perspective and more on the concerns of HP traditionalists. It wasn't necessary anymore to talk a dozen times a day with the dispassionate New York and Boston portfolio managers who owned most HP shares. There was more time to spend with HP retirees and family friends in Palo Alto, Los Altos, Menlo Park, and other Silicon Valley towns. These people didn't own nearly as much stock, but they cherished the old Hewlett-Packard in ways that the institutional investors never did. In this circle, people regarded Carly Fiorina as an interloper barely clinging to power at headquarters, akin to an embattled Third World dictator controlling the capital and nothing else. They wanted her ousted by any means possible. HP retiree Dick Love remembers a conversation just a day or two after the shareholder vote, in which Walter Hewlett remarked, "I don't want to do anything that would hurt HP."

"Walter, she's going to ruin HP if this thing goes through," Love shot back. "It won't be the company that your father and Dave built."

A week after the shareholders' meeting, Hewlett finally decided to sue. He later remembered it as an economic decision, focused entirely on preserving the long-term value of the Hewlett Foundation. His advisers had calculated that stopping the merger could add at least $5 a share to HP's share price, which would amount to $500 million in extra assets for the Hewlett Foundation. All the work involved with the lawsuit would cost his side only about $4 million. Even if the odds of winning were just 1 percent, Walter Hewlett figured, the probabilities and payoffs justified the gamble.

But Walter Hewlett didn't anticipate the wider consequences of betting everything on courtroom proceedings. Carly Fiorina's behavior would be on trial, but indirectly, Hewlett's record would be under scrutiny, too. By going to court in Delaware, where Hewlett-Packard was incorporated, he was inviting both sides to lash into each other's character, motives, and conduct over many months. The moment that *Hewlett vs. Hewlett-Packard* entered the legal docket, the two sides wouldn't be mere opponents debating the merits of the Compaq deal. They would become enemies, locked in an all-out struggle for personal legitimacy.

As Walter Hewlett headed down the path to a lawsuit, he denied other directors even a courtesy call to let them know what was coming. "Communication had pretty much broken down," he later observed. At a board meeting on March 27, he said only that he was keeping his options open with regard to the shareholders' vote. Board members thought his intentions were benign enough that they commissioned a statement for release the next day, announcing Hewlett's return to the board. At 5:30 A.M. on March 28, HP attorney Matt Jacobson was preparing to issue that statement when he saw news of Hewlett's suit cross the news wires. All of a sudden, Jacobson realized, Hewlett's prospects had been dashed.

Over the next few days, HP directors had to decide: Do we still want him on the board? The overpowering answer was: *No way!* Sam Ginn was so flabbergasted he was speechless; he had been telling other directors that he thought his talk with Hewlett went "wonderfully." Dick Hackborn called Carly Fiorina and muttered, "I am so sorry about this." By the following Monday, Hewlett's name had been stricken from the list of board nominees. All through the proxy contest, it had been barely possible to work together, but a lawsuit would poison boardroom dynamics. Directors couldn't open their mouths in any debate without worrying, *Are we having a blunt conversation, or providing raw material for someone else's lawsuit?* In a statement after his ouster, Walter Hewlett expressed surprise that his lawsuit would cost him his board seat. Everyone else saw it as inevitable.

More shocks followed. On April 10, an anonymously leaked version of Carly Fiorina's prevote voice mail for Bob Wayman appeared in a word-for-word transcript on the front page of the San Jose *Mercury News.* The intercepted message made for spicy reading, with Fiorina talking bluntly about the prospects of Deutsche Bank and a less-substantial shareholder, Northern Trust, voting no. She then advised Wayman that "we may need to do something extraordinary for these two to bring 'em over the line." Lively as the call itself was, the most astonishing thing to many readers was that HP executives' private conversations weren't secure anymore. Someone was sneaking into Wayman's phone links—or perhaps into the entire HP voice-mail system.

Wayman was aghast. In a memo to HP employees hours after the *Mercury News* story ran, he said he felt "personally violated" by the leak. "We spent countless hours presenting the business value of our position up until every vote was cast," he said. "But we never, ever crossed any ethical or legal lines. The only good news about participating in a trial is that the facts will come out, the truth will be heard, and our honor will be restored." In pretrial depositions, HP attorneys repeatedly asked Hewlett's top proxy-fight tactician, Dan Burch, whether he had been aware of Fiorina's message before reading about it in the *Mercury News*. "No," he said on eight occasions. In a June 2002 interview for this book, Burch speculated that a disgruntled employee intercepted the call. He didn't sound too disturbed by it. Such snooping "isn't likely to backfire" in a proxy contest, Burch said. "It's considered usual. It doesn't usually offend too many people."

For the first time, strategists in the Fiorina camp began to see ways that the trial might strengthen their standing with employees, the great neglected group of the entire proxy contest. Whether employees had voted yes or no on the deal, almost all of them believed they worked for an unusually ethical corporation. At Hewlett-Packard, it wasn't considered fair play to pad expense accounts, snatch company supplies for personal use, or steal credit for other people's work. Hacking into the company's voice-mail system, no matter what the objective, wasn't the HP Way at all. Members of the Hewlett team disavowed knowledge of the intercepted call, and HP's efforts to track down the hacker eventually petered out. Even so, in cafeteria and watercooler chatter, it felt much easier to side with an angry Bob Wayman—whose roots at HP went back to 1969—than to justify an anonymous hacker's actions.

In pretrial maneuvering, meanwhile, HP's outside lawyers prepared a wide-ranging attack on the credibility of Walter Hewlett himself. They would be allowed to quiz Hewlett for hours under oath, in a closed-doors deposition at Wilson Sonsini's offices. Ostensibly, the exam would focus strictly on lawsuit-related issues, but as a practical matter, nothing was off limits. Walter Hewlett could be grilled about his wealth, his vacation habits, his boardroom attendance, and his truthfulness. The right man for the job was Steven Schatz, a quick-witted lawyer with a raspy voice and a reputation as the pit bull of Wilson Sonsini. Earlier in his career, Schatz had made headlines as a public prosecutor by battling a music promoter accused of income tax evasion in connection with selling various Beatles albums. By the time Schatz was done, the promoter was headed for prison.

"Carly wanted me to depose Walter," Schatz later recalled. "I had to learn stuff quite quickly that was new to me. I explained that other attorneys knew the case in much more detail. But it was very important to Carly that Walter be rigorously deposed."

On April 17, Schatz jabbed away at Hewlett for nearly eight hours. Did

Hewlett think other HP directors were people of integrity? Did he have a regular job? Where was he during the crucial board meetings of July 2001? The questions were scattershot, but the pressure was relentless. The HP hardliners were in command now; Walter Hewlett would be recast as a cranky dilettante who didn't like the HP-Compaq deal but couldn't really explain why. Even though the deposition itself wouldn't be made public until months after the trial, the sharpest barbs could be shared with influential journalists wondering what the suit was all about. By the time Schatz focused on the key factual issues of the case, Hewlett's answers were painfully guarded and hazy. "What I was or wasn't told about Deutsche Bank I couldn't tell you," Hewlett said at one point. Several hours later, asked whether he had read his own lawsuit before it was filed, Hewlett said, "I may have; I'm not sure."

For once, Hewlett couldn't count on much help from his advisers. Steve Neal sat beside him for the deposition and periodically objected to Schatz's tactics. But there wasn't any judge to rule on the objections; Schatz could proceed any way he wanted, with Neal's interjections being noted only in the official transcript. At 6:55 P.M., the ordeal finally ceased. Ever gentlemanly, Hewlett thanked Schatz for "running a very civil process." In later conversations with friends, however, Hewlett said he found the Schatz interrogation one of the most unpleasant and intimidating parts of the entire proxy contest.

Meanwhile, Walter Hewlett's lawyers were hunting hard for the other side's vulnerabilities. Under Delaware law, they could demand that Hewlett-Packard turn over internal documents that might have bearing on their case. The company did so, and before long, couriers were unloading box after box of private HP and Compaq files at Cooley offices. Of the 34,000 pages produced, more than 10 percent consisted of nothing more than articles from the San Jose *Mercury News*, *The Wall Street Journal*, and other publications, all labeled HIGHLY CONFIDENTIAL. The boxes also included a handful of HP and Compaq memos that showed fascinating signs of stress and anxiety within both companies' executive ranks in the weeks before the shareholder vote.

HP's attorneys at Wilson Sonsini worried at first about Carly Fiorina's ability to hold up in a trial. *We need to protect the quarterback*, attorney Boris Feldman told himself during trial preparation. After a face-to-face meeting with Fiorina, however, he breathed a lot easier. She grasped the key issues of the case quickly; she also showed superb instincts about how to keep the upper hand in an adversarial exchange. When Feldman asked if she'd been on the witness stand before, the answer was yes. Fiorina had been tested repeatedly at AT&T and Lucent; she had always won her cases. Feldman didn't bother calling Lucent's general counsel, Rich Rawson, for details, but if he had, Rawson would have raved about her courtroom savvy. "She is almost the perfect witness," Rawson later said. "She is articulate, she is reliable, and in a high-stress situation, she can do something very few people can. When the other side's lawyer is trying to rattle her, she has a great ability to show quiet disdain."

On April 23, the trial began in Delaware Chancery Court, with Chief Judge William B. Chandler III presiding. Both sides regarded him as a fastidious, deeply moral judge who could rule decisively in their favor. A former law professor, Chandler once fined himself $500 for missing a conference call with lawyers. Already in this case, he had let people know in early April that he was missing Sunday church services to hear pretrial motions. For more than one hundred lawyers, journalists, and takeover-stock traders, the trial was a can't-miss event. The moment the courtroom doors opened, people stampeded toward the few available seats. Worried that they wouldn't get in, many of the attendees had hired students or couriers to stand in line for them all night. After a few preliminaries, Stephen Neal stepped forward to spell out the basis for his case.

Neal's opening statement was brilliant. Barely acknowledging his team's inability to build a convincing case on the vote-buying claim, he turned almost all his attention to the Hewlett camp's other assertion: that HP's business was falling apart in February and March 2002 and that the company wrongly concealed those problems from shareholders. Neal's key evidence consisted of a half-dozen memos that even HP's lawyers referred to as "bad documents." In late February, Compaq's chief financial officer, Jeff Clark, wrote in an e-mail: "We have a mile to go on this. Second half of 2002 is a pure disaster." Around that time, Compaq's CEO, Michael Capellas, wrote in his diary: "Case study for years. At current course and speed we will fail." Most tellingly in Neal's eyes, two of HP's internal cost-cutting documents, known as "value-capture updates," showed eroding prospects in February and March of 2002. All the while, of course, Carly Fiorina had been appearing in front of investors, telling them that merger integration was on schedule, or perhaps even ahead of plan. Add it all up, Neal contended, and "the results of this vote should be thrown out. . . . The information was material, it was persistently adverse . . . and it was persistently undisclosed."

Partway through Neal's remarks, takeover-stock specialist Larry Yavner bolted from his bench near the back of the courtroom and ran out the door. He had heard enough. Slipping into a bathroom to avoid detection by court security officers, he pulled out his cell phone and phoned his firm's trading desk in Connecticut. The HP-Compaq merger might unravel in court, he declared. Neal's opening statement was explosive, and if it presaged a Hewlett victory, there wasn't a minute to lose. Sell Compaq, he directed.

After that spectacular start, however, Stephen Neal and Walter Hewlett were in retreat for the rest of the trial. In the HP team's opening response, Steven Schatz argued that the "bad documents" reflected only momentary despondency on the part of executives who eventually rallied to achieve their goals. In many cases, he asserted, success with other parts of merger integration more than offset the trouble spots that Neal had found. Schatz's delivery wasn't nearly as polished as Neal's, and many people in the courtroom found his style jarring. All the same, he was providing a road map for what ultimately would be a relentlessly effective HP defense.

At 11:08 A.M., Neal called Fiorina as his first witness. Within minutes, they were locked in a highly technical argument about HP's calculations for cost synergies and revenue loss in the merger. Back and forth they jousted for nearly three hours. Neal argued that HP was falling badly short of the goals it had promised to investors in December 2001, and that as the proxy contest neared its finish, the company was failing to update the financial community. He could be taunting at times, jolly at others, but always with a sense of showmanship. Some of his best courtroom successes over the years had come in jury trials, and it was easy to see why.

Fiorina didn't give an inch. Again and again, she told Neal that he didn't understand the company's financial goals or the merger-planning process properly. She called him *Sir* occasionally, but she also let glimmers of exasperation slip into her voice. No one in the gallery found her engaging, but she was aiming her remarks at the only person in the room who really mattered: Judge Chandler. When Neal kept pursuing what she regarded as a wrongheaded line of questioning, she parried with quick dismissive answers—and let him know that that was all he could expect. "I'm going to frustrate you by answering in exactly the same way," she told him at one point.

Late in the afternoon, HP's full counterattack began. At 3 P.M., Neal sat down and Wilson Sonsini's Boris Feldman rose to question Fiorina. Now she was relaxed and expansive. She spelled out the eighteen-month history of the Compaq deal, making time to include Dick Hackborn's role, the early back-and-forth with Michael Capellas, and the belief that the merger might be even more cost-efficient than shareholders had been told. When Feldman alluded to the grimmest value-capture report, from March 2002, she explained that such troughs were a hallmark of every planning process she had ever been involved in over the past twenty-two years. Top executives set big targets at first. Operating managers push back initially and propose less-ambitious numbers. Then, eventually, the operating managers figure out how to achieve the boss's goals.

As Fiorina's testimony wrapped up, stock traders pushed HP and Compaq shares closer together once more. Her rebuttal was coherent and plausible to the market. Some people grimaced at the way she spoke of lower-level managers who weren't meeting top corporate goals; she accused them of "sandbagging," a common term for setting obviously low targets that can later be exceeded. That sounded very different from the trusting company that Bill Hewlett and Dave Packard built. But Fiorina wasn't trying to boost employee morale; she wanted the judge to understand how HP executives did things. During a brief court recess, *Fortune* magazine writer Adam Lashinsky passed Fiorina in the hall and told her, "The spread has been cut in half."

Fiorina knew exactly what he meant. "Good!" she said, with a smile.

If Walter Hewlett and Stephen Neal wanted to persuade Judge Chandler that Fiorina was hiding anything, they would need a lot more firepower in the following two days. But from day two onward, the more witnesses that Neal examined, the more rickety his case sounded. During an examination of HP's chief financial officer, Bob Wayman, Neal got millions and billions mixed up. He tried to laugh it off, only to have Wayman interject, "I can't do that or I'd lose my job." Later, the financial tangle got even worse when Compaq CFO Jeff Clark took the stand. First Neal tried to do a revenue calculation in his head and missed the right number by $2 billion. Then he said operating *profit* when he meant *revenue*. Finally, Neal mounted a series of arithmetic questions meant to trap Clark in an embarrassing answer. But as the calculations spun out, Clark ended up $400 million away from where Neal expected him to be. Minutes later Neal sat down, chagrined, without having used all his allotted time to grill the witness.

Hewlett-Packard director Phil Condit wrapped up that portion of the trial, offering analogies that buttressed the company's case even further. As chairman and chief executive officer of Boeing, he observed, he himself had carried out a giant merger with McDonnell Douglas in 1997. As those two companies came together, he said, lower-level managers often saw modest problems that appeared huge in their eyes. They were a bit like crew members on an ocean liner who might look out a single porthole and believe that their view represented everything going on in the world. "The job of senior management is to integrate all those views," he explained. In effect, CEOs such as himself and Fiorina were captains of the ship—capable of seeing the big picture when their aides couldn't.

Throughout the trial, Walter Hewlett watched quietly from the first table in the courtroom, just twenty feet away from the judge and witnesses. His gestures were sparing at first; he generally looked upbeat. By the time Clark testified, Hewlett was taking off his glasses, rubbing his eyes, running his fingers through his hair, and periodically slouching down in his chair. He looked like a blackjack player at the end of a marathon session in Las Vegas, being wiped out at 3 A.M. by one losing hand after another.

At the end of the second day, Hewlett stepped onto the witness stand to tell his own story. His delivery was painfully labored, with many *ers*, *ums*, and repeated words. But he wanted to press on and get some vital things on the record. Prompted by friendly questions from Stephen Neal, Walter Hewlett talked about the Hewlett Trust and Foundation, how he decided to fight the merger, and how he had wanted to stay on the board even after the merger was approved. With evident bitterness, he retold the story of being invited into his father's office by Dick Hackborn and Jay Keyworth in November 2001, only to read about that private meeting later on.

Once Neal sat down, it was Schatz's turn to show Judge Chandler the side of Walter Hewlett that the HP legal team wanted revealed. Schatz's first dozen questions meandered through topics covered in the deposition, and Hewlett's answers this time were more careful and precise. Then Schatz asked a complex question that touched on Hewlett's decision to sue and on what Hewlett thought was going on inside HP at the time.

"I'm sorry," Walter Hewlett replied. "I . . . I flipped out while you were asking the question. Can you ask it again?"

The courtroom erupted in laughter. And Steve Schatz had what he wanted: a highly quotable one-liner that could be cited from now on, whenever Hewlett-Packard wanted to argue that Walter Hewlett wasn't poised enough to deserve serious consideration. Even if Hewlett's closest allies still regarded him as a hero, such ten-second gaffes would sway journalists and their countless readers, including many HP employees and customers. No one was more attuned to that perception than Fiorina herself.

At some point during Hewlett's testimony, she leaned over to Larry Sonsini and whispered, "I've been waiting eight months for this."

Fiorina's three days on the stand weren't perfect either. On the second day of testimony she inadvertently knocked the witness's Bible off its perch. As it clattered to the floor, she looked mortified and said, "I'm truly sorry." At another juncture, Neal's questions irritated her enough that she lashed out: "You're accusing the CEO of a publicly traded company of lying!" It stopped his line of questions; it also became the lead quote in most of the news stories the next day.

Overall, Fiorina proved that she could withstand everything the other side threw at her—and eventually attract sympathy for her resoluteness. On the final day of testimony, Neal brought her back as a witness on a minor point and asked her to review a document he was holding in his hand. As Neal leaned unusually close to her, Wilson Sonsini attorney Boris Feldman leapt up and asked, "Could he give the witness a little room, Your Honor, instead of joining her in the witness-box?" When the laughter subsided, Judge Chandler told Neal to hand over the document and, by implication, to keep his distance.

Neal's only remaining hope involved reviving the vote-tampering allegations associated with Deutsche Bank. To get anywhere on that charge, he needed clear evidence that Hewlett-Packard had bribed or coerced Deutsche Bank in an effort to win its vote. He had pressed that point in his pretrial deposition of Fiorina, asking her what she meant by telling Wayman in the March 17 voice mail that "we may have to do something extraordinary" to win Deutsche Bank's loyalty. But her answers didn't help his case. "I didn't know precisely what I meant," Fiorina replied. Most likely, she said, the company would enlist either a director or a top executive to pitch the deal in person. She acknowledged telling Deutsche Bank executives after the vote that she looked forward to doing business with them. But then she coyly added, "I say that to all customers." Adding up his evidence on the vote-buying claim, Neal conceded in his opening statement that he had only "circumstantial" evidence of any malfeasance.

Partway through the trial, Deutsche Bank's attorneys informed both sides that an audiotape existed of the bank's last-minute vote struggle the morning of March 19. Thanks to the unexpected diligence of a bank employee in Europe, Neal would be able to produce a word-for-word record of Hewlett's opening pitch, the response by Fiorina and Wayman, and Deutsche Bank's deliberations at the end. Would the tape reveal shocking misconduct? Or business as usual? It was time to find out who was telling the truth.

To Hewlett-Packard's delight, the transcript showed Fiorina wrapping up the call with all the good manners and bland pleasantries of a Dale Carnegie graduate. "Gentlemen, we appreciate your time," she had told the investors. "I need to go and try to get ready for a shareowner meeting. We very, very much appreciate your willingness to listen to us this morning. This is obviously of great importance to us as a company. It is of great importance to our ongoing relationship. We very much would like to have your support here. We think this is a crucially important decision for this company."

A few minutes after she hung up, as Deutsche Bank executives continued their deliberations, New York-based Dean Barr issued some blunt advice to his counterparts in Germany, who were inclined to vote no. "I'm not trying to put undue pressure," Barr said, "but make sure you have a very strong documented rationale for why you voted the way you did." He invoked the names of two top Deutsche Bank executives who, he said, regarded the whole matter as "extremely sensitive." One of the German portfolio managers, in effect, threw up his hands at that point. "I don't want to be smarter than you people in New York," he said. "If the majority of you come to the conclusion that it's better for our customers to vote in favor, I try to change our vote here."

As fascinating as the glimpse into Deutsche Bank's deliberations was, the trial was about to end with a whimper, not a bang. The deeper that both sides dug into the factual record, the clearer it was that Fiorina had conducted the proxy contest legitimately. She had lobbied voters hard and used her own judgment in deciding what to tell outsiders about the merger's prospects. But those were time-honored privileges of incumbents in any battle. All the other revelations—the politicking within Deutsche Bank, the secret qualms among top members of the HP-Compaq team— ultimately weren't going to change anything. The deal was done, and Fiorina had prevailed.

For Walter Hewlett, it was time to walk off the stage. He had charted an amazing path the past nine months, dissenting quietly at first, then becoming louder and stronger until some of his oldest friends couldn't recognize him. He had fought hard for the version of the HP Way that mattered most to him, and he had very nearly won. But now he had lost the shareholder vote and his board seat. All he could control was his exit. As he left the Delaware courtroom, he did a remarkable thing. He lingered by the third-floor stairwell for a few minutes and talked with a few journalists about running. All of a sudden, his voice was friendly and confident. He reminisced about buying some of the first New Balance running shoes ever made, when he was a college student in the early 1960s and the company consisted of one small store near the Harvard campus. He asked journalist Michelle Quinn about her training regimen and offered pointers that could help her run faster. The nervous, stammering man on the witness stand was gone. Walter Hewlett was about to suffer a crushing courtroom defeat, but he was leaving Delaware unbowed. This time his effort would be in the record books forever; people would know how hard he fought. He could go home with an easy conscience.

When Judge Chandler released his opinion a week later, he gave Hewlett-Packard all the vindication that it craved. On the proxy-contest disclosure issue, he wrote: "The plaintiffs have been unable to prove that HP misrepresented or omitted material facts about integration in the proxy contest. Instead, the evidence demonstrates that HP's statements concerning the merger were true, complete, and made in good faith." And on the Deutsche Bank allegations, he said he found nothing in Fiorina's voice mail, the conference-call transcript, or other evidence to prove that HP had been engaged in a vote-buying scheme. Chandler didn't view Deutsche Bank's own conduct nearly as kindly, noting that pro-Fiorina commercial bankers were in repeated contact with supposedly objective investment managers. "This fact raises clear questions about the integrity of the internal ethical wall that purportedly separates Deutsche Bank's asset-management division from its commercial division," he wrote. But that was Deutsche Bank's problem, not Hewlett-Packard's.

At Cooley Godward, Walter Hewlett's lawyers digested the ruling in stunned disbelief, still clinging to the belief that they had presented a strong enough case to win. Finally they accepted what had become obvious to everyone else: It was time to capitulate. A day after the ruling, they announced that there would be no further appeals or vote challenges. The now-official tally of the proxy contest would stand, with HP's 838 million votes for the merger narrowly beating back the 793 million votes against, in a margin of 51.4 percent to 48.6 percent.

For Carly Fiorina, the victory amounted to her finest work since coming to Hewlett-Packard—and it nearly annihilated her. After starting the proxy contest in an almost-hopeless position, she had built a strategy to work her way back to parity and beyond. She and her team members had executed crisply and well, day after day, often in harrowing circumstances.

They had tightened up their message, beaten back the critics, fought by the rules, and ultimately rallied just enough voters to win. Along the way, she and Bob Wayman, Larry Sonsini, Allison Johnson, and dozens of other advisers had become friends for life. They had worked together from dawn until midnight, brainstorming, bantering, and caring. Now that the battle was over, the teamwork and camaraderie felt just as exhilarating as what HP's pioneers had enjoyed in the 1950s.

In an unwitting salute to old HP traditions, the key members of the winning proxy-contest team staged a raucous dinner in San Francisco soon after the trial's end, with a sassy awards ceremony right after the meal. Bob Wayman was likened to Clint Eastwood in the movie *Dirty Harry,* snarling the actor's famous taunt to hoodlums: "Go ahead, make my day." Carly Fiorina was likened to Joan Allen in the movie *The Contender,* silently enduring endless slights from small-minded people trying to stop her advancement. Only the portrayal of Walter Hewlett crossed the bounds of fair play. He was depicted as Michael Douglas in the movie *Falling Down*— a bitter loser with a gun, wandering through Los Angeles with no clear purpose in mind. To Fiorina and her advisers, Walter Hewlett would always be a mystery.

As much fun as it was to celebrate for an evening, Hewlett-Packard's hardest work lay ahead. Shareholders had barely given Fiorina the go-ahead to try the biggest merger in high-tech history. Now she and her executives faced immense challenges in proving that the combined company really could succeed. Archrivals such as IBM and Dell Computer were stronger than ever. The high-tech sector was mired in its worst slump in decades, making customers reluctant to buy anything. Many of HP's employees were dispirited by the prospect of 15,000 layoffs in connection with the merger. Enormous new battles lay ahead, in which HP's leadership needed to win the loyalty of customers and employees. Failure was a distinct possibility. Even the optimists believed it would take years before the HP-Compaq merger could pay off.

To have any realistic chance of success, Carly Fiorina needed time. She also needed the support—or at least the sympathetic understanding—of some of her proxy-contest opponents. HP's critics and rivals were muttering that the postmerger company would be hobbled indefinitely by its own in-house strife. Fully 48 percent of votes in the proxy contest were cast against the merger, and the showing within HP's own workforce was even more troubling. People with detailed knowledge of voting patterns said that a majority of HP's U.S. employees ended up opposing the deal. Only strong support from European, Latin American, and Asian employees allowed HP to say that most of its employees worldwide had sided with management. Concerns about Fiorina's leadership were hardly put to rest by those outcomes. Someone needed to step in and play the role of healer.

The final twist to the proxy-contest story was about to play out in Los Altos, home of the Packard Foundation. All through April 2002, the foundation—HP's largest shareholder—had been watching the trial far more closely than outsiders realized. The foundation's general counsel, Barbara Wright, had traveled to Delaware to be an on-the-spot observer. She sat quietly next to Walter Hewlett's wife throughout the sessions and deflected outsiders' questions about her role. "We felt it was important to be here," Wright told journalists, with a gentle smile that closed off further conversation. But twice a day, Wright phoned back to Silicon Valley to tell colleagues how the trial was going. Her steady message: "Carly is in control."

So on the morning of Friday, April 26, Packard Foundation leaders met to debate their next step. Walter Hewlett's suit was doomed. The HP-Compaq merger would go through. Now people who had opposed the deal faced a crossroads. They could keep voting no on shareholder issues every chance they got, telling the world that they had lost confidence in current leadership and wanted Carly Fiorina out. Or they could swallow hard, and decide that for the next year or two, cooperation mattered more than anything. Even if the merger wasn't perfect—even if it wasn't their first choice for HP's future—it might be time to cheer on management and hope for the best.

Among the foundation trustees, Lew Platt wanted to keep fighting. To some extent, so did Dean Morton. The former HP executives had come to regard the merger as a grievously wrong step, and the harsh words exchanged in the proxy contest had soured both men on the company where they had worked for decades. "There isn't anything that's ever going to heal it for me," Platt later remarked. On the morning of April 26, their next chance to wage war with Carly Fiorina was just a few hours away. All of HP's directors were up for renomination, with shareholders due to cast their ballots that afternoon. It was an unopposed race this time, without any way to vote the current board out of office. Even so, a fusillade of Abstain or Withhold votes would be seen as a sign that the shareholders' uprising wasn't over. The Hewlett interests planned to keep voting against management. So did many HP retirees and some employees who were especially disturbed by the company's direction. To Platt, it would be inconsistent now to do anything except keep opposing the Fiorina administration.

Susan Packard Orr disagreed. "Our future is tied to the success of the company, no matter what," she reminded board members. The family foundation still owned more than 200 million shares of HP, and that stock needed to rally hard if the Packards hoped to achieve their dreams of helping sick children and protecting the environment. Fighting an endless guerrilla war against Carly Fiorina wasn't going to help.

By 11 A.M., Susan Orr had won. The full board was ready to endorse Fiorina and all the other directors. In the course of the debate, Susan Orr had taken on the mantle of both her parents. She wasn't the shy, deferential daughter anymore, letting older men make the key financial decisions. She was crusading for the social issues that mattered so much to Lucile Packard. In doing so she was showing her father's legendary resolve, championing a point of view until other people's hesitations were swept aside. Even former leaders of Hewlett-Packard eventually yielded this time.

There was only one problem: No one at foundation headquarters had a paper ballot. For weeks the foundation's chief financial officer, George Vera, had been planning to vote via the Internet. But the foundation's decision had taken so long that the online polls had closed. Old-fashioned paper ballots would be accepted for four more hours, but no one in Los Altos could find one. So Vera called HP's general counsel, Ann Baskins. "We're going to vote yes," he explained. "Can I get a ballot?" Come on over, she replied. Vera dashed into his car and sped over to HP headquarters. When he got there, Baskins scurried down the stairs to greet him.

A few minutes later, Fiorina and Baskins headed to the shareholders' meeting together. As their car reached Interstate 280 and started heading south, Baskins briefed Fiorina on the Packard Foundation's decision. Baskins did her best to deliver the news as matter-of-factly as possible. But both women knew something special had just happened.

At last, Carly Fiorina had won the loyalty of someone in the inner circle of Hewlett-Packard's founding families. Her dealings with the Hewlett family had been an endless series of misunderstandings and troubled exchanges, going back to her first meeting with the gravely ill Bill Hewlett in November 1999. The enmity between her and David Woodley Packard ran even deeper. To the Hewlett and Packard sons, she would always be the interloper. But maybe the sons weren't the most important heirs to watch. Susan Packard Orr, as chair of the Packard Foundation, now spoke for 218 million shares of HP, more than any of the other heirs. She had emerged as a Silicon Valley leader in her own right: a trustee of Stanford University, a powerful board member of the children's hospital, and host of the annual

Palo Alto Christmas party that no one wanted to miss. From their very first meetings in 1999, the two women seemed to understand and respect each other.

Now, on the highway, Fiorina pulled out her cell phone and called Orr to say thank you. They talked for a few minutes, joking briefly about getting together for a drink some time, once the merger was fully official. It wasn't quite a social call; it wasn't quite a business call, but it was a warm enough chat for Fiorina to hope that she had found a lasting ally. After the phone call finished, Fiorina wanted to savor a single remark again and again.

"Susan said, 'We aren't just voting yes on the board,'" Fiorina recounted. "She said, 'We want you to know that we support the direction in which you're taking the company.'"

Chapter 12

CAN CARLY MAKE IT?

W hen Hewlett-Packard opened its doors to Carly Fiorina in 1999, the company was intensely inbred and proud of it. Employee turnover averaged just 5 percent a year. Top management consisted almost entirely of people who hadn't worked anywhere else since college graduation. Executives facing thorny decisions sometimes walked over to file cabinets and fished about until they found a transcript of Dave Packard's comments from a decade earlier. They sought guidance from his words as if they were reading scripture itself. Devotees of the HP Way had created a quasi-religious order that was both glorious and stifling.

People who cared about Hewlett-Packard wanted to modernize this heritage without destroying it. Management classics such as *Theory Z* and *Built to Last* praised Hewlett-Packard as a company with a timeless commitment to management excellence, yet the company was losing its way in the marketplace. The HP Way itself stopped being a beacon to other corporate leaders; in fact, a 1997 attempt to explain it to another company's chief executive made such a poor impression that the listener was tempted to sell Hewlett-Packard short. Something needed fixing in a hurry. Company directors came to believe that only an outsider could save Hewlett-Packard from itself. From July 1999 onward, people held their breath and hoped that Carly Fiorina, the most powerful businesswoman in America, could find a wise way to balance new and old.

Ultimately, however, there was no middle path. The proxy battle over the HP-Compaq merger raged with such intensity because the underlying issues couldn't be compromised. The people who cherished the home-grown culture of Bill and Dave weren't amenable to seeing it overhauled with outsiders' ideas. The founding families couldn't occupy nearly one-third of the directors' seats without exasperating the professional managers who wanted to be answerable only to a boardroom of their peers. The leadership style of a big-company strategist couldn't be reconciled with a loose grouping of small divisions founded by independent-minded engineers. At the time of Carly Fiorina's arrival, Hewlett-Packard was riddled with fundamental contradictions. Nothing could be resolved until one way of doing things became dominant. The more that well-intentioned people tried to deny the inability of old and new to share control, the more they unwittingly created extra tinder for the final, inevitable blowup.

Someone needed to sweep aside all the halfhearted compromises and declare: "This is what Hewlett-Packard will stand for. You may love it or you may hate it, but you will never forget it!"

The champions of new and old were destined to clash. Their initial flash point hardly mattered, and the HP-Compaq merger was as good a battleground as any. Once a few deeply concealed differences made it into the open, everything else was bound to follow. As a result, Carly Fiorina and Walter Hewlett became far more than boardroom opponents in the midst of a $20 billion takeover battle. They weren't reenacting *Barbarians at the Gate,* even though the dollar amounts approached that legendary fight for control of RJR Nabisco. In this case, a private boardroom disagreement quickly turned into an enormous public struggle for HP's soul. When people slipped notes onto Walter Hewlett's windshield, telling him "your father would be proud of you," or when Carly Fiorina told the company's only African American director that she couldn't ever quit, "because then *they* would win," the signature themes of the contest were set.

Each side believed it was in the midst of a heroic crusade to protect its way of life in a dangerous world. Within Silicon Valley, something took place that invited parallels to John Glenn and Yuri Gagarin vying to be the first man to orbit the earth. Two proud, utterly alien cultures had been glowering at each other for a long time. It was time for each tribe to pick its proudest standard bearer and send that person into a single-warrior contest.

Then Carly Fiorina won.

By rights, victory should have been euphoric. After nearly three years of struggling, Fiorina at last got her chance to reshape Hewlett-Packard into the kind of company where she could be most effective. Just as planned, the combined HP-Compaq emerged as one of the world's largest enterprises, with at least $70 billion a year in revenue and the number-one positions in a half-dozen of its key markets. It now had the potential to bulldoze its way past smaller rivals simply because it had more salespeople, more advertising dollars, and more reinforcement from consultants and third-party vendors that wanted to support the vast HP ecosystem. As the biggest competitor around, Hewlett-Packard could redefine industry practices to its advantage. It could win simply by showing up. Fiorina had learned how to play that game extremely effectively at AT&T and Lucent. Finally, she could do the same thing at Hewlett-Packard.

What's more, Fiorina for the first time was surrounded by fellow newcomers who didn't mind redefining Hewlett-Packard her way. The Compaq acquisition brought sixty-five thousand fresh faces into the company. Most of these employees had job-hopped already; they were comfortable settling into new assignments and getting the job done, without agonizing over each cultural adjustment. The executives who came from Compaq's PC division already appreciated the importance of being number one in a market segment. The managers who came from the old Digital Equipment knew how to push and elbow against the likes of IBM. In meetings with these new team members, Fiorina could relax and enjoy being back with her kind of people. As she readily acknowledged a few months after the deal became effective, "part of what we've done in the merger is inject new DNA."

Yet the victory took its toll. Anyone who spent time with Fiorina could see that she had become a warier person, jolted by the proxy contest and the economic slump. She was mindful of strangers or even apparent allies who could hurt her. Months after Judge Chandler exonerated her, she still scheduled long, off-the-record conversations with journalists so she could argue about details of takeover coverage, trying to prevail on tactical issues that everyone else had forgotten. At a Gartner Group research conference in October 2002, when someone asked her a mild question about the printer business's outsize contributions to HP's overall profitability, she sarcastically replied: "I guess we should have spun it out like many people suggested." She had beaten Walter Hewlett at the ballot box and in the courtroom. Even so, she couldn't shake him in her own mind.

Fiorina was straining, too, to become a different kind of leader. She wasn't the fast-paced outsider anymore, or the daring rebel standing alone. She had become the face of established authority. Aides at Hewlett-Packard described her as "stoic," a word that evoked outright laughter from her Lucent friends, because it was so at odds with the young evangelist they remembered. But it was true. In Fiorina's first three years at Hewlett-Packard, she had been a strategic whirlwind, creating most of the opportunities and problems that she now faced. In her fourth year, it was time to stop taking the company on new journeys. She needed to stand still, repair her own mistakes, and exhibit the day-by-day precision of a skilled operating executive. That was her best hope of making Hewlett-Packard stronger for the merger.

In a revealing moment in 2001, Fiorina returned to the Stanford campus to deliver the commencement speech. The Compaq deal was just starting to brew; she was already an embattled CEO. Back at her old campus, addressing several thousand freshly minted graduates, Fiorina talked with stunning candor about dropping out of law school, trying to find her way, and eventually making it to the top of Hewlett-Packard. The audience, including former president Bill Clinton (there to see his daughter, Chelsea, graduate), was spellbound. Yet for all the bravery evident in both her life and that speech, Fiorina came across as astonishingly caught up in her own story. In the half-hour talk, she used the word "I" 129 times while thanking only one person, her husband, by name for his support. Sentence after sentence began: "I showed up . . . I never looked back . . . I hit my stride." At that moment, all of her life's work was being organized around a single question: "Can Carly make it?"

As the ultimate steward of Hewlett-Packard's fate after the Compaq merger, Fiorina was starting a fresh chapter of "Can Carly make it?"—but this time with an unexpected twist. There isn't anything heroic or dangerous about the day-to-day work of merger integration. It is a long, slow process that involves getting thousands of prosaic details right. Is the San Diego lab talking to the Massachusetts lab? How do we want to use the Proliant brand name? Which factories do we keep open? Which do we close? The most effective leaders in this arena roll up their sleeves, immerse themselves in the small stuff, and share credit assiduously. It is the ultimate team project, without any room for narcissism. To succeed in this world, Carly Fiorina needed to become a different person.

"I always thought it would be nice if Carly gathered some scar tissue," said Dick Munro, the retired chairman of Time Incorporated, a few months after the HP-Compaq proxy contest was over. He had seen Fiorina swagger earlier in her career, when they both sat on the Kellogg board. Now, from a distance, Munro welcomed her newfound caution. "She had overwhelming self-confidence then, and she was probably right most of the time," he recalled. "But she had a sharp edge. When she got to Kellogg, I said to myself: 'Someday, Carly, you're going to get yours. You're going to learn that you're not always right. You'll encounter the same frustrations that all the rest of us face. And if you're lucky, it will make you a better person.'"

Going forward, the only scorecard that mattered for Fiorina—and Hewlett-Packard—consisted of the merged company's achievements. "If the company performs well, people will see that as demonstrating the competence of Carly and her team," conceded former CEO Lew Platt. "But if they have trouble, you'll have cannon fodder for years to come." Chief executives of other computer companies said it would take at least two years before anyone could offer a verdict on whether all the anguish was worth it. The merger was transforming Hewlett-Packard in so many ways that it would take eight quarters or more of head-to-head competition against IBM, Dell Computer, and others to know whether bigger was better. In fact, the answer might always be murky. Was the 1901 merger that created U.S. Steel a good idea? Historians were still debating that one.

Even so, anyone who kept an eye on Hewlett-Packard had some early hunches. Journalists and Wall Street analysts, in particular, couldn't help themselves. The most impatient observers revised their views every time HP's stock price twitched. The merger was failing. It was succeeding. It was anyone's guess. Others waited for decisive evidence of recovery or deterioration in the HP's newly amalgamated computer businesses. The shrewdest gauge, however, lay in the career choices of the top few hundred people at the company. If they were sticking around, or if the talent pool was getting better all the time, the merger had a good chance of emerging as a winner. If the best people were bolting—as had happened years earlier when Hewlett-Packard bought Apollo Computer and Compaq acquired DEC—then the merger's early promise was likely to slip away.

For one jubilant day in May 2002, investors gave Carly Fiorina a big thumbs-up. Eight days after the dismissal of Walter Hewlett's lawsuit, Fiorina stepped onstage in Cupertino to celebrate the birth of "the new HP." Roars and cheers from more than two thousand employees welcomed her. "Are we ready or what?" Fiorina shouted. Four times, the audience bellowed back: "We are ready!" She was back in the Flint Center, the place where shareholders denounced her at the culmination of the proxy contest. This time Fiorina didn't need to hide behind the safety of the podium. She strode back and forth across the stage, beaming with self-assurance. Nobody booed; instead, her remarks were interrupted by applause and the joyous toots of toy horns and other noisemakers. Appearing onstage with her was the company's new number-two executive, Compaq's old boss, Michael Capellas. They shared an exuberant hug onstage; he beamed when she called him "my partner and my friend." The day of that celebration, the company's shares jumped 6 percent, settling at $20 apiece.

A month later, however, the stock had retreated to $17. The economic backdrop was getting steadily worse, and HP was being hammered by high-tech woes that a pep rally alone couldn't solve. In August, the company reported an 11 percent drop in revenue for the combined company and combined operating losses of more than $600 million for the personal-computer and enterprise-computing businesses. Only because of relentless cost cutting was the company able to meet Wall Street's profit targets. Computer executives vowed to do better, but it was hard to see how they could improve results decisively without a pickup in the overall economy. "I'm just not hearing a compelling story here about why we should invest in the company anytime soon," a Boston money manager declared. By midsummer, the stock dipped as low as $10.75. Even after the previous year's terrorist attacks on the World Trade Center, HP stock didn't trade this poorly. If the Compaq merger was supposed to fix HP's weakest operations, the company had a long way to go.

After another three months, the mood had brightened a bit. Fiorina in October 2002 told analysts that Hewlett-Packard was winning nearly 70 percent of its face-offs against Sun and IBM for key enterprise customers' business. That amounted to one of the Palo Alto company's best showings in years. Lehman Brothers analyst Dan Niles upgraded his opinion of the stock, based on the belief that HP's services business was finally picking up momentum. The printer business stormed the market with more than a dozen simultaneous new-product launches, including some $79 and $49 printers that were meant to wipe away Lexmark's inroads into that low-end business. Did any of that amount to a decisive advance for the combined company? No one knew. But in the hair-trigger world of investor sentiment, HP enjoyed a few weeks of Wall Street's newfound love.

On the crucial issue of top managers' loyalties, things looked good at first. Computer-storage company EMC poached one relatively senior HP executive, but that was the closest thing to a high-profile defection in the merger's early months. Everyone else decided either that they liked working at the combined company—or that there wasn't much alternative. In the tech slump, few major companies were hiring.

Michael Capellas, however, began to chafe. No matter how people positioned things, taking the number-two job at Hewlett-Packard was a big step down from running Compaq. At public events where he and Fiorina both spoke, she took command and left him waiting for cues to interject a few thoughts. Within the enterprise-computing business, where Capellas might have been expected to weigh in with big ideas, midlevel managers reported that he had become almost invisible a few months after the merger. If Capellas was working on important projects, they couldn't find traces of his involvement. Six months into the merger, Capellas decided he had endured enough. He announced his resignation, signaling that he planned to become chief executive of WorldCom instead. He was about to take command of a tarnished telecommunications company in the midst of bankruptcy proceedings. Perhaps he could turn it around, though, and at the very least, he would be his own boss. "Once you've been a CEO, that's part of what's in your blood," he explained. "Now is the time to look for the next challenge." Accustomed to running his own show at Compaq, Capellas had no desire to stick around and play Abelard to Fiorina's Heloise.

Perhaps the Capellas departure was inevitable. On the day it was announced, Fiorina did her best to shrug it off, telling aides that his brief tour of duty had been expected all along. All the same, it sent HP's stock skidding more than 10 percent. She couldn't afford more defections.

Other top executives from Compaq appeared to thrive in the new Hewlett-Packard. Compaq alumnus Peter Blackmore brought a more aggressive style to the enterprise-computing business. Month by month, Compaq managers increased their prominence in the combined company's sales organization. Fellow Compaq alum Shane Robison became one of Fiorina's most dependable lieutenants. Officially he was chief technology officer, a somewhat nebulous position. But he increasingly took responsibility for Hewlett-Packard's efforts to introduce its high-end computers to industries, such as biotechnology, that had been elusive to date. Some HP employees grumbled that Compaq was secretly taking over their company. It was an exaggeration, but it underscored an important point. The new HP was mixing up its gene pool, hybridizing what it hoped would be the best elements of both its predecessor companies.

Longtime HP executives did the best they could to make peace with redefined responsibilities. Among them was Duane Zitzner, who had been overseeing the back end of HP's entire computer operations before the merger. Once Blackmore took command of the enterprise business, Zitzner had to make do with running just the personal-computer operations. He was a common target of teasing by colleagues, and a nickname that Fiorina had conferred on him—"Duane-O"—didn't bolster his stature. But he believed that by late summer 2002, he had whittled HP's operating costs to the point that they were lower than Dell's. His division briefly surpassed Dell as the top seller of PCs in the United States, only to forfeit that title three months later as Dell kept expanding faster than anyone else. Zitzner wasn't about to give up the fight, though. He went toe to toe with Dell in seeking giant orders from the Internal Revenue Service and Home Depot, and came away a winner both times. "I'm not going to make this revolutionary jump," he declared. "We just need to keep marching down the road, being very methodical."

Vyomesh Joshi, the high-energy chief of the printing business, stepped into the spotlight when Dell announced that it wanted to get into the printer business, long regarded as the untouchable stronghold of Hewlett Packard. Dell decided to partner with Lexmark, the one-time IBM printer company, which had become a serious HP rival in the sub-$100 printer category. Joshi professed to be unworried, arguing that the printer business was much more complex than Dell realized, and that without deep investments in new technology, the Texas company couldn't stay competitive for long. Dell officials snapped back that much of HP's technology really amounted to ways to make printer cartridges hard to copy or recycle—puffing up the prices of those products. Michael Dell declared that he would help consumers save money on ink and laser cartridges. "We aren't quaking in our boots," Fiorina replied, in what seemed sure to be the first in a long series of taunts and counterattacks between the two companies.

Ann Livermore, who had championed the aborted plan to buy PricewaterhouseCooper's consulting business a year after Fiorina arrived at Hewlett-Packard, got one last chance to revisit that acquisition prospect in the summer of 2002. IBM was on the brink of buying PwC, and investment bankers wondered if Hewlett-Packard wanted to enter a bidding contest. Livermore and Fiorina quickly decided that the answer was no. They had plenty to do as it was, and they didn't think the business was all that attractive anymore, given the overall slowdown in the information-technology sector. IBM quickly scooped up the consulting shop for $3.5 billion. It was a stunning markdown from the $18 billion that PwC had hoped to fetch two years earlier, and a reminder how much the financial markets had soured on the high-tech sector.

For Hewlett-Packard's directors, the proxy contest became a closed chapter, thrilling to recall at times but not really pertinent to their work at hand. New alliances were forming in the boardroom, thanks to the arrival of four former independent directors from Compaq: telecom executive Larry Babbio, prominent attorney Sanford Litvak, venture capitalist Tom Perkins, and broadcast executive Lucille Salhany. Fiorina jousted good-naturedly with Perkins, who had worked at Hewlett-Packard in the 1960s and was chock full of opinions about almost anything. But she could rest easy about most directors' loyalties. Babbio, in particular, had been one of her biggest fans during her Lucent days. He was the executive in 1998 who urged *Fortune* magazine to anoint her as the most powerful woman in American business.

In interviews, HP directors urged journalists to take a long view of the merger and to accept the fact that it would take years to know the outcome. Fiorina and the rest of HP's leadership team had set a multitude of initiatives in motion. They wanted Hewlett-Packard to exploit the clout that came with being number one in many of its markets. They wanted the combined company to stop posting losses in its PC and enterprise-computing businesses. Finally, they wanted smaller but enticing areas such as service and storage to become bigger profit centers. Add it all up, and Fiorina and company were a bit like eighteenth-century merchants sending a half-dozen ships on long trading voyages. If all the ships came back full of valued cargo, the gambles would pay off wonderfully. Everyone would be rich. If some of the ships made it back, the merchants could continue a tolerable life and try again before long. Only if nothing made it back would the merchants be ruined.

Walter Hewlett, meanwhile, struggled to accept defeat in the proxy contest and to figure out how he wanted to integrate that experience into the rest of his life. His moods ranged from bitter to serene. Most often he gave the impression of someone biding his time, waiting to see if a bigger role might lie ahead in a few years. He stayed active on the Agilent board, where he was a respected and appreciated director. He turned down newspaper interview requests on the first anniversary of the Compaq bid, but he indicated he might give an occasional speech about shareholder activism. In the privacy of his living room, he told people what he didn't like about Fiorina. In doing so, he chose his words as carefully as if he were still a director, occasionally praising things she did well.

Only when asked about the HP board did Walter Hewlett reveal anger that wouldn't die. "I feel like this board of directors declared war on this company," he said at one point. "They declared war on the shareholders, on the employees, and on the founding families." Hewlett spoke about the HP Way as something that had "gone underground for now. But it's a proven way to run a company. It will be back." If a new slate of directors ever wanted him to return to the HP board, he added: "I could probably be very helpful."

For the Hewlett and Packard foundations, an upturn in the company's fortunes couldn't come fast enough. Not only were they still the company's largest shareholders, but they also remained painfully sensitive to zigzags in HP's stock price as they tried to set their operating budgets. Paul Brest, president of the Hewlett Foundation, admitted to checking the stock price two or three times a day, hoping a rebound would bolster his grant-making authority again. He could take small cheer from days when the stock was above $15; that was certainly better than $11. In the early months after the merger's completion, though, HP stock remaining stubbornly below its year-earlier levels, leaving the foundations no choice but to recast their budgets with longlasting austerity in mind.

The Packard Foundation made the deepest cuts, slashing its 2003 budget to just $200 million, less than one-third what it spent three years earlier. Foundation CEO Dick Schlosberg laid off more than 30 percent of his staff and jammed his big science and education programs together into one greatly shrunken initiative. What had once appeared to be Dave Packard's greatest legacy—a mammoth foundation rivaling Bill Gates's—no longer even made the top-ten list in the United States. "It's unbelievable," a stunned Schlosberg told a reporter.

All the same, Susan Packard Orr kept the faith. In a Silicon Valley speech four months after the merger's completion, she spent most of the time talking about a nonprofit advisory company she chaired. But she wryly acknowledged that people had come to hear her speak only because they wanted answers to three questions: How to get a Packard Foundation grant, why the foundation hadn't sold its HP stock at the top of the bull market, and what she really thought about Carly Fiorina. Visit our Web site for grant advice, she said. On the foundation's investment strategy, remember that "Father told us to hold on to the stock." As for the final question, Orr's answer was a masterpiece of optimism and diplomacy:

"I hope she hits a home run."

The people struggling hardest to get their bearings were Hewlett-Packard's alumni, who had thought for decades that they understood the company as well as anyone. Men such as John Young, Lew Platt, and Dean Morton had assembled beautiful mental models that couldn't anticipate the collapse of the old ways of doing things. The existence—let alone the importance—of a lawsuit called *Hewlett v. Hewlett-Packard* left them absolutely stupefied. Even Dick Hackborn began reworking his favorite diagrams to assemble a unified explanation for everything he had witnessed and done. "What are the lessons from all this?" he asked a few months after the HP-Compaq merger finally took place. It wasn't a rhetorical question. For once, Hackborn didn't have all the answers.

In the most jarring turn of events, the HP Way suddenly lost its once-magical appeal. Thousands of employees still believed in engineering excellence, teamwork, and respect for the individual, but it didn't add up to an omnipotent creed anymore. Much of the significance of the HP Way derived from employees' *belief* that it was significant. Even if everyone subscribed to a slightly different version of the HP Way—even if the soft-hearted variants weren't really helping run the business effectively—employees felt a great sense of unity and strength from this shared doctrine. It was akin to the Bill of Rights or the Lord's Prayer. It was always there, comfortable and familiar. Then came that fateful morning when Alan Miller and Larry Sonsini sized up the votes on the Compaq merger and declared that Carly Fiorina's deal had won by a "slim but sufficient" margin.

The vote counters had broken the spell. If the most ardent champions of the old ways couldn't fend off Carly Fiorina's merger, even with the Hewlett and Packard families solidly behind them, then the golden age was over. The HP Way had turned into a cul de sac. The final word came from David Woodley Packard. Just after the merger's completion, he announced the death of his father's company by posting a three-foot-high R.I.P. notice in the movie-poster case just outside his Palo Alto movie theater. The stark black-and-white notice was meant to infuriate Fiorina's aides, which it did. All the same, the accompanying text was unforgettably poignant.

"The HP Way touched many people's lives," David Woodley Packard wrote. "Most of us expected that it would last forever—that it would prove as timeless as a Frank Capra movie. But those entrusted with the duty to safeguard it have exercised their legal right to make another choice. *Dura lex, sed lex.* The law is harsh, but it is the law. HP employees are now on a new ship, being taken on a new voyage. The company has even changed its stock symbol to HPQ to stress that the 'old' HP is gone. For the sake of the surviving employees, of course, I hope for a good outcome. But it is hard to imagine that their leaders can invent something better than what they left behind."

So how was it possible for Hewlett-Packard, a company so firmly anchored in its heritage, to become so astonishingly different in such a short period? Were the old assessments totally wrong? Were they largely right but somehow missing a few key insights? If other factors mattered even more than Bill and Dave's legacy, what were they?

The answers start with the pressures felt on any founder-driven business after the pioneers fade from the scene. Thirty years ago, there wasn't any firm on Wall Street with more swagger than Salomon Brothers. In the advertising world, Ogilvy & Mather epitomized witty, distinctive work. In journalism, the *Los Angeles Times* was such a towering presence in Southern California that it attracted a half-dozen biographers over the years. Each of those enterprises seemed enduringly successful and distinctive. They were the Hewlett-Packards of their industries: proud, meticulous, and totally in step with their founders' values. People who worked there couldn't imagine that their unique cultures would ever be diluted by mega-mergers.

Today, none of these companies stands alone. Salomon Brothers has been absorbed by Citigroup. David Ogilvy's old ad agency has taken shelter inside a British conglomerate known as WPP Group. Even the great California newspaper of the Otis and Chandler families sold out, becoming part of Chicago's Tribune Companies. In each of these cases—and thousands of similar ones during the past few decades—business turmoil, heightened competition, and sometimes a bit of leadership fatigue made it time to do a deal. The arguments in favor of consolidation were just too hard to resist. Big companies mustered the largest sales forces, the heftiest expansion budgets, and the cheapest sources of capital. Big companies could overpower the competition simply by showing up. In tough times, big-company mergers squeezed out costs with awesome speed. Again and again, the pioneers gave way to the consolidators. Each time, there was intense wistfulness about the end of an era, but before long, everyone bowed to the inevitable.

Some of the most clear-sighted comments about this process came from Hugh Burroughs, a longtime program officer of both the Packard and Hewlett foundations. He had seen HP's founding families up close, spending twenty years appreciating how deep the cult of Bill and Dave ran in Palo Alto. Then he stepped outside. At the time of the HP-Compaq takeover battle, he was running a small foundation in Los Angeles set up by Berry Gordy, the founder of Motown Records. Early in his career, Gordy thought his independent label could reshape the whole music industry by itself. But after nearly thirty years in the business, he sold Motown to a much bigger conglomerate, explaining that "in today's economy, the big get bigger and the small get extinct." There was an inexorability to the whole process, Burroughs said. "It's the same basic story at Motown, HP, or companies everywhere. If you want to stay competitive, you've got to merge. The days of being a freestanding business are over."

For Carly Fiorina and the HP board, there was no reason to cry about this transition. In the summer of 2001, they could see more clearly than anyone that Hewlett-Packard wasn't well positioned in the computer industry.

They wanted to move fast while HP still had the cachet and the stock-market valuation to be the nominal acquirer, rather than the company selling out. When Carly Fiorina, Dick Hackborn, Phil Condit, Pattie Dunn, and their boardroom peers debated the Compaq acquisition in the summer of 2001, they knew they weren't about to enter paradise. The increased exposure to the personal-computer business wasn't ideal. The economic backdrop was problematic, and the merger integration challenges were formidable. While the surviving entity would remain in Palo Alto and be called Hewlett-Packard, it was clear that combining forces with Compaq would create a profoundly different enterprise. Yet the transaction was worth doing anyway. It provided a shot at fixing HP's troubled enterprise computing business. It strengthened the company's position in computer services and storage. It brought in some aggressive executives who knew how to sell, which had eluded Hewlett-Packard for a long time. Most of all, it beat the alternative of sitting still and doing nothing as HP's own computer businesses eroded.

Given the challenges that Hewlett-Packard faced, the Compaq merger was perfect enough.

In the heat of the proxy contest, however, Carly Fiorina promised something more. She evoked the founders' spirit, making people think once again about the days a half century ago when Bill Hewlett and Dave Packard were creating the best outfit on earth. The Compaq deal, she contended, would rekindle the energy and genius that made Hewlett-Packard great in the first place. It was brilliant campaign rhetoric, but it created an impossible set of expectations that would bedevil her company—and her own public standing—for years to come.

Ultimately, the Hewlett-Packard of 2002 wasn't the same company as the garage startup of the 1930s or even the small instrument company of the 1950s. It couldn't be. Hewlett-Packard had become so big that it needed to be run by entirely different principles. It wasn't selling to the engineer at the next bench anymore; it was trying to connect with mass markets around the globe. It wasn't enjoying 40 percent operating profit margins that allowed it to show a big heart to individual employees and still make a lot of money. It was fighting for supremacy in some of the world's most competitive industries, where the winners ran ruthless businesses on 11 percent operating margins and the losers perished.

On a more personal level, Carly Fiorina wasn't the same kind of leader as Dave Packard or Bill Hewlett. She couldn't be. The founders had an unshakable credibility that came from having done every job themselves when the company was tiny. They had been research scientists, salesmen, janitors, and factory foremen. When they practiced management by walking around, they were admired and beloved before they opened their mouths. In addition, their company was small enough in its prime that it was possible to lean over a partition, say hello to some workers, and eventually get to know almost everyone. Carly Fiorina couldn't do that. HP's 140,000-person payroll was so huge that if she stopped all her other duties and tried only to meet each employee for a brief, one-on-one chat, she wouldn't get to the end of the roster until she was seventy-four years old. She had no choice but to exercise most of her influence by speeches, white-board presentations, and mass e-mails. She was the superbly trained professional manager who led with detachment, the sort of person who inevitably took command after the founders left.

During her visits to HP Labs, Fiorina made peace with this role. She knew that a big part of her job was to identify the company's next great ideas while they were still tiny—and to help champion them as potential products or even full-fledged divisions in the years ahead. When she met with scientists, she asked them lots of appropriate questions about potential customers, marketing strategies, and release dates. She could help them succeed. But she wasn't Bill Hewlett, a man with thirteen patents, able to brainstorm with his researchers about the internal circuitry of a new product. She wasn't Dave Packard, slipping into the plant at night to destroy a poorly built oscilloscope. They were perfectionists; she was a pragmatist. She knew what would work in the modern world, going back to the days when she grabbed a shabby red circle from the discard pile and turned it into Lucent's wonderfully effective logo.

Given enough time, Fiorina believed, she could make everything right again. True, HP's earnings had fallen in half since she arrived, and the stock price was way down. But she was fighting her way through the same tech-sector slump that tormented all her competitors, and she was holding her own a bit better than most. Her brightest scenarios were four or five years in the future, when the Compaq merger would be fully digested. She could imagine sitting down to write the annual letter to shareholders and telling people that Hewlett-Packard was an undisputed leader in the fields it participated in. This would be the company that customers thought of first when hard problems needed solving. Employees would be proud to work there. And the company would lead once more by virtue of its character as well as its capabilities.

In the abstract, Dave Packard and Bill Hewlett were still her heroes. In a reflective moment at the end of one dinner, Fiorina thought about Packard's classic management principles of the 1950s—some of which foreshadowed hers—and remarked, "It's the only way to run this company." After the HP-Compaq merger battle subsided, though, she largely stopped talking about the founders. It was as if she had put them back on the mantelpiece, safely protected with dust covers. In wide-ranging conversations about the state of American business, she brought up two different companies, unbidden, as examples of enterprises that got it right. They were Microsoft and IBM, the powerful pragmatists.

"Technology is more than an engineer's game," she said. "That's where Microsoft has been brilliant. If you think about technology companies that have really led, they didn't fall too much in love with the technology." Eventually, she believed, the rest of Silicon Valley would catch on.

Notes

All of the principal living characters in this book sat for extended in-person interviews. Carly Fiorina was interviewed six times between May 2002 and November 2002; Walter Hewlett was interviewed four times in that same period. Both of them provided unfettered access to their proxy-contest advisers. In addition, HP directors, executives, and rank-and-file employees talked at length about the aspects of the company they knew best. HP alumni and competitors added valuable perspectives.

Documents and videotapes, both public and private, played a vital role in many chapters. Oral histories helped capture the early days of Hewlett-Packard with clarity. Newspaper and magazine articles chronicled many of HP's wisest and weirdest moments. The most commonly cited publications are *The Wall Street Journal,* the San Jose *Mercury News, The New York Times, BusinessWeek, Fortune,* and *Forbes.* HP's in-house magazine, long known as *Measure* and briefly renamed *Invent,* was an important source as well. The court records of *Hewlett v. Hewlett Packard* provide rare glimpses into the company at a period of maximum stress.

All interviews are by the author except as noted. Supplemental interviews are by Elizabeth Corcoran (EC), Brian Eule (BE), and Blair Tindall (BT).

Reconstructions of specific meetings are based on accounts of the participants themselves, cross-checked with one another wherever possible. Bill Hewlett and Dave Packard created a culture of candor and storytelling, which is an enormous benefit to any author. People connected with Hewlett-Packard remember a lot, and their memories are strikingly consistent. The notes below indicate the key sources for each reconstruction and any meaningful variations among them.

PROLOGUE

Page
1 **"Pack it in babe":** columnist Christopher Byron, writing in *The New York Observer,* May 28, 2001.
1 **"better if she left":** *The Wall Street Journal,* February 11, 2002.
1–4 Directors' dinner March 14, 2001. This account is based on in-person interviews with Carly Fiorina, Pattie Dunn, Bob Knowling, and Dick Hackborn in August and September 2002. Phone conversations with Phil Condit and Jay Keyworth in October and November 2002 clarified crucial details.
1 **squab and sugar snap peas:** e-mail exchange in October 2002 with Rosemarie Thomas, an HP aide to the board. She recalled that waiters "could not clear the dishes because the directors were in very intense discussions."

CHAPTER 1: The Best Outfit on Earth
5 The ruined oscilloscope. This account is based on in-person interviews with HP retirees Bill Terry and Alan Bagley in May and June 2002, supplemented by phone in-

terviews with HP retirees Bob DeVries and Eric Hammerquist in June 2002. Terry recalled Packard's note saying: "This isn't nearly strong enough." I have relied on Hammerquist's version, finding him most precise on all other details. Hammerquist left Hewlett-Packard a few years after the incident and enjoyed a long and productive career at another electronics company.

5 **"a proud, enthusiastic bunch":** Bernard Oliver oral history, p. 35. Interviews conducted by Arthur Norberg, Charles Babbage Institute, University of Minnesota.

6 World War II and American character: Stephen E. Ambrose, *The Victors* (New York: Simon & Schuster, 1998) and *Band of Brothers* (Simon & Schuster, 1992).

7 Dave Packard's nicknames. Both were cited by Alan Bagley in a May 2002 interview; Eleanor Hewlett Gimon alluded to "Pappy" in an August 2002 interview, saying it was a coinage by her father, Bill Hewlett.

7 Dave Packard's school board exchange: Bagley interview, May 2002.

8 **"Hewlett allowed you":** as quoted in David Jacobson, "Founding Fathers," *Stanford Magazine,* July/August 1998.

8 Hewlett's thirteen patents: "The End of an Era," *Invent,* March/April 2001, p. 23.

8 **"I'm probably most proud":** James C. Collins and Jerry I. Porras, *Built to Last* (New York: HarperCollins, 1994), p. 1.

9 Packard as ham-radio enthusiast: This and many other biographical details appear in David Packard, *The HP Way* (New York: HarperCollins, 1995). Other useful primary sources include some reminiscences by Dave Packard, *The Scientist,* September 5, 1988, "How HP Got Started," *Measure,* December 1979, and Frederick Terman's oral history, Stanford University Libraries.

9 Hewlett's campus mischief: San Jose *Mercury News,* January 14, 2001; interview with Eleanor Hewlett Gimon in August 2002.

10 Terman as matchmaker: In a profile of Frederick E. Terman that appeared in *Reader's Digest,* December 1962, the growth of Hewlett-Packard is described, at which point Dave Packard is quoted as saying, "Fred Terman is the daddy of the whole works."

13 Ely's quest for a computer: phone interview with Paul Ely, June 2002.

14 Bill Hewlett as tortilla courier: *Invent,* March/April 2001, p. 8.

15 Indignation about HP ad: *The Analytical Engine,* August 1995. The anecdote is recounted by Joe Schoendorf, a prominent venture capitalist and former HP employee.

16 Santa Rosa storeroom: This anecdote is cited as a useful parable in *Built to Last,* p. 211, based on the authors' 1990 interview of Bill Hewlett. "True or not, the stories illustrate how HP management worked," the authors concluded.

17 Dave Packard's missteps in Washington: "The Pentagon's Powerful No. 2 Man," *BusinessWeek,* March 21, 1970.

17 **"I gave up smoking":** Bagley interview, May 2002.

17 Hewlett gripping the lectern: interview in May 2002 with former HP executive Sy Corensen.

18 Weekends at the ranch: an excellent description was provided at Bill Hewlett's memorial service, January 20, 2001, by family friend Arjay Miller. His remarks appear on the HP Web site as www.hp.com/hpinfo/newsroom/hewlett/memorial.htm

18 Hewlett on women's opportunities: *Palo Alto Times,* November 1, 1974.

20 Promoting from within: interview with Bob Boniface, July 2002.

20 Racing to assemble the terminal: The best account appears in *BusinessWeek,* June 9, 1975. John Young in a July 2002 interview confirmed the anecdote, though he insisted that the race wasn't meant to signify anything.

21 **"When I started visiting":** interview with Young, July 2002.

22 Packard's ambivalence about PCs: interviews with Jay Keyworth and Walter Hewlett in July 1992. Both men were HP directors in the late 1980s.

23 Packard lumbering up the stairs: phone interview (EC) with Randall Williams-Gurian, April 2002.

24 Young as turnaround specialist: "Suddenly, Hewlett-Packard Is Doing Everything Right," *Business Week*, March 23, 1992.

24 The founders' version: "It Had to Be Done and We Did It," *Forbes*, April 26, 1993.

25 **"I've been traveling":** This reconstruction is based chiefly on the recollections of HP director Jay Keyworth, who was interviewed in person in July 2002 and September 2002 and by phone in October 2002. Walter Hewlett, in a July 2002 interview, provided extra detail about the founders' concern over HP's leadership and its competitive standing vis-à-vis Microsoft and Intel.

CHAPTER 2: The Man Who Said No

26 Fairview Avenue ambience: personal observation on an August 1992 visit.

26 Hackborn's prescience about printers: in-person interview in August 2002 with former HP executive Rick Belluzzo; telephone interviews in August and September 2002 with former HP executives Douglas Carnahan, Ray Smelek, and Steve Gomo.

27 Hackborn's biography and subsequent details: *Richard Hackborn Oral History*, HP Archives, May 8, 1998; "Dick Hackborn: History of Success," *Measure*, May/June 1991

27 Negotiations with Canon: interview in June 2002 with Don Hammond.

28 Clashes at 1984 meeting: Former HP executive Ray Smelek, in a September 2002 phone interview, recalled this as an especially feisty meeting. Hackborn in his oral history described it as "a battle," adding "it's reputed to be a bigger battle than it really was." The quote: "You're running the show" is from the Hackborn oral history and is loosely attributed to all three of HP's leaders at the time.

28 Failure of Hackborn's first project: *Measure*, May/June 1991, p. 13.

28 Printers and toilets: *Wall Street Journal,* September 8, 1994.

30 **"one of the most creative":** Michael Maccoby, *The Gamesman: The New Corporate Leaders* (New York: Simon & Schuster, 1977), p. 124. Some fifteen years later, *New York Times* reporter Andrew Pollack unmasked Jack Wakefield's true identity in an article headlined "HEWLETT'S CONSUMMATE STRATEGIST," *New York Times,* March 10, 1992.

31 **"For a job like this":** Bill Hewlett's comment was recalled in a June 2002 interview with Walter Hewlett.

32 Lew Platt's debut: In an August 2002 interview, Platt recalled John Young's support and Dave Packard's advice. In a September 2002 e-mail exchange, Platt recounted Hackborn's congratulations.

33 Platt as single parent: San Jose *Mercury News,* September 23, 1999.

34 Standing ovations for Platt: telephone interview with former HP director Tom Everhart in May 2002.

34 Debate about SAP installation: The account is based on a June 2002 telephone interview with former HP vice president Dick Love. Platt in a November 2002 e-mail exchange confirmed the disagreement, adding that he believed Love's proposal would have involved shouldering other operating groups with overly expensive versions of the SAP software.

35 Packard memorial service: An excellent account appeared in the San Jose *Mercury News*, March 30, 1996.

36 Man-on-the-moon analogy: *BusinessWeek*, September 30, 1996.

37 Dueling lobbyists: cited in a September 2002 interview with Gary Fazzino, HP's head of government and public affairs.

37 Platt/Hasan lunch: The account is based on a September 2002 telephone interview with Malik Hasan and a November 2002 e-mail exchange with Lew Platt.

38 Belluzzo's move to Silicon Graphics: *Wall Street Journal*, January 26, 1998.

38 **"maintenance mode":** *BusinessWeek*, July 13, 1998.

39 **Platt was stunned:** interview in August 2002 with Lew Platt.

40 Platt's tougher orders: *BusinessWeek*, July 13, 1998.

41 Walter Hewlett and spin-offs: In a June 2002 interview, Walter Hewlett said he grew interested in spin-offs after meeting George Hatsopoulos, the founder of Thermo-Electron, a Massachusetts company known for cleaving off divisions as they became substantial. "That started me to thinking that maybe Hewlett-Packard ought to spin off something," Walter Hewlett said.

41 David Woodley Packard's objections: cited in interviews with four HP directors.

42 Personality tests at HP: The steam-bath and cigarette questions were cited in *Forbes*, December 13, 1999.

42 Directors cooling on Platt: Eight members of the HP board in Lew Platt's final year, including Platt himself, have commented about this period in in-person or phone interviews. The Fery/Platt exchange was recounted by Jack Brigham in a September 2002 interview. Fery in a June 2002 phone conversation declined to talk about Hewlett-Packard. Platt's remark "Why fight it?" was made in an August 2002 interview.

43 **Hackborn hadn't campaigned:** interview in September 2002 with Jay Keyworth.

44 **"a great athlete":** interview in May 2002 with Jeff Christian.

45 **"a media personality":** Lew Platt, as quoted in *Fortune*, March 29, 1999.

CHAPTER 3: Give Me a Chance!

46 Kevin Kelly's prophecy: In an essay titled "New Rules for the New Economy," Kelly wrote: "(T)he dynamics of networks will continue to displace the old economic dynamics until network behavior becomes the entire economy," *Wired*, September 1997.

46 **"You learn":** interview in September 2002 with Carly Fiorina.

46 **"It rendered all the fat":** The quote comes from Carly Fiorina's commencement address to Stanford University's graduating class of 2001, delivered June 17, 2001.

47 **"It left me cold:** ibid.

47 **"professional and elegant":** The quote comes from a telephone interview in June 2002 with Kathy Fitzgerald.

47 **"raise holy hell with Carly":** interview in August 2002 with Bob Knowling.

47 **That's wrong, Fiorina argued:** interview in July 2002 with Lucent general counsel Rich Rawson; interview in September 2002 with Carly Fiorina.

48 Lucent road show details: multiple telephone interviews in April 2002 with Jeff Williams; telephone interview in June 2002 with Lucent chairman Henry Schacht; and a telephone interview in July 2002 with former Lucent investor-relations specialist Mary Ann Niebojeski. Also helpful was coverage in *The Wall Street Journal*, particularly the March 31, 1996 "Heard on the Street" column and a Lucent corporate videotape, *Road Show Highlights*.

49 **"Up, Up and Away":** interview in September 2002 with Carly Fiorina. The song begins: "Wouldn't you like to ride in my beautiful balloon?"

50 Fiorina's editing of speeches: Lucent executives shared a draft copy—with discernible editing changes—of her talk on "The Communications Revolution." Fiorina in a November 2002 interview confirmed that the changes were hers.

50 *Rocky* **movie posters:** telephone interview in August 2002 with Bill Marx.

50 Strip-club encounter: described in a September 2002 telephone interview with Lucent executive Carole Spurrier; confirmed in October 2002 by Carly Fiorina.

51 Ascend meeting and the socks: first described in hazy terms by multiple Lucent employees and Ascend alumni (BT). Confirmed by Carly Fiorina in a September 2002 interview.

52 Babbio's endorsement of Fiorina: interview in September 2002 with Larry Babbio.

53 Schacht on recruiters: telephone interview in June 2002 with Henry Schacht.

53 Christian's approach: described in Jeffrey E. Christian, *The Headhunter's Edge* (New York: Random House, 2002). In-person interviews with Christian in May 2002 and Fiorina in August 2002 added important details.

55 Finalists' list: interviews in August 2002 with search-committee members Sam Ginn and Lew Platt; interview in September 2002 with Dick Hackborn.

56 Lane's candidacy: telephone interview in November 2002 with Ray Lane.

56 Zander's critique of HP: telephone interview in October 2002 with Ed Zander.

57 Fiorina/Platt exchange: interview in July 2002 with Carly Fiorina; interview in August 2002 with Lew Platt.

57 Fiorina/Ginn exchanges: interview in July 2002 with Carly Fiorina; interview in August 2002 with Sam Ginn.

58 Fiorina's test results: *Measure*, September/October 1999.

58 Bill Marx's assessment: telephone interview in August 2002 with Bill Marx.

59 **four-hour lunch:** first reported in *BusinessWeek*, August 2, 1999. Interviews with Carly Fiorina in July 2002 and Dick Hackborn in September 2002 provided many extra details.

61 **"the next Jack Welch":** Dick Hackborn's comment was cited by Walter Hewlett in a June 2002 interview and confirmed in an August 2002 interview with HP director Pattie Dunn.

62 Patio dinner: July 2002 interview with Carly Fiorina.

CHAPTER 4: Rules of the Garage

64 E-mails about garage ad: HP's marketing department compiled a summary of more than two hundred staff e-mails, of which more than 90 percent were rated "excellent" or "very good." One critic labeled the ad "a triumph of fluff over substance." At least seventy employees called the ad great, awesome, superb, or brilliant.

65 Note from the Clintons: described in a September 2002 interview with Gary Fazzino; confirmed in a November 2002 interview with Carly Fiorina.

66 Myers-Briggs ratings: The contrast between Carly Fiorina and many traditional employees was first pointed out in a May 2002 interview with Yvonne Hunt, head of employee communications at HP.

67 **"perfect enough":** The phrase and its prevalence were cited in a September 2002 interview with Webb McKinney.

68 **"Leadership is a performance":** *Forbes*, December 13, 1999.

68 **Fiorina's pay package:** disclosed in Hewlett-Packard's report to shareholders for

the quarter ended July 31, 1999, as filed with the Securities and Exchange Commission. The valuation of the restricted stock was confirmed in a November 2002 e-mail exchange with HP manager James Otieno.

68 **HP's fleet of corporate aircraft:** A picture of one of HP's early corporate jets appears in *The HP Way*. In an e-mail exchange in November 2002, HP aviation specialist Ken Peartree confirmed the Gulfstream III's tour of duty. In a September 2002 interview, former HP general counsel Jack Brigham discussed the Platt-era retrenchment of corporate jets. The purchase of two Gulfstream IV aircraft was reported in *Forbes*, December 13, 1999.

69 Two versions of the Rules campaign: The early version appears in the November/December 1999 issue of *Measure*, on the cover; the later version appears in an inside photo. In a May 2002 interview, Steve Simpson of Goodby Silverstein provided additional details.

70 Mice in the garage: Details come from a July 2002 telephone interview (BT) with Michael McHugh.

71 **'How committed are you . . . ?':** August 2002 interview with Carly Fiorina.

71 Hewletts' lunch invitation: ibid.

71–72 Fiorina/Hewlett lunch: The reconstruction is based on in-person interviews with all five guests. Arjay Miller in May 2002 provided the fullest details about Bill Hewlett's remarks. Carly Fiorina in August 2002 said she hadn't been able to make out his words but was told he said "Get me out of here." Alan Bagley in May 2002 recalled Bill Hewlett saying: "Gotta go." Edwin van Bronkhorst and Bob Boniface remembered fewer details.

73: **"Her main secret":** e-mail exchange in July 2002 with Nigel Taylorson.

73 The Kellogg boardroom: telephone interviews in May 2002 with Richard Munro and in June 2002 with Harold Polling.

74 Fiorina/Gutierrez exchanges: telephone interview in August 2002 with Carlos Gutierrez.

74 Seascape meeting: The reconstruction is based on a July 2002 interview with Debra Dunn, an August 2002 interview with Carly Fiorina, and a September 2002 interview with Vyomesh Joshi.

75 **"I was a deer":** *Wall Street Journal*, August 22, 2000.

76 HP's bureaucracy: interview in June 2002 with Dan Plunkett.

76 HP's employee turnover: Rates for the Platt and Fiorina eras were cited in a September 2002 interview with Susan Bowick, HP's head of human resources.

77 **an ascetic temple:** interview in September 2002 with Vyomesh Joshi.

78 The inevitable "Oh, shit!" day: interview in May 2002 (EC) with Eric Schmidt.

79 **"one damn spank server":** Duane Zitzner's comment was first reported by ZDNet.com journalist Mary Jo Foley in a September 12, 2000 Web posting. Zitzner in a November 2002 interview added details on the Superdome launch.

CHAPTER 5: *Inside the Boardroom*

80 Platt/Fiorina travels: interviews in August 2002 with Carly Fiorina and Lew Platt.

80 Platt in executive session: This reconstruction is based on interviews with seven HP directors at the time. Platt in an August 2002 interview confirmed the two direct quotes initially recalled by other directors. Ginn's comment—and his decision to speak first—was recalled by fellow director Jay Keyworth in a July 2002 interview. Ginn in an August 2002 interview had fewer details about the meeting but concurred with others' accounts.

82 Fiorina/Hackborn encounter: This reconstruction is based on an August 2002 interview with Carly Fiorina and a September 2002 interview with Dick Hackborn.

84 Packard's concern about raiders: interview in May 2002 with former HP executive Dean Morton; interview in August 2002 with Eleanor Hewlett Gimon.

84 Ligatures: David Woodley Packard in a February 1998 interview spelled out his views on ligatures. Lew Platt in an August 2002 interview and Dick Hackborn in a September 2002 interview said David Woodley Packard shared those concerns among directors.

84 Ph.D. dissertation: Stanford news release February 27, 1969, announcing that the university would acquire a copy of David Woodley Packard's dissertation.

85 **"a direction I was not meant to stretch"**: San Jose *Mercury News*, February 2, 1987.

85 **grassroots connections:** interview in June 2002 with Walter Hewlett.

86 **"a board in transition":** Hackborn oral history, p. 112.

88 Creating a new market: interview in August 2002 with Sam Ginn.

88 The board's strategic focus: Condit testimony in *Hewlett v. Hewlett-Packard*, April 25, 2002.

89 Board chemistry: Lucent PR chief Kathy Fitzgerald in a July 2002 interview recalled Henry Schacht's advice.

89 **create an apparent business crisis:** *Measure*, May/June 1991. In that article, Rick Belluzzo is quoted as saying: "One of Dick's lessons from history is that strong cultures don't change without a crisis. To jump-start a business, it's not uncommon for Dick to create a crisis." The article's next quote was from Hackborn himself, who said: "At HP, when people know they have a problem, they perform beyond all expectation."

90 **"the agenda was clear":** interview in June 2002 with Larry Sonsini.

91 **"I dropped that stock":** interview in September 2002 with Walter Hewlett.

92 HP interest in Kodak: interview in August 2002 with Carly Fiorina.

95 Fiorina/Capellas exchange: In a September 4, 2001 news conference, the two executives mentioned their 1999 encounter in Washington. Fiorina in an August 2002 interview and Capellas in a September 2002 interview added details.

CHAPTER 6: The Billionaire's Legacy

98 The Watsons' saga: Tom Watson, Jr., and Peter Petre, *Father, Son & Co.* (New York: Bantam Books, 1990).

98 Bill Hewlett as father: Several of these stories were shared publicly by family members at the memorial service for Bill Hewlett on January 21, 2002. Eleanor Hewlett Gimon in an August 2002 interview provided extra insights.

99 **"no special consideration":** Bill Hewlett's comment was recalled by Walter Hewlett in an interview with *Measure*, May/June 1987.

101 **"four kids to struggle":** *Wall Street Journal,* March 6, 1998.

101 Contributions to Stanford: *Palo Alto Weekly,* October 14, 1998.

102 Tribute to Bill Hewlett: "The End of an Era," *Invent*, March/April 2001.

103 Fiorina's expression of awe: In a Hewlett family videotape of the service, Carly Fiorina is visible for about two seconds as the camera pans the audience while David Woodley Packard is speaking. She is spellbound.

105 **"Someday those grandchildren":** interview in May 2002 with Flora Family Foundation chairman Herant Katchedourian.

107 **kitchen table:** *Wall Street Journal*, March 6, 1998, which is the source for many subsequent details about the Packard Foundation's evolution.

108 **"This is your project":** Dave Packard's comments were recounted in an August 2002 telephone interview (BE) with Lawrence Crowley.

110 Coast Dairies visit: recalled by Michael Mantell in a September 2002 telephone interview (BE).

111 **"a spectacular time":** interview in May 2002 with Dean Morton.

111 **three magic sentences:** interviews in August 2002 with Stephen Peeps, head of the Packard hospital foundation, and in September 2002 (BE) with Harvey Cohen.

112 At odds with his sisters: The different approaches to grant making were highlighted in "The New Packard," *Philanthropy*, August/September 2001.

113 **"degraded popular culture":** San Jose *Mercury News*, July 2, 1989. The Judy Garland epiphany is regularly cited in profiles of David Woodley Packard, appearing in interviews he granted for the *Mercury News* profile of 1989 and a similar piece in the *San Francisco Chronicle*, January 20, 1990.

114 Budgets could stretch: interview in June 2002 with Dick Schlosberg.

114 Portfolio diversification: interviews in May 2002 with Arjay Miller and Laurie Hoagland, investment chief of the Hewlett Foundation.

CHAPTER 7: *Three Questions*

117 **"the next IBM":** interview in September 2002 with Michael Capellas.

118 Easily fixable missteps: *San Francisco Chronicle*, November 14, 2000.

118 Fiorina's criticism of McGinn: cited in an August 2002 interview with HP director Pattie Dunn, confirmed in an October 2002 interview with Carly Fiorina.

119 **"We had less clarity":** interview in September 2002 with Bob Wayman.

119 **"navigating through the fog":** *BusinessWeek*, April 9, 2001.

120 **"not an optional journey":** The quote comes from an HP videotape of the Mexico City presentation in March 2001, titled "Conversations with Carly: Priorities 2001."

120 **'Don't worry Margaret':** interview in July 2002 with Margaret Youngblood, an executive at Landor Associates. Her firm helped design the famous Lucent logo.

121 The pay-cut debate: interview in September 2002 with Susan Bowick.

122 HP's layoffs: Statistics about people and dollars involved were announced by Hewlett-Packard. Details about employee reaction are based on interviews with more than a dozen HP employees (BE) and managers. Some of them shared copies of documents given to them at the time of termination.

123 **Silicon Valley charity ball:** telephone interview in June 2002 with Michael Malone.

124 Genesis of *Financial Times* story: telephone interview in July 2002 with Louise Kehoe; interview in August 2002 with Suzette Stephens.

125 July 19 board meeting: This reconstruction is based on interviews of all eight directors in the room at the time. Carly Fiorina also provided a copy of her PowerPoint presentation. Direct quotes from Carly Fiorina, Sam Ginn, and Pattie Dunn were provided by the participants themselves and confirmed in substance by at least one other director.

128 July 20 board meeting: This reconstruction is based on interviews with all nine directors in the room, plus observers Duane Zitzner and Larry Sonsini. The quote "I wish you'd been here yesterday" is remembered by Pattie Dunn, Carly Fiorina, and Walter Hewlett, but no one is certain which director said it.

129 **"Walter, don't you dare":** Carly Fiorina's exact words were cited in a July

2002 interview with Walter Hewlett. In an August 2002 interview, Fiorina confirmed the substance of her remarks.

131 Michael Capellas's background: An especially thoughtful portrayal appeared in *BusinessWeek,* September 4, 2000, in a cover story headlined "Compaq's Rockin' New Boss." The "toughest job" quote is from that article.

131–32 **"As you start to slide":** interview in September 2002 with Larry Babbio.

132 **"lipstick on a pig":** interview in September 2002 with Bob Wayman.

133 **"I'm disappointed":** This and many other details of the two CEOs' interplay come from interviews in September 2002 with Carly Fiorina and Michael Capellas. Compaq's decision to break off talks briefly in early August was disclosed in Securities and Exchange Commission filings by both companies in connection with the merger plan.

133–34 Heloise and Abelard: McKinsey executive Robert Uhlaner, in a July 2002 interview, said his firm had chosen blander code names, which didn't meet with Carly Fiorina's approval. She came back with the famous medieval couple.

134 Hewlett/Sonsini exchanges: These reconstructions are based on interviews in June and August 2002 with Larry Sonsini and on interviews in July and November 2002 with Walter Hewlett.

CHAPTER 8: Walter Hewlett's Rebellion

136 **barbecue was sizzling:** This and subsequent details are based on interviews in May 2002 with Arjay Miller and Jim Gaither and on a July 2002 interview with Walter Hewlett.

138 **"you ought to get a lawyer":** interview in May 2002 with Jim Gaither.

138 Lawyers who listened: This reconstruction is based on in-person interviews in May 2002 with Stephen Neal and in July 2002 with Walter Hewlett. Keith Flaum in a July 2002 telephone interview added important details.

140 Hewlett/Fiorina phone call: This account is based on interviews in July 2002 with Walter Hewlett and in August 2002 with Carly Fiorina.

141 **"Look at my personality":** interview in July 2002 with Walter Hewlett.

142 The John Paul Jones analogy: The journalist was Michelle Quinn of the San Jose *Mercury News,* who in a July 2002 phone conversation recalled the exchange. Walter Hewlett confirmed it in a November 2002 interview.

143 Training horses for the Mellons: interview in June 2002 with Dan Burch.

143 **"Let's stick to the high road":** cited in an April 2002 interview with Todd Glass and Dan Katcher, two members of Joele Frank's public relations firm.

144 **"Walter never looked up":** interview in August 2002 with Bob Knowling.

144 Visiting Bill Hewlett's office: A partial account of this exchange appeared in *BusinessWeek,* February 11, 2002. Major additional details come from interviews in July 2002 with Walter Hewlett and September 2002 with Jay Keyworth as well as personal observation in September 2002 of the office itself.

146 *I've just lost $1 billion!:* This comment and subsequent details come from an interview in June 2002 with Dick Schlosberg.

147 Packard Foundation deliberations: This account is based on interviews with three decision makers at the Packard Foundation as well as on a July 2002 interview with Walter Hewlett.

148 The Orr/Fiorina call: This reconstruction is based on an in-person interview in June 2002 with Dick Schlosberg, an in-person interview with Carly Fiorina in September 2002, and a telephone interview with George Vera in July 2002.

149 Analysts' pessimism: The quotes are from the *Houston Chronicle,* December 8, 2001 and the San Jose *Mercury News,* December 8, 2001.

150 Walter Hewlett on the road: This portrait is based on interviews in May 2002 with Spencer Fleischer and Tully Friedman and on interviews in June 2002 with Dan Burch and Larry Dennedy, another member of the proxy-soliciting team. Dennedy recalled the fuel-leak incident as terrifying. Fleischer portrayed it as stressful but under control.

151 **"my sword and my shield":** interview in July 2002 with Walter Hewlett.

153 **"Why talk about that?":** interview in May 2002 with Laurie Hoagland.

CHAPTER 9: The Crusade of Her Life

155 Fiorina's South Korea speech: The summary and quotes come from an HP videotape of that meeting, titled "Carly Fiorina Coffee Talk in Korea," October 16, 2001.

156 Firefighter analogy: The comparison arose in the speech titled "Technology, Business and Our Way of Life: What's Next?" that Carly Fiorina delivered in Minneapolis September 26, 2001. In that speech, she said, "While perhaps some critics do not yet see the full benefit of the merger, the role of leadership is sometimes to take bold actions that defy conventional wisdom." She then cited three acts of heroism on September 11. Immediately afterward, she said: "As business leaders, as we are faced with questions of life and death rather than how much our stock is worth, the significance of our business contribution to the world may be increased. And that is a good thing."

156 **"building the future":** Carly Fiorina's speech, titled "Imaging and Invention in a Digital Age," was delivered at the Consumer Electronics Show, Las Vegas, January 8, 2002.

156 **"an outsider with a big dream":** Carly Fiorina's speech, titled "Fueling Innovation and Opportunity with Linux," was delivered at the Linux World Conference, New York, January 30, 2002.

157 **"my legacy":** Fiorina's comment was made in an October 2001 interview with Reuters. It was aired in an early November 2001 Reuters article about the merger's prospects, which ran in many publications, including the *Seattle Times,* November 7, 2001.

157 Employee attitudes: HP's own surveys were cited in a May 2002 interview with Yvonne Hunt, head of internal communications at the company. David Woodley Packard hired the Field Research Corporation to survey HP employees in Fort Collins, Colorado; Boise, Idaho; and Corvallis, Oregon. Field officials randomly surveyed a total of 940 employees at all three locations; they said findings for each site had a margin of error of five to six percentage points in either direction.

158 Sunday-morning conference call: This reconstruction is based on interviews in September 2002 with Carly Fiorina and Dick Hackborn.

158 **"lightning speed":** *New York Times,* December 12, 2001.

159 **newfound resolve:** interview in May 2002 with Marty Korman.

159 **a 15 percent prospect:** interview in September 2002 with Michael Capellas.

160 Alan Miller's visit: This reconstruction is based on interviews in June 2002 with Steve Pavlovich and in July 2002 with Alan Miller.

161 **"I've already made up my mind":** telephone interview in June 2002 with Lewis Sanders.

162 David Woodley Packard's ad: *Wall Street Journal,* January 23, 2002.

163 **a war-room caucus:** The reconstruction is based on interviews in June 2002 with Allison Johnson, Charles Charnas, and other members of the team.

163 Fiorina/Sonsini conversations: as described in interviews in June 2002 and August 2002 with Larry Sonsini.

164 Fiorina's investor meetings: interview in September 2002 with Matt L'Heureux, a Goldman Sachs executive advising HP; court testimony by Carly Fiorina in *Hewlett v. Hewlett-Packard.*

164 Jeff Bezos's phone call: interview in September 2002 with Carly Fiorina.

164–65 Poor morale: *Wall Street Journal,* November 16, 2001.

165 The Vancouver visit: An ominous account of this meeting was posted by a former HP employee on the Internet in March 2002. In an e-mail exchange in November 2002, an HP spokeswoman offered a more benign version.

166 **Fiorina's annual performance review:** This account is based on in-person interviews in August 2002 with Pattie Dunn, Bob Knowling, and Sam Ginn as well as on a September 2002 e-mail exchange with Dick Hackborn and Walter Hewlett's pretrial deposition in *Hewlett v. Hewlett-Packard.*

167 Confused shareholders: interview in June 2002 with Steve Pavlovich.

168 **"musician and a paleontologist":** The genesis of this phrase was discussed during interviews in June 2002 with Allison Johnson and in July 2002 with Alan Miller.

170 Not hurting Fiorina: The Lew Platt comment was recalled in a June 2002 interview with Dan Burch.

171 Aides crowding into Fiorina's office: The reconstruction is based on a September 2002 interview with Matt L'Heureux and an e-mail exchange in October 2002 with Allison Johnson. Fiorina in a September 2002 interview said she briefly had stepped out of the room to call a major institutional shareholder. She confirmed returning to the room to say, "Now we're ready . . ."

CHAPTER 10: Into the Counting Room

173 Campaign spending in 1976: The Federal Election Campaign Acts of 1974 and 1976 allotted major candidates $22 million apiece in federal funds. Candidates Jimmy Carter and Gerald Ford were allowed to supplement that by $12 million in donations. That total of $34 million per candidate doesn't include general spending by both political parties or specific outlays for the party conventions. Whichever way one sorts out the numbers, though, the financial parallels between a presidential campaign and the HP-Compaq proxy contest are striking.

173 Outlays by HP and Hewlett: Bob Wayman, HP's chief financial officer, disclosed the company's $75 million total shortly after the proxy contest was resolved, San Jose *Mercury News,* May 15, 2002. A spokesman for Walter Hewlett in February 2002 pegged his side's total spending at $32 million, San Jose *Mercury News,* February 14, 2002. In a July 2002 interview, Walter Hewlett said the Delaware court case cost him about $4 million beyond that.

174 **"We wanted to disclose that":** interview in May 2002 with Stephen Neal.

175 Walter Hewlett's itinerary: as cited in Spencer Fleischer's travel calendar, which became part of the evidentiary record in *Hewlett v. Hewlett-Packard.* Fleischer in an October 2002 telephone interview said that all but two of the appointments logged into the calendar actually took place as planned. His amendments are reflected in the text.

176 MacKenzie's solicitations: The intense vote-getting effort by both sides was first

chronicled by *The Wall Street Journal,* March 15, 2002. Important extra details came from personal observation and an interview in June 2002 with Dan Burch.

176 Innisfree's solicitations: interview in July 2002 with Alan Miller.

177 **more than $100 per voter:** Mike Lynch, "Proxy Battle," *Reason Online,* March 7, 2002.

178 **"I can't ever do that, Bob":** The conversation was recalled in an August 2002 interview with Bob Knowling. Carly Fiorina acknowledged it in a September 2002 interview.

178–79 Zitzner's e-mails: They became part of the evidentiary record in *Hewlett v. Hewlett-Packard.* The "Chicken Little" retort is from Carly Fiorina's pretrial deposition, April 20, 2002.

179 Bill Gates and stress: An important early account of the pressures felt by Gates appeared in *The Washington Post,* December 29, 1998. The quote: "It's all closing in on me" appears in John Heilemann *Pride Before the Fall* (HarperCollins, 2001). In a November 2002 interview, Microsoft spokeswoman Marianne Allison-Ward said the Heilemann account hasn't been disputed by Microsoft.

180 Approach to Lew Platt: The outlines of the approach appeared in the *Financial Times,* March 2, 2002. Interviews in May 2002 with Tully Friedman and in August 2002 with Lew Platt added significant details.

182 **a New Jersey airstrip:** Spencer Fleischer provided considerable detail as a witness testifying on April 25, 2002 in *Hewlett v. Hewlett Packard.* Corroboration comes from Dan Burch's deposition in the case.

184 Predawn crowds March 19: personal observation. Warren Hargrave's comments were made to the author that morning. Andreas Hotea's comments appeared in *Investor's Business Daily,* March 20, 2002.

185 HP's message to Deutsche Bank: A transcript of this call was introduced as evidence in *Hewlett v. Hewlett-Packard.*

185 **Hewlett was working the phones:** The Hilton description is based on personal observation (author and BE). Walter Hewlett's phone calls and results are described in his deposition in *Hewlett v. Hewlett-Packard.*

186–87 The shareholders' meeting: The account is based on personal observation, March 19, 2002 in the press tent, supplemented by a videotape of the proceedings and detailed coverage in the San Jose *Mercury News,* March 20, 2002.

189 **Miller's best judgment:** interview in July 2002 with Alan Miller.

189 **Sonsini quickly passed:** interview in August 2002 with Larry Sonsini.

189 Events in the counting room: This reconstruction is based on in-person interviews in June 2002 with Larry Sonsini and HP executives Alison Johnson, Charles Charnas, Matt Jacobsen, and Steve Pavlovich, supplemented by HP's photos of the scene and by multiple phone interviews with Alan Miller and Dan Stoller, a New York attorney advising Compaq.

191 **pens barely stirred:** personal observation

CHAPTER 11: Searching for Vindication

192 The *Marathon* documentary: The thirty-minute film shows Walter Hewlett training with Erich Segal, who at the time was a young assistant professor of English at Harvard. Segal later gained fame as the author of *Love Story.*

192 The 1965 Boston Marathon: Walter Hewlett in a September 2002 interview recounted his misfortune in that race.

193 **gathered at Neal's law offices:** A full account appears in Dan Burch's deposi-

tion in *Hewlett v. Hewlett-Packard*. Spencer Fleischer in a September 2002 telephone interview added details.

194 **"Go see Walter":** Carly Fiorina's remark was recalled by Sam Ginn in an August 2002 interview.

194 Ginn/Hewlett exchange: This account is based on an interview in August 2002 with Sam Ginn and on interviews in July 2002, September 2002, and November 2002 with Walter Hewlett.

195 **Even if the odds:** interview in July 2002 with Walter Hewlett.

197 **"Carly wanted me":** interview in July 2002 with Steven Schatz.

198 *protect the quarterback:* interview in June 2002 with Boris Feldman.

199 **Chandler once fined himself:** *New York Times*, April 14, 2002.

199 **Neal's opening statement:** Court transcripts and personal observation provide the basis for this section and the following five pages.

199–200 **Yavner bolted from his bench:** personal observation.

203 Fiorina/Sonsini exchange: interview in August 2002 with Larry Sonsini.

207 **"Carly is in control":** Susan Wright's comment was recalled by George Vera, chief financial officer of the Packard Foundation, in a July 2002 telephone interview.

207–8 Packard Foundation deliberations: This reconstruction is based on in-person interviews with Dean Morton in May 2002, Dick Schlosberg in June 2002, and Lew Platt in August 2002, as well as on a phone interview with George Vera in July 2002.

209 Fiorina/Orr exchange: This reconstruction is based on interviews in September 2002 with Ann Baskins and Carly Fiorina.

CHAPTER 12: Can Carly Make It?

210 **Management classics:** William Ouchi, *Theory Z: How American Business Can Meet the Japanese Challenge* (Boston: Addison-Wesley, 1981), and James C. Collins and Jerry I. Porras, *Built to Last* (New York: HarperCollins, 1994).

212 **"inject new DNA":** interview in October 2002 with Carly Fiorina.

213 Commencement speech: Carly Fiorina, "The Process of Distillation: Getting to the Essence of Things," Stanford University, June 17, 2001.

213 **"scar tissue":** telephone interview in May 2002 with Dick Munro.

213 **"If the company performs well":** interview in August 2002 with Lew Platt.

214 **birth of "the new HP":** The celebration is documented on an HP videotape of Carly Fiorina's address at the Flint Center in Cupertino, May 7, 2002.

216 **"Once you've been a CEO":** *Wall Street Journal*, November 12, 2002.

216 Zitzner's outlook: interview in November 2002 with Duane Zitzner.

218 **"They declared war":** interview in July 2002 with Walter Hewlett.

219 Paul Brest checking stock price: San Jose *Mercury News*, September 3, 2002.

219 **"It's unbelievable":** San Jose *Mercury News,* September 20, 2002.

219 Susan Packard Orr's speech: "Funders' Fair Presentation," September 12, 2002.

221 **"the same basic story":** telephone interview in April 2002 with Hugh Burroughs.

224 **"the only way to run this company":** interview in September 2002 with Carly Fiorina.

224 **"more than an engineer's game":** interview in October 2002 with Carly Fiorina.

Acknowledgments

On the outermost edges of my memory is a five-minute meeting with Bill Hewlett in the spring of 1977, when he visited the Stanford campus. He was in his midsixties and I was just nineteen at the time, too young for me to realize an opportunity slipping away. The exact words of that conversation are lost with the passage of time, but one image remains enduringly clear. It is of Hewlett-Packard's cofounder standing on a sunlit patio, surrounded by a dozen undergraduates, and grinning quietly as the brightest ones talked about the future of computing. This was how Bill Hewlett found new ideas. It was my first introduction to what company insiders knew as "management by walking around."

The best moments in the development of this book occurred as the listening habit took hold. Five years ago, Jerrold Lucey, M.D., first alerted me to the deeper dramas of the Hewlett and Packard legacy. More recently, *Fast Company* editors Bill Taylor and Alan Webber have passed along more good ideas than I can count. Fellow journalists Louise Kehoe, Quentin Hardy, Michelle Quinn, and Mark Boslet generously shared contact lists and insights. Among early readers of draft chapters, Bernie Wysocki, Keith Hammonds, Charles Fishman, Jack Corcoran, Joan and Edward Anders, Sue Shellenbarger, and Keith van Sickle all helped make the writing brighter, clearer, and more accurate.

Researchers Brian Eule, Blair Tindall, and Catherine Pligavko were dependable, smart, and sometimes outright heroic as they helped keep this project on track amid very tight deadlines. At Hewlett-Packard, Suzette Stephens, Anna Mancini, and Heather Wagner opened doors and created a climate of trust. Harlean Morawietz's transcripts and Julie van Haase's news clippings were a great boon. Many HP alumni, including Alan Bagley, Dean Morton, and Dave Kirby, shared decades of wisdom as they helped me understand the company's heritage.

At Portfolio, editors Adrian Zackheim and Bill Brazell were a joy to work with. Tory Klose and Leni Grossman performed miracles in getting this book into type in record speed. My agents, Kim Witherspoon and

David Forrer, shepherded this project along with their usual care and skill. They believed in this idea even when it started as a seven-hundred-word e-mail, written when no one knew whether Carly Fiorina or Walter Hewlett would win.

As important as all those contributions were, one person did far more than anyone else to make this book come to life: my wife, Elizabeth Corcoran. From her own writing career at *Scientific American, The Washington Post,* and *Forbes*, Betsy knows Hewlett-Packard as well as anyone. She was a patient coach on the fine points of computer technology, a tireless reader of drafts good and bad, and a brilliant interpreter of the puzzle pieces that I brought home each day. She found Jack Wakefield, six weeks into this project. Later on, her counsel helped everything from the book's overall structure to the line-by-line narration of the proxy contest. She's the best.

Index